IN THE
STEPS
OF JESUS

We want to hear from you. Please send your comments about this book to us in care of zreview@zondervan.com. Thank you.

ZONDERVAN®

In the Steps of Jesus
Copyright © 2006 by Peter Walker

Published by Lion Hudson Publishing plc., Mayfield House, 256 Banbury Road, Oxford OX2 7DH, England. www.lionhudson.com

This edition published by special arrangement with Lion Publishing in 2007 by Zondervan, *Grand Rapids, Michigan 49530*

Library of Congress Cataloging-in-Publication Data

Walker, Peter.
       In the steps of Jesus : an illustrated guide to the places of the holy land / Peter Walker.
            p. cm.
       Includes bibliographical references.
       ISBN-13: 978-0-310-27647-0
       ISBN-10: 0-310-27647-0
       1. Jesus Christ — Travel. 2. Bible. N.T. Gospels — Geography. 3. Palestine — Description and travel. 4. Israel — Description and travel. 5. Palestine — Antiquities. 6. Israel — Antiquities. I. Title.
       BT303.9.W35 2007
       226'.091—dc22

                                                                                      2006037475

The edition printed on acid-free paper.

Interior design by Lion Hudson

Printed and bound in China

13 · 10 9 8 7 6 5 4

IN THE STEPS OF JESUS

AN ILLUSTRATED GUIDE TO THE PLACES OF THE HOLY LAND

PETER WALKER

ZONDERVAN.com/
AUTHORTRACKER
follow your favorite authors

For Georgie,
multis quam gemmis pretiosiori
(Prov. 8:31 and D.O.P. 8:3.1)
with thanks and much love

Contents

Introduction

Travel broadens the mind, they say. Presumably it can also deepen the mind, or even change it. Going to places we have never gone to before, seeing the world through the eyes of others, learning to listen to their stories (both from the past and the present), we can return to our original starting point with new vision or expanded horizons.

This feature of common human experience was no doubt at work in ancient times whenever people travelled for any reason other than strict necessity. To paraphrase the famous opening lines of Chaucer's *Canterbury Tales*, 'When the spring is in the air… people long to go on pilgrimages.' Today the equivalent might be travelling for conferences or purely for a holiday, so it is no wonder that in our own age the travel industry continues its relentless expansions. Many people, it seems, have a 'travel bug'.

This book is written for such people – including those who would love to travel but are unable to do so for some reason. It is patterned as a journey round various places in the Bible lands and will itself take you on a journey – to a part of the globe that, historically, has been one of the most visited places on earth. Modern political troubles

in the region frequently act as a disincentive for would-be travellers. If that is you, then this book is designed expressly to help bring something of the region back to you.

So this can be, if you wish, a 'travel guide for the non-traveller'. There may of course be readers who find these pages an incentive to travel to the places mentioned, but there will be others who receive its challenge in a different way – as an invitation to make a mental, perhaps more personal, journey. In the absence of physical travel there is always the liberating possibility of travel within our minds.

Behind the places mentioned here there lies a story, and behind the story stands an enigmatic figure – probably the most famous person ever to set foot in this region. In some ways this figure from the first century AD remains a shadow. People often visit this region hoping to learn more about him (almost in search of him, it seems), but they can sometimes return home sharply disappointed. For, unlike a great builder such as Herod the Great, this person did not leave any physical remains that we can see or touch in the area. The physical land does not, in that sense, bring him any the closer.

Nor did he himself ever write anything. Contrast this with another first-century figure from the region, Josephus. As the Jewish commander of rebel troops in Galilee, he first

Satellite view northwards over the Sinai Peninsula towards the fertile green of the 'Promised Land'.

Luke: the man behind the message

The New Testament contains two books written by Luke: an account of the life of Jesus (one of the four 'Gospels', which means 'good news'); and an account of the activities of the first Christians, especially the apostle Paul (the 'Acts of the Apostles'). These make up nearly 40 per cent of the New Testament. What do we know about this man who contributed so much to the writing of the Bible?

Paul's companion

From Paul's letters we learn that Luke was one of his travelling companions, who visited him during some of his imprisonments. Paul describes him when writing to the church in Colossae as the 'beloved physician' (Colossians 4:14). So he was a medical doctor of some kind. Some have wondered if he is the unnamed 'brother' whom Paul sends with Titus to Corinth, describing him as 'praised by all the churches for his service to the gospel' (2 Corinthians 8:18). Is this a reference to the fact that Luke was already gathering a body of oral and written material that summarized the life and teaching of Jesus (the beginnings of his Gospel)?

From the book of Acts we can deduce a little more. On some occasions the author suddenly breaks into the first person: for example, 'we boarded a ship...' (Acts 27:2). From these we can establish when Luke was travelling with Paul. He may have been a native of a place called Troas (near ancient Troy, on the north-west coast of what is now Turkey) – at least this is where he first joined Paul, travelling across to Philippi with him (Acts 16:10–40). He then seems to have stayed in Philippi before rejoining Paul's companions as they made their way to Jerusalem (Acts 20:5–6). Luke remained in Palestine throughout Paul's two-year imprisonment in Caesarea (Acts 23–26) and then joined him on the journey to Rome, which included being shipwrecked off Malta (Acts 27–28).

Writing his story

We do not know what happened to Luke after arriving in Rome. Quite possibly he met Mark (the writer of another Gospel) while he was there (in Colossians 4:10 Paul refers to Mark just a few verses before he refers to Luke). Meeting Mark may have spurred him to spend time preparing his own material for publication.

Probably Luke had used his time in Palestine (AD 57–59) to research the people and places associated with Jesus and the apostles, perhaps even producing a first draft of his Gospel. We do not know when he produced his 'final edition'. Many scholars suggest dates as late as AD 85, but a date ten or even twenty years earlier is preferable. Possibly Luke's Gospel was given its final shaping just after the destruction of Jerusalem in AD 70, which Luke may have seen as an integral part of the story he was telling – the dramatic story of what resulted from Jesus going up to Jerusalem.

Luke's writing is of a recognizably high quality. His calibre as a historian – though frequently disputed – conforms to the best standards of ancient historiography. He writes in a polished Greek style (it was probably his mother tongue). At the same time his language seems to have preserved the Jewish flavour of many of his sources. He uses phrases that make more sense in a Semitic language than in Greek: for example, 'and it came to pass'.

Luke, then, is our guide as we follow in the steps of Jesus. Many have found him to be an accessible and dependable guide.

---

fought against the Romans and then went over to their side, later writing lengthy volumes about that war and more generally about the antiquities of the Jewish people. Through his writings we gain a great deal of precious historical information; but we also gain access to the person and thought of Josephus the author, as he seeks to defend himself and to justify his changing of sides. Not so with this other Jewish man from first-century Galilee. Not for nothing have some spoken of 'the shadow of the Galilean'.

What we do have (which sometimes makes scholars of the classical world slightly envious) is no less than *four* accounts of his life and teachings, written down by others within a generation or so. Much briefer than the writings of Josephus (and written by authors far less preoccupied with justifying themselves), the Gospels are concise and sharply to the point. They are ruthlessly focused on their subject matter, determined to do all that lies in their power to bring this recent historical figure to life.

Although all four of the gospel writers are quoted in this book, there will be a special focus on one of them – the only non-Jewish author among them, a medical doctor called Luke. There are several reasons for this choice. First, his narrative is filled with a

Luke's perspective on Jesus

Luke has a particular gift for conveying emotional colour and warmth. His portrait of Jesus is perhaps the most 'human', and in it we see a wide variety of people responding to Jesus in their different ways. Luke's Gospel refers more frequently than the other Gospels to women (they may indeed have been his sources), and it tells several stories from a female perspective: for example, his account of Jesus' birth is told from Mary's viewpoint. From this some have sensed that Luke was not just a 'beloved physician' but also a brilliant psychologist. Perhaps his close dealings with people in their medical difficulties gave him a special sympathy and an understanding of human weakness.

In keeping with this, Luke emphasizes the way Jesus included all people within his care. No one is automatically excluded or 'beyond the pale' – whether rich or poor, male or female, Jew or non-Jew (or 'Gentile'). This last point may have meant a lot to Luke personally. Almost certainly he was himself a Gentile by birth. At the same time he may already have been attracted to the ethics and belief of Judaism, even before he heard the message about Jesus. There were many such 'God-fearers' on the fringes of the synagogue in the ancient world. When the apostles began preaching the gospel and announcing that Gentiles could now enter the kingdom of God *as Gentiles* (without first needing to be circumcised, for example), this was indeed 'good news'.

So Luke writes to encourage other Gentile readers that they too now belong in God's family, and that Jesus in his earthly ministry had a welcoming attitude towards non-Jews (hence, for example, Jesus' story of a good Samaritan in Luke 10:25–37). He emphasizes that Jesus' message was all about 'salvation' and the 'forgiveness of sins' (Luke 2:11; 7:48; 24:46–7). The climax of a key episode within his Gospel (focused on Jesus' encounter with a dishonest tax collector called Zacchaeus) is Jesus' clear statement that he 'came to seek and to save that which is lost' (Luke 19:10). Indeed Luke devotes the whole of chapter 15 to the theme of the joy experienced when people who had been lost are now found – the high point of which is Jesus' parable in which a 'prodigal son' is welcomed home by his delighted father.

So Luke's Gospel is an extended invitation to people of any background to consider themselves welcome in the company of Jesus.

particularly human colour – he takes us artfully and imperceptibly into the thought-world of ordinary people of the time as they try to make sense of, and respond to, the person who has turned up in their midst. Next, he has the feel of a genuine historian, someone who is interested in showing how his story is anchored in the real world and in mapping it squarely onto the known world of his readers. Thirdly, being himself by birth an outsider to the world of Judaism, he is particularly good at helping others who feel 'on the outside' to know that they can enter into this Jewish story and not get lost. They are warmly invited to come in and see for themselves.

Yet the primary reason is this: Luke too had the 'travel bug'. He wrote a sequel to his Gospel (now called the book of Acts) in which it becomes clear that he himself was often on the move, travelling from northern Greece to Jerusalem and then from Palestine to Rome. He had made a physical journey – both towards Jerusalem and then away from it. And in his writings he gives us his insights from that journey and invites his readers (even if they cannot emulate his physical travel) to make a spiritual journey, both to Jerusalem and then away from it. His invitation still stands.

So we will travel with Luke and see where it leads us. Luke begins his Gospel with a short prologue, after which he takes us immediately to the Temple in Jerusalem. Here, deep in the heart of the Jewish world, he recounts the strange events unfolding among faithful Jewish men and women who have been waiting all their lives for Israel's God to fulfil what they understand to be his promises to them. Luke wants us to see that the story he is about to tell is itself a 'story within a story'.

For the figure at the centre of his narrative is part of a much larger picture, an age-long history going back more than a millennium – the history of Israel. Indeed he appears to have seen himself as the ultimate fulfilment and climax of that story – the person who would single-handedly turn the course of that history into something new, who was himself the central hinge or turning point in the narrative. From now on, nothing would be quite the same again. A new age was dawning; a whole new era had begun.

Then (after various important 'ports of call' such as Bethlehem, Nazareth and the desert) we begin an extended journey up from Galilee to Jerusalem, which scholars have helpfully called Luke's 'Travel Narrative'. This journey occupies far more narrative space in Luke's account than in the other Gospels (indeed, over 40 per cent of his story). Luke wants us to make this journey to Jerusalem ourselves, to sense its importance, while all the time asking ourselves how the events that will soon take place in Jerusalem could possibly prove to be so significant in history – so epoch-making. Things indeed 'come to a head' in Jerusalem – there are tears, conflict, misunderstandings, underhand dealings,

Key dates around the time of Jesus

The following list gives an overview of the key relevant dates before and after the ministry of Jesus. Some dates must remain uncertain. For discussion over the date of Jesus' birth, see page 22. The other possible date for Jesus' crucifixion is AD 33. If Jesus was crucified on a Friday, which coincided in the Jewish calendar with the 'day of Preparation' for Passover, then this only occurred on either 7 April AD 30 or 3 April AD 33. The earlier date is preferred below.

37 BC	Herod the Great takes control of the area.
27 BC	Octavian assumes title of 'Augustus' and 'Emperor'.
5 BC	Birth of Jesus in Bethlehem (in April?).
4 BC	Death of Herod the Great (in March). Territory divided between his three sons, also known as 'Herod': Archelaus (Idumea, Judea and Samaria); Antipas (Galilee and Perea); Philip (Trachonitis). Serious rebellion crushed by Romans under General Varus.
AD 6	Archelaus deposed and exiled; Judea now under direct Roman rule (Coponius serves as first 'prefect'). Revolt led by Judas the Galilean.
AD 14	Reign of Emperor Tiberius begins (until AD 37).

AD 26	Pontius Pilate arrives as governor of Judea. Herod Antipas moves capital of Galilee from Sepphoris to Tiberias.
AD 26	Ministry of John the Baptist.
AD 27–30	Ministry of Jesus.
AD 30	Crucifixion of Jesus.
AD 31/32	Paul's conversion on the road to Damascus.
AD 34–35	Paul's visit to Jerusalem (then leaving for Tarsus).
AD 36	Pontius Pilate brutally squashes a revolt by the Samaritans and is recalled to Rome.
AD 38	Herod Agrippa appointed to succeed Philip and Antipas.
AD 39	Caligula (emperor from AD 37–41) attempts to place his own statue in the Jerusalem Temple, causing fierce Jewish resistance (Josephus, *Antiquities* 18.8).
AD 41	Herod Agrippa takes control of Idumea, Judea and Samaria and is given title of 'king'; he begins the new 'third' wall on Jerusalem's north side (Josephus, *Antiquities* 19.7). Claudius reigns as emperor until AD 54.
AD 44	Death of Herod Agrippa (Acts 12:1–23); Rome sends out 'procurators'.

AD 49	'Apostolic Council' in Jerusalem (Acts 15:1–29); riots in Jerusalem, leading to fierce massacre (Josephus, *War,* 2:12).
AD 52	Felix serves as procurator until AD 59.
AD 54	Reign of Emperor Nero begins.
AD 57–59	Paul and Luke visit Jerusalem (Acts 21); Paul arrested and imprisoned in Caesarea Maritima; Festus arrives as procurator (AD 59–61).
AD 62	Under High Priest Ananus, James (Jesus' brother) is put to death (Josephus, *Antiquities* 20.9).
AD 64	Great fire in Rome; Nero's persecution of Christians.
AD 66	Outbreak in Caesarea of First Jewish Revolt against Rome; Jerusalem Christians flee the city (perhaps to the city of Pella).
AD 67–70	Roman siege of Jerusalem under General Vespasian.
AD 70	Vespasian's son, Titus, destroys the Temple in August (followed in September by his burning of Upper City).
AD 74	Fall of Masada

tragedy and confusion – but there is also an unexpected 'twist' at the end of the story which then propels it into a whole new dimension.

No wonder, then, that Luke wrote a sequel to answer the vital question, 'What happened next?' If the climax of one story proves to be the hinge-point in another larger story, then the story must be continued. But for now he leaves his readers with two pictures: a couple of people travelling away from Jerusalem, trying to make sense of what has just taken place in the city; and, at the very end of his book, some people back in Jerusalem's Temple (the place where it had all started), who are full of new joy and eagerly waiting for the next instalment in the story. Their travelling days, it turns out, have only just begun.

This is the story we will be following in these pages. The chapter sequence tries (wherever possible) to reflect Luke's own sequence. Like Luke's writings too, we hope there will be a sequel to this present volume in which we can see what happened next and trace the various journeys that were made from Jerusalem out into the wider world. But for now this present volume will end on something of a 'cliffhanger'. It will take an open-ended approach which, rather than attempting to force 'closure', will leave some questions waiting to be answered.

For, although our travelling will end close to Jerusalem (near where the journey started), we may find that during the course of the journey we have been given much to reflect on. Familiar things may be seen in a new light. We will have come full circle, with the end point of our journey proving to be the same as the place from which we started, yet there may be something different about it; and it itself may beckon to be the start of a whole new journey, if we are willing. So we may find (even if we have never physically left our seats) that we have indeed been travelling in our mind's eye – a kind of travel that indeed 'broadens the mind'.

Making the most of this book

Each chapter focuses on a particular place or area associated with the life of Jesus. Within each chapter there is an opening main section that explores what that place was like in his day. Here we are aiming to explain Jesus' ministry in its original context, and to see if there are any particular factors associated with that place's previous role in the biblical story which can add an extra layer of meaning to our understanding of what Jesus said and did there. Those readers who want to keep their focus squarely within the biblical text (whether they are interested in the latest in gospel studies or the themes of biblical theology) might select only these opening sections. Effectively, each section offers an overview of that place as it appears in the whole Bible (indeed some of these were inspired by needing to give such overviews to fellow-travellers when in the actual places). They can be read in sequence and will keep you following closely the themes of Luke, our first-century guide.

This biblical overview is followed by a quite separate second main section which aims to explain and interpret what people would see if they visited that site or area today. Necessarily this involves an outline of anything significant that has affected that landscape in the 2,000 years since the time of Jesus. So this is where we look at issues such as: archaeology; the possible authenticity (or not) of the site; the evidence of later Christian pilgrims or historians. At this point Luke is left far behind as we trail through the 'ups and downs' of the post-biblical period. This might be of real

Josephus on John the Baptist and Jesus

Josephus was writing in Rome at the end of the first century AD. His two major works (the *History of the Jewish Wars* and the *Antiquities of the Jews*) give us a key window into understanding the Jewish world at the time of Jesus. They also confirm many aspects of what is portrayed in the Gospels. Here is what he wrote about John the Baptist and Jesus:

John the Baptist

Now some thought that the destruction of Herod's army came justly from God as a punishment for what he had done against John, called the Baptist. For Herod had had him killed, even though he was a good man. John had commanded people to exercise virtue (both righteousness towards one another and piety towards God) and in this way to come to baptism… The crowds gathered around, because they were greatly moved by hearing his words. Herod, however, feared that the great influence John had over the people might put them under his power and incline them to raise a rebellion… So, because of Herod's suspicious temper, John was sent as a prisoner to the castle at Machaerus and was there put to death.

Antiquities 18:5 (cf. Mark 6:14–29)

Jesus

Now there was about this time a wise man called Jesus [if it be proper to call him a man]. For he was a worker of wonderful deeds, a teacher of those who receive the truth with pleasure. He attracted many Jews as well as many Gentiles. [This man was Christ]. And when Pilate, at the suggestion of the principal leaders among us, had condemned him to the cross, those who had loved him at the beginning did not forsake him. [For he appeared to them alive again on the third day, as the divine prophets had foretold these and countless other wonderful things concerning him.] And even now the tribe of Christians, so named from him, has not yet disappeared.

Antiquities 18:3

What Josephus wrote about Jesus has naturally caused much debate. Some of the words (marked above in square brackets) seem more likely to have come from a Christian copyist at a later date. Even so, Josephus seems to have known about Jesus and the early Christians; he seems to have known that his teaching had attracted people outside the nation of Israel, that he was a messianic claimant, and that he had been crucified during the time of Pilate.

---

interest to church historians or non-specialist archaeologists. Importantly, however, these sections are not written on the presumption that readers have visited (or soon will be visiting) these sites. So practical 'tourist' information has been omitted – even though it has been easiest for me to walk around the sites with an imaginary visitor in mind.

Between these two major sections there is at the centre of each chapter a list of key dates that relate to the place under discussion. These include dates from before the birth of Christ (which are particularly relevant to the first, biblical section) and dates that fall after his birth (particularly relevant to the second, post-biblical section). This ties the chapter together, as well as hinting at the Christian conviction that this Jesus may indeed stand at the centre of human history (after all, our Western calendars are still taking their names from him – 'before Christ' and in the 'year of the Lord'). This list of key dates is also where you will find many of the references and quotations alluded to in other parts of the chapter. Hopefully at a glance you will be able to see here the whole history of that particular site.

Each chapter also contains box features, which give the reader an opportunity to look at the relevant background information in more detail (for example, history, geography, culture or archaeology). These box features include some extended quotations from other ancient sources.

For the New Testament period, we are particularly indebted to the Jewish historian Josephus. As indicated earlier, Josephus knew Galilee and Jerusalem well. He was the military commander for the Jewish rebels in Galilee at the start of the First Jewish

The door in the southern transept of Constantine's Church of the Nativity in Bethlehem. The Greek wording means 'light' and 'life', words used in John's Gospel to describe Jesus.

Revolt and was one of Rome's 'most wanted' men – dead or alive. In dramatic circumstances (described in his *War* 3:8) he went over to the Roman cause, predicting (rightly) that his captor Vespasian would be the next emperor. Twenty years later he wrote a full account of the war and also a more general book on Jewish history (*Antiquities*). He wrote at vast length (several of his 'speeches', for example, contain more words than the sum total of all Jesus' teaching as preserved in the Gospels); he was prone to some exaggeration in his numbers and especially wanted to blame the 'Zealot' party for the Jewish uprising (making out that they were a small minority who had had a disproportionate influence over the rest of the Palestinian Jews who were not really anti-Roman). Even so, he provides the best evidence outside the Gospels for what was going on in this region during that period. To read Josephus is to be made aware that the gospel writers did not set their story in some fanciful world but in a real world, verifiable from other sources. It is also to be reminded what a politically volatile place Palestine was in Jesus' day and to lose some of the common idea that it was a place of sweet calm or quasi-mythical 'disembodied bliss'. Reading Josephus enables us to hear the gospel writers (and Jesus) better – in a far more real, even gutsy, way.

For the later period there are some extended quotations from those who visited the region within the age of the early church. Eusebius (c. AD 260–339) lived in Caesarea on the coast. He is famous for his ten-volumed *Ecclesiastical History* (a Christian equivalent perhaps to Josephus' earlier work, without which our knowledge of the early church period would be virtually minimal). He was also the bishop of Palestine in the critical era when Constantine came to power throughout the whole Roman (later Byzantine) empire. At the end of his life he would write the emperor's biography (the *Life of Constantine*), but he also wrote numerous books on the Bible and local matters: a history of the *Martyrs of Palestine* (Christians in the Holy Land experienced a major imperial persecution between AD 303 and 310); a *Commentary on the Psalms*; and an alphabetical gazetteer of biblical places (the *Onomastikon*). This last book (first published around AD 290) gives us vital clues in identifying the authentic gospel sites, showing us how they were being remembered (or otherwise) during the first 300 years after Jesus.

Other quotations from the later period include extracts from the Bordeaux Pilgrim (seemingly a rather simple-minded man who kept a brief travelogue of his visit in AD 333) and Egeria (probably a Spanish nun, who kept a much fuller and more extended diary of her three-year long visit to the East in AD 381–84). There is a focus too on Cyril (c. 315–84), the enthusiastic bishop of Jerusalem throughout the middle of the fourth century, who delivered his eighteen *Catechetical Lectures* to some baptismal candidates in the church of the Holy Sepulchre in Lent AD 348; also on Jerome (the biblical scholar who lived in Bethlehem from AD 384).

The reason for including these extracts is that, as any visitor to the gospel sites today can soon testify, the Holy Land has been massively affected by the Christians of this early Byzantine period. The landscape was altered dramatically in their day. This was the generation in which gospel sites, previously buried or disused or forgotten, were first marked with churches. In terms of archaeology we cannot get back to the time of Jesus without first passing back through the time of the Byzantines. Those who want to follow 'in the steps of Jesus' find that – whether they like it or not – others have got there before them. Yet few visitors to the Holy Land have access to the great texts that survive from this period. I hope this book will now remedy this and give you a whole new lens through which to view the land of Jesus' birth.

Finally, readers will note that there are comparatively few references to events within the last hundred years. This has been a deliberate choice, as focusing on the complex recent politics of this region would itself spawn a whole library of new books. I have touched on these issues myself in *The Land of Promise* (2000) and *Walking in his Steps* (2001) and there are numerous works by others (some of which are listed in the further reading section) that deal with the political and theological questions raised by modern Israel/Palestine. (Indeed the issue of finding a single, suitable name for the land of the Bible shows the extent of the problem: 'Israel', 'Palestine', the 'Holy Land', the 'Land of the Holy One' – each has had its problems, both in the first century and in the present day).

The fact that these contemporary concerns are not discussed here should not be taken as a sign that I think them unimportant or somehow imagine that people should visit Jerusalem today without being made painfully aware of the issues. Such 'cocooned' and 'sanitized' visits do take place and in their own way they only contribute further to the very problems that they are trying to pretend away. Suffice it to say that a concentrated focus (as here) on the ministry of Jesus in its original context might contain within it some key insights which, if heeded, might unlock some of the painful paradoxes in the land of the Bible today.

A personal journey

Speaking personally, it has been exciting to draw together in this book the fruit of many years of guiding people round the land, carrying out academic research and teaching about the ministry of Jesus in the land of the Bible. I first visited Jerusalem in 1981 and was immediately captivated by its questions. Two periods of doctoral research followed, one looking at Jerusalem and the gospel sites in the Byzantine period (especially the contrast between Eusebius and Cyril), the other examining the same issues in the New Testament period. More recently my interests have taken me further back to biblical theology (how do we bring together the Old and New Testaments on any particular subject?) and to studying the various writing strategies of the Synoptic Gospels (especially Luke). All these strands find some expression in what follows.

I am grateful to numerous people who have helped me along the way: family and friends, colleagues at work. Readers may readily identify the personal influence of many of the writers listed in the further reading section. I continue to be recognizably indebted to Jerry Murphy O'Connor for his unrivalled archaeological guide, *The Holy Land*, through its numerous editions. To him and many other conversation partners on this journey, my many thanks. It is an exciting road on which to be walking.

Though written originally to help those who may never have the opportunity to visit the Land, the book has proved useful, so I am told, by those actually visiting these Gospel sites; others have spoken of valuing being able to read a chapter through immediately before or after visiting the relevant site.

The edition contains a few minor changes – chiefly reflecting some alterations on the ground in the area. The major addition is the inclusion of a plan for the present church of the Holy Sepulchre (see p. 189); somehow, with my enthusiasm for the fourth-century Constantinian church, this was overlooked. The church is indeed a confusing one at the best of times, so hopefully the first-time visitor will now be able to make more immediate sense of it.

Finally, it is very pleasing that the book has already appeared in several other languages. I trust it will prove a reliable and insightful guide for everyone who reads it and for many years to come.

My hope, then, is that you too will join the many of us on the road, and that through these pages you may be able to share in some of this adventure, as together – in whatever way and wherever we are – we seek to travel 'in the steps of Jesus'.

Peter Walker
Wycliffe Hall, University of Oxford
January 2009

Ancient Israel (1003–587 BC)

c. 1003 BC	King David founds Jerusalem.
c. 970 BC	King Solomon dedicates the Temple in Jerusalem.
722 BC	Fall of Samaria and the Northern Kingdom of Israel.
587 BC	Fall of Jerusalem to Nebuchadnezzar.

The Persians (538–332 BC)

c. 538 BC	First Jews return from Babylonian exile.
458 BC	Return of Ezra (followed in 445 by Nehemiah).

The Greeks (332–168 BC)

c. 168 BC	Antiochus Epiphanes desecrates the Temple.

Independent Jewish Kingdom (168–63 BC)

168–64 BC	The Maccabees revolt.

The Romans (63 BC–AD 313)

c. 63 BC	Pompey brings Roman rule and himself enters the Jerusalem Temple.
37–4 BC	Reign of Herod the Great.
AD 66	First Jewish Revolt.
AD 70	Fall of Jerusalem.

AD 132–35	Second Jewish Revolt under Bar Chochba.
AD 135	Emperor Hadrian refounds Jerusalem as 'Aelia Capitolina'.

The Byzantines (AD 313–637)

AD 325	Emperor Constantine summons the Council of Nicaea.
AD 333	Visit of 'Bordeaux Pilgrim' to Holy Land.
AD 335	Eusebius of Caesarea gives oration at the Dedication of the church of the Holy Sepulchre.
AD 348–84	Cyril as bishop of Jerusalem.
AD 361–63	Reign of 'Julian the Apostate', who gives permission for Jewish rebuilding of the Temple.
AD 381–84	Visit of Egeria; Jerome founds a monastery at Bethlehem.
AD 451	Council of Chalcedon: Jerusalem becomes a 'patriarchate'.
AD 614	Sack of Jerusalem by Chosroes of Persia.

The Arabs (AD 637–1099)

AD 637	Caliph Omar captures Jerusalem.
AD 691	Abd al-Malik builds the Dome of the Rock.
1010	Caliph el-Hakim desecrates the Holy Sepulchre.

1048	Emperor Constantine Monomachus restores the Holy Sepulchre.
1054	The Great Schism between the Eastern and Western Church.

The Latins (1099–1187)

1099	The First Crusade.
1187	Battle at Horns of Hattin; Saladin takes Jerusalem.
1188–92	The Third Crusade.

The Mamluks (1247–1517)

1291	Fall of Acre.
1453	Fall of Constantinople.

The Ottoman Turks (1517–1917)

1537–42	Suleiman the Magnificent rebuilds Jerusalem's walls.
1808	Fire destroys much of the Holy Sepulchre.
1841	Anglicans and Lutherans found joint bishopric in Jerusalem.
1897	Zionist conference in Basle.

The British (1917–1948)

1917	Balfour Declaration.

Map of Palestine in Jesus' day

chapter number of places
covered in book

0 — 60 km
0 — 40 miles

Sidon

Mt Hermon

Tyre

Caesarea Philippi
(Banias)
⑦

Ptolemais
(Acre)

Lake
Semechonitis

*Mediterranean
Sea*

UPPER
GALILEE

GAULANITIS

TRACHONITIS

Bethsaida-Julias

GALILEE

Gamla

BATANEA

Sea of
Gennesaret
⑤

Tiberias

AURANITIS

Sepphoris
② Cana
Nazareth

Yarmuk

Gadara

Caesarea
Maritima

DECAPOLIS

Pella

Plain of Sharon

⑥
Samaria
(Sebaste)

Gerasa
(Jerash)

Jabbok

Joppa
(Jaffa)

Samarian Hills

JUDEA

PERAEA

Rabbah
(Ammon)

Bethel Hills

Lydda
(Lod)

⑧ Jericho
(Tel es-Sultan)

⑭

⑩ ⑪

Emmaus
(Nicopolis)

⑫ ⑬

④ ③

Jerusalem

⑨

Qumran

Mt. Nebo

Bethany

Bethlehem ①

Herodium

Asphaltic
Sea

Machaerus

Ashkelon

Hebron

Arnon

Masada

The Negev

Besor

Zered

Bethlehem

In those days Caesar Augustus issued a decree that a census should be taken of the entire Roman world…

So Joseph also went up from the town of Nazareth in Galilee to Judea, to Bethlehem the town of David, because he belonged to the house and line of David. He went there to register with Mary, who was pledged to be married to him and was expecting a child. While they were there, the time came for the baby to be born, and she gave birth to her firstborn, a son. She wrapped him in cloths and placed him in a manger, because there was no room for them in the inn.

And there were shepherds living out in the fields nearby, keeping watch over their flocks at night. An angel of the Lord appeared to them… 'Do not be afraid. I bring you good news of great joy that will be for all the people. Today in the town of David a Saviour has been born to you; he is Christ the Lord. This will be a sign to you: You will find a baby wrapped in cloths and lying in a manger.'

Luke 2:1–12

Open fields south of the hill-town of Bethlehem. The rugged terrain here (with ancient walls, terraces and watch-towers) gives way to the barrenness of the Judean Desert, a few miles to the east.

Humble beginnings

*'But you,
Bethlehem, are
by no means
least amongst
the princes of
Judah...'*

**Matthew 2:6 (quoting
Micah 5:2)**

It was a small village, perched on some rounded hills overlooking the desert to the east. Six miles (ten kilometres) south of Jerusalem, it was an obvious stopping-point for those travelling on the ancient 'Way of the Patriarchs' that ran along the ridge of hills – from Shechem in the north to Hebron in the south. The village's name, Bethlehem, means 'house of bread': clearly it was a useful place at which to stop for supplies on your journey, a place surrounded by wheat fields and arable land.

It is in this small, ancient village that the story of Jesus begins. In some senses, as we shall discover, his story begins much further back in the mists of time and in other places. Yet this was the place of his birth – some time around the year 5 BC.

Bethlehem BC

This event has given tiny Bethlehem a reputation and significance out of all proportion to its size. Yet it was not without some interesting history in its own right. Several stories associated with key Old Testament characters are connected with Bethlehem:

- Jacob and his family travelled along the 'Way of the Patriarchs' (from Bethel to Mamre). However, just outside Bethlehem (also known as Ephrath), his wife Rachel died while giving birth to Benjamin (the 'son of my right hand'). So she was buried there, her tomb marked by a pillar (Genesis 35:16–20).
- The story told in the book of Ruth is located here. Ruth was originally from Moab (to the east) but had married into a Hebrew family. When her husband

died, she chose to travel with her grieving mother-in-law, Naomi, back to Naomi's hometown of Bethlehem. Here she met and married Naomi's relative, Boaz, and became the grandmother of King David.

- One of Israel's greatest prophets, Samuel, came to Bethlehem to visit the family of a man called Jesse. He anointed Jesse's youngest son, David, to succeed Saul as king of Israel.

- Later in David's life, Bethlehem was occupied by the Philistines and David expressed his longing to drink some water from its well. Three of his 'mighty men' stole into the town to fetch the water, but he refused to drink it, offering it to God instead (2 Samuel 23:13–17).

- Thereafter Bethlehem was associated with great King David and, as expectations grew that God would send another king like David, the prophet Micah predicted that, even though Bethlehem was 'small among the clans of Judah', yet from here would come a 'ruler of Israel, whose origins are from of old' (Micah 5:2–4).

So Jesus' birth in this village turns out to be very fitting. In biblical memory Bethlehem had already been a place both of danger (for Rachel, for David's men) and of joy (the birth of Benjamin, the anointing of David, the focus for hope in the Messiah). When both her sons died, Naomi (which means 'blessing') had wanted to be called 'Mara' (which means 'bitterness'); but her bitterness had been turned to joy. So too now Jesus' birth is seen by Luke as an occasion for 'great joy', but that joy is tempered by suffering. For example, his birth triggers off Herod's massacre of innocent children (Matthew 2:16–18). And a little later in Luke's story Mary is told that her child's life will result in the 'falling and rising of many in Israel'; indeed a 'sword will pierce your own soul too' (Luke 2:34–35).

Sunset over Bethlehem. The Church of the Nativity lies behind the more recent churches. Beyond are the low hills of the Judean Desert and then in the distance are the higher hills of TransJordan beyond the Dead Sea.

Bethlehem was also the place remembered as the original home of King David, the great ruler who had once been a shepherd. Now shepherds are told to go into the 'town of David' to see Jesus, who in due course will be described in the New Testament as the true 'son of David', the long-awaited Messiah and the 'great Shepherd'.

Thirdly, Bethlehem was already a place associated with divine reversal. David had been a child, the youngest son, when God called him. God had overturned human expectation in the choice of his king: if humans look on outward appearances, the Bible writer comments, 'the Lord looks at the heart' (1 Samuel 16:7). Now in Jesus we see something similar: a humble birth in a tiny village, but the one born here will in due course be spoken of throughout the world.

The star of Bethlehem

The Christmas nativity story is so well known. Yet many of its supposed details, popularized by children's nativity plays and advent calendars, have little basis in the original accounts in the Gospels. For example, there was no 'stable' – instead Jesus may have been born in a cave at the back of a house (see page 24). It is also most unlikely that the shepherds and the Magi visited the infant Jesus at the same time. And the 'Magi' were not 'three kings': we do not know how many there were, and they were evidently astronomers or (more likely) astrologers, not kings.

These later accretions can then cause a cynicism about other parts of the story: are they also mere fancy? One aspect of the story, often criticized, is the 'star' seen by the Magi. Matthew 2:7–9 says that this was a star that had recently appeared, that travelled through the sky and that came to rest over Bethlehem.

Yet there are good arguments for seeing this 'star' as a comet. Chinese records indicate that three significant comets appeared around this time (in 12, 5 and 4 BC). Of these only the middle one fits the chronology. We know Jesus was 'about thirty' in AD 29 (see Luke 3:23), so the comet in 12 BC is too early; the one in 4 BC is too late, since we know that Herod the Great (who responded so negatively to the news of Jesus' birth) had died before the end of March 4 BC. The Chinese records indicate that the comet that appeared in 5 BC (unlike the others) was a 'tailed comet'; it appeared in the east and was visible for 70 days.

So this comet of 5 BC could well have been Matthew's 'star', which was originally seen by the Magi in the east in the morning sky, but by the time they had reached Jerusalem two months later it had moved round to the south. Bethlehem is south of Jerusalem, so as they approached Bethlehem the comet could well have appeared over Bethlehem. The description of its 'stopping over' the town is used by writers such as Dio Cassius and Josephus to refer to other comets, which were seemingly suspended over cities such as Rome or Jerusalem. The tail of the comet may have risen up vertically from its 'head', giving the strong impression that it was focused over a particular place.

In fact there were other astronomical events in the previous few years that may have triggered the Magi's interest: a conjunction of Saturn and Jupiter in the constellation Pisces in 7 BC (which only occurs every 900 years); and a conjunction of Saturn, Jupiter and Mars in Pisces in 6 BC (which, in Pisces, occurs even less frequently). When the comet then appeared in the constellation of Capricorn, this would have been a third and final signal, according to the Magi's understanding, that a significant king was about to be born in Israel. Only then did they set out.

The identification of Matthew's star with a comet goes back as far as Origen in the third century – though it has sometimes been dismissed on the (false) grounds that comets were thought in ancient times only to be omens of bad news. Recent astronomical study, however, suggests that it could make very good sense after all.

If this is the case, we may be able to venture a more accurate date for Jesus' birth. The comet first appeared between 9 March and 6 April 5 BC; so it would have been May/June at the earliest before the Magi arrived in Jerusalem. Although Jesus could have been born some considerable time before this, there is an assumed connection in Matthew's account between the first appearing of the star and the birth date of Jesus (Matthew 2:7). If so, Jesus may well have been born around Passover time in 5 BC (Passover fell that year on 20 April). The 2,000th anniversary of his birth would then have fallen in April 1995.

This would tally with the account of the shepherds being 'out in their fields by night' – a detail that rules out the winter months (December through to February) and which probably points to the lambing season. The choice of 25 December only became fixed in the calendar of the Western Church in the early fourth century, a date chosen by Christians because it aptly replaced the pagan festival of *sol invictus* (the 'invincible sun').

It is more likely however that Jesus was born in April, around Passover time. Mary and Joseph would have taken the infant Jesus to be presented in the Temple when he was around six weeks old, and then returned to Bethlehem. Some time later they were visited by the Magi, but they were warned about Herod's intentions to kill Jesus so they swiftly fled to Egypt.

Christmas Questions

Several things about Jesus' birth will remain uncertain. For example, there is the problem of dating: when exactly was he born? Or again, why did Mary travel with Joseph even though she was in the advanced stages of her pregnancy? Travelling down from Nazareth by mule or donkey would have taken five or six days. Presumably Joseph could have come on his own. So the fact that Mary travelled with him may indicate that she too had property in the area of Bethlehem in her own name, which needed to be registered in the Roman census. If so, this would mean that her father had died leaving no sons, and that Mary was his eldest daughter. Joseph travelled with her for obvious reasons – but probably because he too had property in the area, and also needed to countersign Mary's document as her legal guardian.

And why was there 'no room in the inn' when they arrived? One reasonable explanation is quite simply that Bethlehem was overcrowded, with many others also returning to this ancient village for the census. There may have been many such 'descendants of David' (or 'Davidides') scattered around the country. Indeed there may have been a cluster of them in Nazareth, so Joseph and Mary would have been travelling south as part of a small company.

But there is an alternative interpretation. Luke's phrase may be seen as a sign of discretion – the inn was 'no place' for a woman to be giving birth to her child. If so, the

'Does not the Scripture say that the Christ will come from David's family and from Bethlehem, the town where David lived?'
John 7:42

Key dates: Bethlehem

c. 1350 BC	Bethlehem mentioned by the king of Jerusalem in one of the *Amarna* letters.	AD 125	*Protoevangelium of James* 18 refers to Jesus' birth 'in a cave'; a little later Justin Martyr says the same in *Dialogue with Trypho* 78.	c. AD 384	Jerome establishes a monastery here and refers to a church recently built 'at the shepherds' fields' (*Epistle* 46:12).
c. 1020 BC	Samuel's visit to anoint David, son of Jesse (1 Samuel 16:1–13).	AD 135–325	Hadrian's expulsion of the Jews from the area around Jerusalem. Bethlehem deserted and covered by a wooded grove dedicated to a rural god (Jerome, *Epistle* 58).	c. AD 530	Basilica's renovation by Emperor Justinian, adding one bay, the narthex and the three apses seen today.
c. 920 BC	Town fortified by David's grandson, King Rehoboam (2 Chronicles 11:5–6).			AD 614	Church left undisturbed in Persian invasion (because of Magi's familiar dress in the mosaic on the façade).
c. 720 BC	Bethlehem mentioned in Micah's prophecy as 'least among the clans of Judah' (Micah 5:2).	c. AD 230	Origen's *Contra Celsum* 1:51 says that visitors were being shown the 'cave' and the 'manger' of the nativity.	c. 1009	Church left undisturbed despite Hakim's orders (because Muslims had been allowed to use the south transept).
538 BC	Return of 123 Bethlehemites from exile (Ezra 2:21).	c. AD 315	Eusebius says that 'the cave is shown there by the inhabitants to those who come from abroad to see it' (*Proof of the Gospel* 3:2).	c. 1165–69	Renovations (including a new roof, possibly donated by King Edward I of England) in joint project of the Crusaders and Byzantines.
c. 5 BC	Birth of Jesus: conjunction of Saturn and Jupiter in constellation Pisces (May, October and December).	c. AD 326	Queen Helena orders the building of a basilica over the site of Christ's birth (Eusebius, *Life of Constantine* 3:41).	1925	Franciscan church in Shepherds' Fields built by Barluzzi.
5–4 BC	Visit of the 'Magi' and 'massacre of the Innocents' by Herod the Great (Matthew 2:1–18).	AD 333	Bordeaux Pilgrim refers to the basilica built in Bethlehem by Constantine.	1948	Refugee camps established around Bethlehem.
4 BC	Death of Herod the Great (Josephus, *Antiquities* 17:8).	AD 339	Dedication of the Church of Nativity on 31 May.	1995	Bethlehem brought under separate Palestinian control.

supposedly churlish 'innkeeper' (as featured in many nativity plays!) may have been trying to do Mary a favour: in other words, 'Let me show you somewhere more suitable – somewhere warmer and more private.' And he leads her to the warmest place, at the back of the home – a cave.

This initially strikes us as very strange. Yet many first-century homes were built from natural caves, and in cold weather this was where you would also keep your valuable livestock. Almost certainly this was the cosy place – not a stable, located instead in a wind-swept field – where Mary brought her firstborn child into the world. And soon she laid him to rest in a nearby feeding-trough (or 'manger').

It was indeed an inauspicious start, a humble point of entry. The fact that Mary was not yet properly married, being only 'pledged' in marriage to Joseph, would only have added extra shame and ignominy to the scene.

A humble entrance into the world

Luke's Gospel highlights the humble circumstances of Jesus' birth. So it is not surprising that, in his account, the first people to visit Jesus are some local shepherds. In Matthew's Gospel, by contrast, we sense the author's focus on the royal nature of Jesus' birth. The visitors mentioned by Matthew (perhaps arriving significantly later – since Herod issues orders for the massacre of all children up to the age of *two*) are more exotic. They are mysterious 'magi' from the East who have come looking for the 'king of the Jews' and bringing appropriate gifts of gold, incense and myrrh.

Yet Luke too makes clear that there is more going on here than meets the eye. For the appearance of the angels with their powerful message makes clear that this is a birth quite unlike any other: this child is God's appointed 'Saviour'. For Luke, as a Gentile, the good news is that he is not just the Jewish Messiah (the 'Christ') – he is also the 'Lord', whose coming will bring blessing and 'peace on earth' for 'all people'. The event may seem a tiny one in a backward province, far away from Caesar Augustus. But Luke wants his readers to recognize Jesus as the true Lord of the whole world. This will be a divine reversal on a massive scale. For in this baby, as other New Testament writers will say, we see God himself entering his own world in human form: 'the Word became flesh' (John 1:14).

If so, Bethlehem turns out to be the place in which eternity entered time and the created world was invaded by its Creator. A tiny, insignificant place, but within its 'dark streets', as the carol says, shines an 'everlasting light'.

Right Terraced olive-groves near Bethlehem. Many such terraces date back more than three millenia.

Far Right Aerial view of King Herod's Herodium, his refuge near Bethlehem.

Bethlehem Today

Bethlehem today is a sprawling Arab town, flanked on either side by the towns of Beit Jala (to the west) and Beit Sahour (below it towards the desert on the east). Although only 6 miles (10 kilometres) south of Jerusalem, the journey can take much longer, because of the checkpoint that must be negotiated on entering what has become a Palestinian enclave. This 'security' wall, built in 2004, tells its own powerful, sad message. Those who experience any difficulty going through the wall might spare a thought for those within the Bethlehem area who would dearly love to be able to leave the region occasionally but who are prevented from doing so by curfews and restrictions. The wall can make Bethlehem seem like an open prison.

Modern visitors to Bethlehem often go first to the area of the so-called **Shepherds' Fields** (on the edge of Beit Sahour). From here there is a good view back up to the slopes of Bethlehem, giving a sense of how the village naturally lay on the 'Way of the Patriarchs' running along the ridge of the country southwards towards Hebron. From here too the features of the Church of the Nativity are clearly visible, giving an indication of where the first-century village would have been and how it was perched on the hillside overlooking the fields.

There is also a good view to the east, in particular of the distinct conical shape of the Herodium (the natural hill in the desert that King Herod developed as his 'bunker'). The fields nearby show how the vegetation becomes more sparse as you move further to the

Bethlehem

25

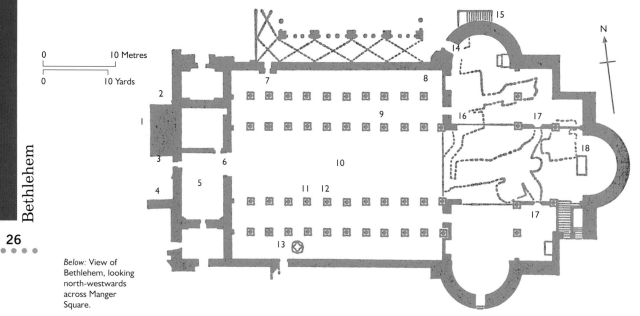

Below: View of Bethlehem, looking north-westwards across Manger Square.

The Church of the Nativity. (1) Buttress; (2) Sixth-century lintel; (3) Entrance; (4) Sixth-century lintel; (5) Narthex; (6) Armenian carving; (7) Entrance to Franciscan cloister; (8) Aisle closure; (9) St Cathal; (10) Fourth-century mosaic floor; (11) St Canute; (12) St Olaf; (13) Fourth-century baptismal font; (14) Entrance to Franciscan church; (15) Entrance to caves; (16) Fourth-century mosaic floor; (17) Entrance to Nativity cave; (18) Greek Orthodox altar.

east. There are also a few remaining examples of ancient terracing, which enabled farmers to increase the fertility of this otherwise quite inhospitable soil.

Various sites have been used over the years to help visitors imagine the location of the shepherds at the time of Jesus' birth: there are properties owned by the YMCA, by the Latin Catholics and by the Greek Orthodox. The last of these is probably on the site of the fourth-century church mentioned by Egeria (and later by Arculf in AD 670), which had been built on the site of a cave. It was rebuilt in the fifth century and has survived intact. Later, with the development of a monastic settlement, another chapel was built over its roof, but it still allowed visitors to look down into the cave below. Meanwhile the area owned by the Catholic Franciscans was also a monastic settlement in the Byzantine period. On the site today there is a small church containing colourful murals designed by Barluzzi. There is also

a large cave which gives a good idea of the natural shelters that may have been used by the shepherds on that night.

Visitors making their way back up into Bethlehem will eventually enter Manger Square. Facing eastwards they are confronted by the impenetrable walls of an Armenian convent on the right and the Catholic Church of St Catherine (set back a little to the left). In between lies the **Church of the Nativity**, built originally by Constantine early in the fourth century and then renovated by Justinian in the sixth. Spared from attacks on several occasions, it can lay claim to being the longest continuously used church in the world.

The outlines of earlier **entrances** to this historic church can clearly be seen in the masonry. These include Justinian's vast lintels from the sixth century and the medieval arch, designed to prevent Crusaders from entering the church on horseback. Now, however, all visitors must stoop through a tiny doorway created in the Turkish period – perhaps an appropriate entrance point, some might think, for a church commemorating a great act of humility.

Once inside, the unadorned dignity of the church is impressive. Its length and open style give a good idea of Byzantine church architecture. Below the floor (under some wooden trapdoors) the beautiful mosaics of the earlier Constantinian basilica can clearly be seen. Looking up above the pillars, one can see the remains of some **mosaics on the walls**. The lower register depicts the ancestors of Jesus as recorded by Luke on the nave's northern wall, and as recorded by Matthew on the southern wall. Meanwhile the higher register summarizes some key decisions made by the early church: the decrees of six 'provincial councils' are depicted on the northern wall; on the southern wall are the decrees of the first six 'ecumenical' (or worldwide) councils, such as Nicea or Chalcedon. In this way the visitor, both ancient and modern, is being trained to see the true, deeper significance of the birth remembered here. To the 'naked eye' this

The fourteen-pointed star in the Cave of the Nativity – the traditional birth-place of Jesus.

'There is now shown in Bethlehem the cave where he was born and the manger in the cave.'
Origen, *Against Celsus* 1:51

The western façade of the Church of the Nativity: above its tiny door can be seen the outline of a medieval arch.

'For he who was "God with us" had submitted to be born even in a cave of the earth, and the place of his nativity was called Bethlehem by the Hebrews. So the pious empress [Helena] beautified the cave with all possible splendour.'

Eusebius, *Life of Constantine* 3:43

birth was an outwardly simple, ordinary event; but to the 'eye of faith' and with the gift of hindsight, it was unique – the moment of divine entry into the human world.

Going through the south transept, visitors then descend a flight of well-worn stairs into the **Cave of the Nativity**. Bedecked with many candles and asbestos-coated decorations, it can make for a puzzling first impression. In fact it is one of several ancient caves, lying at the back of a first-century village home. And this cave, because it is the innermost, was selected in the fourth century to mark the site of Jesus' birth – indicated by the star formation in the floor on the right.

Initially it may seem a little strange. There is no 'stable' (something that is never mentioned in the Bible); and the 'manger' (situated in the little chapel to the left at a lower floor-level) is obviously far from being the original. Yet there are good arguments for the authenticity of this general area. The tradition that Jesus was born in a 'cave' dates from as early as AD 135, and these caves were indeed at the western edge of the village in the first century. Constantine's builders may then have been acting on good local knowledge, preserved by Christians for several generations. So, quite probably, it was somewhere very near here that Mary gave birth to her firstborn child, Jesus. This is the scene of the incarnation, the mystery of God becoming human.

Quite often, as tourist groups pass through, the cave becomes crowded; but normally a return visit a little later on can find it deserted. In the meantime it is worth going across into the neighbouring Church of St Catherine and down the steps on the right into the so-called **caves of St Jerome**. Jerome, one of the six great 'doctors' of the

Jerome in Bethlehem

One of Bethlehem's more famous residents was Jerome. A great student of classical literature, he travelled from Rome to Palestine in AD 384. This was the era when numerous Christians were visiting the Holy Land and many were deciding to stay. As a result several monastic communities were established for those wishing to study and pray.

Jerome decided to set up his own community in Bethlehem, close to the Constantinian Church of the Nativity. Others soon joined him, including a woman called Paula and her daughter Eustochium, who both helped Jerome to build up a significant and well-respected community.

Jerome is most famous for his translation of the Bible's Old and New Testaments into Latin (known as the 'Vulgate', which means 'popular'). Prior to this time Western Christians had only had the Bible in Greek. During his stay in Bethlehem Jerome studied the original Hebrew text of the Old Testament and consulted with local rabbis, so that he could make an entirely fresh translation. His work stood the test of time and was the authoritative Bible version for Roman Catholics until well into the twentieth century.

Jerome also wrote his own biblical commentaries and translated into Latin some key works of previous Holy Land scholars such as Origen and Eusebius. From these (and also from his numerous letters) we can gain a good idea of what Palestine was like in his time. In his *Epistle* 108, he describes Paula's intensive tour around the 'holy places' associated with Jesus' ministry. He also encourages some of his friends to visit the Holy Land. Others he tries to dissuade, assuring them that they are no nearer to God in Bethlehem than in the 'remote British isles': 'access to the courts of heaven is as easy from Britain as it is from Jerusalem' (*Epistle* 58).

Visitors to the caves next to the Cave of the Nativity are shown what purports to be Jerome's study. Although this may not be correct, it is not impossible that Jerome sometimes worked here. For any who treasure the Bible as the 'Word of God', there can be something powerful about imagining Jerome working at his translation of this 'Word' in the immediate vicinity of the birthplace of Jesus, whom John's Gospel describes similarly as the ultimate 'Word' from God (John 1:1).

Jerome wrote that Paula was 'buried beneath the basilica beside the cave of the Lord' and made arrangements for his own burial there too. Their tombs have not survived but they would have been somewhere in these caves – buried as close as possible to the birthplace of the one they thought of as their 'Lord'.

ancient church and the translator of the Bible into Latin (the Vulgate), set up a monastic settlement near here in the late fourth century. A map on the wall helpfully shows how these caves connect up with the Cave of the Nativity.

Having seen these other caves, those who return to the Cave of the Nativity are often better able to imagine it without its adornment, and can capture in their mind's eye the simplicity of the event remembered here: how the shepherds visited and how Mary, knowing more than she could yet say, 'treasured up all these things in her heart' (Luke 2:19). And many since, knowing who would emerge from these humble beginnings, have been moved to sing in this place the words of a popular carol, 'O come, let us adore him, Christ the Lord!'

Map of Galilee

To Damascus

Jordan

Chorazin

Bethsaida-Juli

Capernaum
(Tel Hum)

Zalmon

Gennesaret

Jotapata
(Khirbet Jifat)

Cana ?
(Khirbet Kana)

Magdala

Gergesa
(Kursi)

Arbela

Sea of
Gennesaret

G A L I L E E

Tiberias

Hippos
(Susita)

Sepphoris

Cana ?
(Kafr Kanna)

Nazareth
(en-Nasira)

Mt Tabor

Sennabris

Philoteria

Yarmuk

To Mediterranean

Kishon

Tabor

Gadara
(Umm Qeis)

Nain
(Nein)

Jordan

Valley of Jezreel

Agrippina

Site of ancient
Megiddo

D E C A P O L I S

To Mediterranean
and Egypt

Herodian/Gentile town/village

Jewish town/village

Major trade routes

Scythopolis

0   10 km

0   8 miles

Pella

Nazareth

Jesus returned to Galilee in the power of the Spirit… He went to Nazareth, where he had been brought up, and on the Sabbath day he went into the synagogue, as was his custom. And he stood up to read. The scroll of the prophet Isaiah was handed to him. Unrolling it, he found the place where it is written:

'The Spirit of the Lord is on me,
because he has anointed me
to preach good news to the poor.
He has sent me to proclaim freedom for the prisoners
and recovery of sight for the blind,
to release the oppressed,
to proclaim the year of the Lord's favour.'

Then he rolled up the scroll, gave it back to the attendant and sat down. The eyes of everyone in the synagogue were fastened on him, and he began by saying to them, 'Today this scripture is fulfilled in your hearing.'

All spoke well of him… 'Isn't this Joseph's son?' they asked. Jesus said to them, 'Surely you will quote this proverb to me: "Physician, heal yourself! Do here in your hometown what we have heard that you did in Capernaum." I tell you the truth, no prophet is accepted in his hometown… There were many in Israel with leprosy in the time of Elisha the prophet, yet not one of them was cleansed – only Naaman the Syrian.'

All the people in the synagogue were furious when they heard this. They got up, drove him out of the town, and took him to the brow of the hill on which the town was built, in order to throw him down the cliff. But he walked right through the crowd and went on his way.

Luke 4:14–30

Childhood locations

'Can anything good come out of Nazareth?!' (John 1:46) So quipped a man called Nathanael when he heard where Jesus had grown up as a child. It was an honest question, as Jesus himself acknowledged, and one that perhaps many in Jesus' day would have thought privately.

For Nazareth was a tiny village, with a population sometimes estimated to have been as little as 100 people. It was dwarfed into insignificance by the nearby city of Sepphoris (the capital of the Galilee region) as well as by some of the larger towns around Lake Galilee (such as Bethsaida, the home town of Nathanael). Even from the perspective of these Jewish towns around the lake, Nazareth was 'off the map' in the eyes of many of Jesus' contemporaries.

View looking south-eastwards over the Church of the Annunciation and the site of ancient Nazareth. The village lay in a hollow surrounded by hills, with the Jezreel Valley beyond to the south.

The early hidden years

Yet perhaps that was the point. This made Nazareth the ideal place for the hidden years of preparation that Jesus needed before his public ministry began. Out of the public eye, it was a quiet village nestling in a hollow in the hills of Galilee. At the same time it was also a place from where the child Jesus could discreetly 'watch the world go by': for, just to the south of the village there was a great vantage point from which to look over the Plain of Jezreel. Here a young boy could see all the commercial traffic as it passed along the 'Via Maris' – the road connecting Galilee and Syria beyond with the Mediterranean and with Egypt.

This village is where Jesus was 'brought up' and where, according to Luke, 'he grew in wisdom and stature, and in favour with God and man' (Luke 2:51–52). Apart from one story about Jesus as a twelve-year-old boy (in which his parents lost him on the return journey from their Passover visit to Jerusalem), we know nothing of these early years in Jesus' life.

Ever since, of course, there has been some fascination about that period, as people have asked about life in this 'holy family': What did Jesus learn from Joseph's trade? When did Joseph die? What was it like having Jesus in your family? Perhaps above all, did the young Jesus show any of the miraculous powers that are evidenced later in his adult ministry? There are some fanciful accounts in the so-called 'apocryphal' Gospels, such as the *Infancy Gospel of Thomas*, that speculate, for example, how Jesus turned wooden models of birds into living creatures. The church, however, took an early decision (around AD 150–200) to dismiss these accounts as late and unreliable. They contented themselves instead with the sparse account in the four 'canonical' (or 'recognized') Gospels. This period in Jesus' life is veiled from us, and we can only imagine what might have taken place.

In fact, of the four Gospels, it is only Luke who comments on this period at all. Quite possibly the reason for this is that he had visited this area of Jesus' childhood during his two-year visit to Palestine with Paul (AD 57–59). If so, he may well have interviewed various people, including Jesus' mother Mary. Certainly his accounts of Jesus' birth and childhood seem to be told from Mary's perspective. So, when Luke records that 'Mary treasured up all these things and pondered them in her heart' (Luke 2:19), he may be giving the reader a signal as to how he (Luke, a Gentile from the Aegean) was able to pass on this story. Perhaps he had got the 'inside story' from Mary herself.

Near Sepphoris, the capital of Galilee

Another reason why Nazareth was a good location for Jesus' childhood has to do with politics. In Jesus' day Galilee was a separate administrative region from Judea in the south (centred on Jerusalem). So when Joseph and Mary returned from Egypt, they came north to Nazareth (rather than to Bethlehem in Judea) because, having been warned by an angel in a dream, they sensed their child would be safer here: he would be further removed from the territory of Herod the Great's violent son, Archelaus, who now controlled Judea. Once again Nazareth's insignificance turns out to be strategic. Jesus needed to be hidden – kept 'below the radar screen', as it were – until the time was ripe.

Galilee was controlled instead by Herod Antipas. Compared to Judea, Galilee was a much smaller area, focused around the hills to the west of Lake Galilee. Geographically it was divided into 'Upper' and 'Lower' Galilee, with the hills in 'Upper Galilee' further to the north rising to over 3,000 feet (1,000 metres). Nazareth was at the southern-most end of 'Lower Galilee', perched in the first line of hills and almost overlooking the Plain of Jezreel (in Judea). It was also only 4 miles (6.5 kilometres) south-east of Herod Antipas's capital, Sepphoris.

'God anointed Jesus of Nazareth with the Holy Spirit and power, and... he went around doing good and healing all who were under the power of the devil, because God was with him.'

Acts 10:38

Sepphoris is never mentioned in the New Testament, so we can only speculate as to whether Jesus ever went there. Intriguingly, we know from Josephus that Sepphoris had been completely razed to the ground by the Romans when they put down an uprising triggered by the death of Herod the Great in 4 BC. Yet Herod Antipas immediately decided to rebuild it. This means that throughout Jesus' young life and into his teenage years, Sepphoris would have been a major building site – the perfect place of employment for someone like Joseph. Joseph was a *tekton* (Mark 6:3) – a word which, though often translated 'carpenter', more properly refers to a worker in stone as well as wood. He was a stonemason, a builder. So the family's move north to Nazareth may also have been inspired by some other considerations – good employment prospects.

Did Joseph commute each day, making the 50-minute walk into Sepphoris from

Ancient Sepphoris

'Varus sent a part of his army to Galilee under a commander called Caius. Caius put those that met him to flight, and took the city of Sepphoris, and burnt it, making slaves of its inhabitants. Varus himself marched to Samaria with his whole army, where he did not meddle with the city itself, because it had made no commotion during these troubles…

Josephus, *War* 2:5

Sepphoris was the capital city of Galilee during Jesus' childhood and was only 4 miles (6.5 kilometres) away from Nazareth. Josephus refers to it as the 'ornament of all Galilee' (*Antiquities* 18:27), perhaps referring to its beauty or its defensive capability. Its name (associated with a Hebrew word *zippor* meaning 'bird') has been taken as a reference to its good position. The Romans recognized it as a key city in the region and in 38 BC it was captured by Herod the Great in the middle of a snowstorm.

When Herod died in 4 BC, Sepphoris became the focus of a Jewish rebellion which was soon put down by the Romans under Varus. Herod Antipas then decided to rebuild the city from scratch, making it his capital.

This means that, when Jesus was growing up, Sepphoris offered great employment prospects for people such as Joseph. The founding of Tiberias (in AD 20) then temporarily eclipsed its importance, but it remained an important centre throughout the first century. Its inhabitants wisely chose not to join in the revolt against Rome in AD 67 and a generation later it was renamed Diocaesarea in honour of the Roman emperors.

Recent excavations have begun to show the extent of Herod Antipas' rebuilding. Much of what can be seen, however, dates to later periods when Sepphoris flourished as a Jewish city. Visitors can see a Roman-styled theatre dating from the early second century AD that could have seated more than 4,000. There is a large mansion from the early third century with a splendid mosaic covering its dining-room floor (known as the 'Dionysus mosaic' because of the figure in the central mosaic). There are also fine mosaics in the sixth-century synagogue and in the lower city. This area shows how much Sepphoris had expanded by the fourth century, with colonnaded streets being laid out at right angles and the building of some aqueducts to bring in water from over 3 miles (5 kilometres) away.

The ancient theatre on the north-east side of Sepphoris.

Nazareth? Did the boy Jesus sometimes go with him? Is this where Jesus first learnt about the building trade, the value of planning well before building a tower (Luke 14:28–30) and the importance of laying foundations on rock, not sand (Matthew 7:24–27)? Is this where Jesus learnt about Greek plays and their use of 'masks'? This gave rise to the concept of 'hypocrites' (from the Greek for stage actor) – a term he would often use during his ministry (see Matthew 23:13). Is this where he first encountered Gentiles and sensed what it meant to be an Israelite living in this frontier state where it was so tough to keep the boundary markers between Jew and Gentile?

We do not know. Some have suggested that the Gospels' silence as to whether Jesus ever visited Herod Antipas' other new city, Tiberias, could indicate Jesus' refusal to enter such pagan centres. On the other hand, there is ample evidence that Jesus actively chose to make contact with Gentiles, so it seems unlikely that Jesus would have ruled out such visits on principle. More probably Joseph and Mary would have allowed him to travel wherever they did.

Even so, they would presumably have taught him quite strictly the traditional ways of keeping oneself 'clean' in the midst of Gentiles. All the more so if Joseph was a 'Davidide' – that is, he belonged 'to the house and line of David', Israel's great king (Luke 2:4). Matthew and Luke give ample evidence for this (Matthew 1:6, 17, 20; Luke 1:27, 32; 3:31). Indeed there is some evidence that Nazareth was a village particularly full of such 'Davidides', who, though materially very poor, ensured they kept their

Mary and Joseph with the baby Jesus. Many artists have portrayed the life of the 'holy family' in Nazareth, often giving them an imaginary setting far removed from the likely original.

descent pure by not marrying outside this 'royal' line. Some scholars suggest that Nazareth had been colonized by Jewish settlers from the south of the country around 100 BC, as part of a deliberate programme to 're-Judaize' Galilee. If so, this provides yet another reason why Joseph and Mary returned here after Jesus' birth in Bethlehem. It was not just their hometown from before their marriage; it was also a place where their fellow-villagers would understand the need to foster and guard any royal claimant growing up in their midst.

Mary's strange visitor

Because Jesus launched his adult ministry down by the lake in Capernaum, there are only three or four episodes in the Gospels associated with Nazareth, and one of these takes place before he was born – the so-called 'annunciation'. This was when the 'angel Gabriel was sent to a town in Galilee called Nazareth' to announce to the young Mary dramatic events that were about to change her life (Luke 1:26–38).

The reader is to imagine this event, frequently depicted in art, taking place in this small first-century village – perhaps in one of the small stone houses, but possibly in a nearby field. There is a popular local tradition of its taking place as Mary visited the well, on the north side of the village.

It is a powerful story, full of surprises, ending with two great statements. On the one hand, the biblical conviction that 'nothing is impossible with God' and, on the other, Mary's commitment and obedience: 'May it be to me as you have said' (Luke 1:37–38). And, given the poverty and insignificance of Nazareth, we are not surprised that Mary sees it all as a sign of God overturning human values: 'He has been mindful of the humble state of his servant... he has scattered those who are proud in their inmost thoughts... but has lifted up the humble' (Luke 1:48, 51–52). Can such a good thing come out of Nazareth? Is this really the place from where God's great master plan is going to be launched on the world?

Nearby Cana

There is also an episode in the Gospels relating to another village, a little to the north-east of Nazareth: the story of Jesus turning water into wine in 'Cana of Galilee' (John 2:1–11). The 'wedding miracle' is justly famous – 150 gallons (570 litres) of great new wine would have kept villagers happy for several days! It saved the host from permanent disgrace. But for John there are deeper meanings: God's overflowing generosity, and the new wine of Jesus' kingdom, which symbolizes the new era that Jesus would bring. There is also an exchange between Jesus and Mary which suggests that this marks a turning point for Jesus. Above all it is the first 'sign' of Jesus' glory, a revelation of Jesus' unique identity and power.

Jesus in Nazareth's synagogue

But for Luke the most important event, as he considers this area of Jesus' childhood, is what happened when Jesus returned one Sabbath and entered the synagogue (quoted on page 31). When Jesus read from Isaiah 61 and then said that this Scripture had been fulfilled in him, you could hear a pin drop. Jesus was saying that these Old Testament hopes found their fulfilment in him, that he was the One who was 'anointed' with God's Spirit, the one who had power to release captives, the one who announced the year of God's favour and good news to the poor.

'Only in their hometowns, among their relatives and in their own homes are prophets without honour'

Mark 6:4

Initially the response was favourable, but things turned nasty when Jesus hinted that this time of long-awaited fulfilment was going to include God blessing the Gentiles (just as God had blessed Naaman the Syrian in the days of Elisha). This did not fit the agendas and hopes of these loyal Jews (including many 'Davidides'). So the villagers turned him out, taking him to the 'brow of the hill'. Quite possibly this might have been the steep drop to the south, overlooking the Jezreel Valley, though it may have been one of the short, sharp drops on one of the terraced hills nearby. Either way, it was a dramatic end for Jesus' 'homecoming' to Nazareth. The local lad was dismissed. Perhaps because they remembered him when he was younger, they were prone to scorn. And Jesus drew out the salutary moral: 'I tell you the truth,' he continued, 'no prophet is accepted in his hometown' (Luke 4:24).

Locating of Cana

The precise location of Cana is disputed, but it will have been somewhere between Nazareth and Lake Galilee. In John 4:46–54 Jesus (located in Cana) pronounces to a royal official that his son, who was dying of a fever in Capernaum, would not die but live. The man heads off and meets messengers coming up from Capernaum with news that his son had recovered at one o'clock the previous afternoon – the exact moment when Jesus had spoken the word. From this meeting (approximately half way between Capernaum and Cana) we can deduce that the total distance between them was perhaps a 6 to 8 hour walk – around 15 to 20 miles (24 to 32 kilometres).

John always refers to the village as 'Cana of Galilee', presumably in order to distinguish it from another town of the same name (perhaps the one much further to the north near Sidon mentioned in Joshua 19:28). By the fourth century, however, the location of Jesus' Cana was unknown. In his *Onomastikon* (written around AD 290) Eusebius hazards a link with the Joshua reference, but in due course visitors to the region chose instead to identify Cana with the village (now known as Kefr Kenna) just 4 miles north-east of Nazareth. This was conveniently nearby, *en route* to the lake, and not far too from Mount Tabor, which around this time was being identified as the scene of the transfiguration (see page 96). The choice appears to have been driven largely by practical convenience, and probably not by prior tradition.

In recent years archaeologists have suggested that a far more likely sight is Khirbet Qana. This is some 8 miles (13 kilometres) north-east of Nazareth. Recent archaeology has revealed a small village, laid out in an orderly manner with a good number of cisterns dotted among the houses. As the crow flies, the distance from Khirbet Qana to Capernaum is roughly 17 miles (27 kilometres).

This is an important story for a variety of reasons. For students of history, it is the earliest ever account of what happened in Jewish synagogues in the first century. There are some fascinating details here about regular Sabbath worship – for example, the attendant bringing out the relevant Scripture scrolls and the invited reader standing to read them.

For Luke, however, this episode serves as a manifesto of what Jesus had come to do. He deliberately places it at the start of his account of Jesus' adult ministry (even though he knows that Jesus has already started his healing work in Capernaum), so that his readers can understand Jesus' purposes straightaway: he has come to bring good news, freedom and sight – not just for those in Israel but also for the Gentiles. The arrival of this good news may cause division, and Jesus may tragically be rejected by many who had the best opportunity to respond, but it is still good news – intended for all.

'Nazareth? Can anything good come from there?' Yes, says Luke, Nazareth was the starting point for

Left: The synagogue recently built within 'Nazareth Village'. Synagogues had one doorway (often facing Jerusalem) and seating on all sides. We can imagine the eyes of all fixed on Jesus as he sat down after reading the Isaiah scroll.

the 'good news' (the 'gospel'), which was intended to be a blessing for all the world. Nazareth may seem like a backwater, totally insignificant in the world's eyes; but this was God's chosen place among humble people from which the gospel has now gone out to the 'ends of the earth'.

And ever since, his followers have embraced these humble beginnings by declaring their allegiance to 'Jesus of Nazareth'. Some even call themselves 'Nazarenes' or are called that by others (*Notzrim* is the Hebrew word use by Jewish people to describe Christians). To follow the One from tiny Nazareth is to accept that sometimes others will see this as vaguely ridiculous: '*Nazareth*? Can anything good come from there?'

Nazareth Today

'Nazareth: from which Christ gained his name "the Nazarene"; and from which we who are now called "Christians" long ago gained the name "Nazarenes". [The village] is still to this day in Galilee… near Mount Tabor.'

Eusebius, Onomastikon 138–140

Nazareth today is a large sprawling town. Apart from a new development (called Nazareth Illit, or 'upper Nazareth' on a hill to the east, which is for Jewish residents), the population is made up of Israeli Arabs (65 per cent Muslim, 35 per cent Christian). The ancient village lies at the centre, on the north-west side of the busy High Street.

In recent years there has been heated controversy over the intended building of a mosque in this area, but at present the **Church of the Annunciation** still very much dominates the skyline, with its large conical dome visible from far away.

This modern church, built by the Franciscans, stands over some ancient ruins that may well have been Jesus' childhood home. It is built with split levels. The large and spacious upper church (with colourful depictions of Mary from different nations all around its walls) is used for regular worship and caters well for the many international

Key dates: Nazareth

4 BC	Death of Herod the Great. Jewish uprising results in destruction of neighbouring Sepphoris.	c. AD 200	Rabbi Judah ha-Nasi leads the Sanhedrin in Sepphoris and oversees compilation of the *Mishnah*.	c. AD 383	Egeria is shown a 'big and very splendid cave in which Mary lived' (Peter the Deacon, section T).
3 BC	Herod Antipas begins rebuilding Sepphoris as his new capital. Return of Jesus' family from Egypt.	c. AD 200	Julius Africanus recounts that some Jewish Christians, associated with Jesus' family, still live in Nazareth (Eusebius, *Ecclesiastical History* 1:7).	c. AD 650	Arculf is shown 'two very large churches' (over possible sites of Jesus' home and the scene of the annunciation).
c. AD 28	Jesus' return to Nazareth synagogue.			c. 1099	Crusaders build a church dedicated to the annunciation over a cave in the centre of Nazareth.
c. AD 58	Possible visit of Luke to Galilee to research Jesus' life and meet some of his relatives.	AD 251	A Christian called Conon (martyred in Asia Minor) states: 'I am of Nazareth in Galilee; I am of the family of Christ, to whom I offer worship from the time of my ancestors' (*Analecta Bollandiana* 18:180).	c. 1620	Franciscans permitted to buy back the ruins of the Annunciation church.
c. AD 95	According to Eusebius, *Ecclesiastical History* 1:7, two grandsons of Jesus' brother, Jude, are brought before the Emperor Domitian, but dismissed as politically innocuous.	c. AD 330	Count Joseph of Tiberias gains permission from Emperor Constantine to build churches in Sepphoris and Nazareth (Epiphanius, *Against Heresies* 30:11).	c. 1730	Franciscans rebuild this church.
				1955	Franciscans demolish this church to make way for the present building (dedicated in 1968).

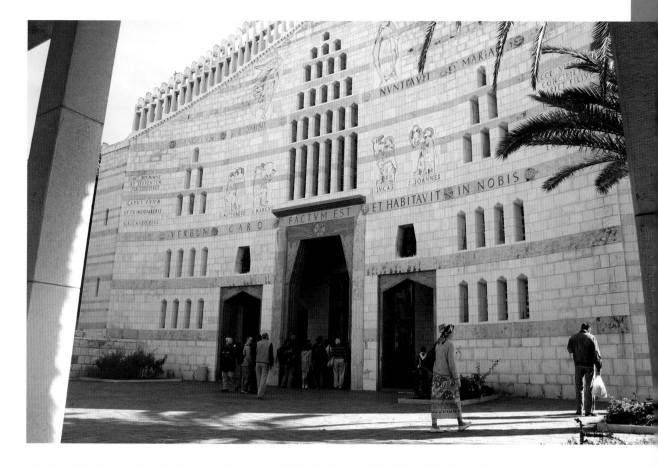

pilgrims. The lower church incorporates some of the features of the Crusader church, and has the atmosphere of a dark, mysterious crypt. It also gives visitors the opportunity to look down to yet another level, where there are clear signs of Byzantine structures centred round some caves. In the fifth century there was a small church here (with an adjacent monastery) which itself contained an earlier (pre-Constantinian?) baptistery. Just to the side is a mosaic floor with an inscription: 'gift of Conon, deacon of Jerusalem'. This probably dates to the early middle of the third century (if Conon is to be identified with the resident of Nazareth of the same name, known to have been martyred in AD 251). Evidently the small caves here were deemed significant by the earliest Christians. We may well therefore be dealing with an ancient tradition that links us to the first century – perhaps the synagogue or (more likely?) the home of Jesus.

Just to the north of the church there is a **museum** which contains numerous artefacts dating back to the first century: one can see here oil presses and house foundations that would have been part of the Nazareth known to Jesus. There are also some inscriptions suggesting that Byzantine Christians viewed this site as a 'holy place'.

Around 150 yards (137 metres) to the west (under the property of the **Sisters of Nazareth**) there are also some ruins that may date back to the first century, though some think they are Crusader: you can see stone walls and the doorway of a home.

The western façade of the Church of the Annunciation, depicting the gospel writers and (above) Gabriel's visit to Mary. The main text above the door is in Latin: 'the Word became flesh and dwelt among us' (John 1:14).

The Nazareth Decree

'It is my will that graves and tombs lie undisturbed for ever… Respect for those who are buried is most important; no one should disturb them in any way at all. If anyone does, I require that he be executed for tomb robbery.'

This so-called 'Nazareth Decree' has aroused considerable interest. Found on a stone slab in the Nazareth area, it was brought to Paris in 1878. It is dated to the first century and appears to convey an order from the Roman emperor – possibly Claudius (emperor from AD 41–54) – in the period when Galilee was brought back directly under Roman rule.

The imperial decree may well have been a response to tomb robbing in general. Yet some have wondered if this was somehow connected to the rumours circulating about the disappearance of Jesus' body from his tomb in Jerusalem. Was this decree set up in Nazareth because this small village was known to have been Jesus' childhood home and had given its name to his followers (the 'Nazarenes')? Had the disciples' teaching about the resurrection reached the ear of the Roman authorities? Jesus' followers were certainly accused quite early on of having stolen Jesus' body (Matthew 28:13–15), so this decree may well have been an early response designed to quash these rumours as soon as possible.

However, even if there is no conscious connection with Jesus of Nazareth, this decree still reveals that the imperial authorities in this period saw grave robbery as an extremely serious crime – indeed as a capital offence. This only makes it yet more unlikely that the (already fearful) disciples would have risked such an act.

The most intriguing aspect of these excavations, however, is a first-century tomb: four or five people can fit inside the burial chamber and just by the low doorway is a rolling-stone. In the time of Jesus this may have been a Jewish necropolis, just outside the village. Some then have speculated that this might have even been the tomb of Joseph. In any event it gives the visitor a very good example of the size and shape of tombs in the time of Jesus. And, given that Nazareth was so tiny in the first century, visitors can be fairly confident that they are walking in areas where Jesus too would have walked in his childhood.

Other things to see in Nazareth include:

The Church of St Joseph

Built in 1914 over a medieval church with an underground chamber, this location became associated in recent centuries with Joseph's carpentry shop.

Mary's Well

This well is situated about 450 yards (400 metres) to the north-east of the Church of the Annunciation (further along the High Street). It was presumably the site of the town's well back in the first century. It is therefore referred to as 'Mary's Well', with some suggestions that the annunciation may have occurred in this vicinity. As a result there is a Greek church nearby dedicated to St Gabriel. This contains some beautiful frescos and gives visitors a very good idea of Orthodox church architecture.

'Nazareth Village'

This recently created village is located on some ancient terraces about half a mile to the south-west of the Church of the Annunciation. This is a great new site to include in a visit to Nazareth.

Life in Jesus' day

Nazareth in Jesus' day would have been tiny. Some think there would have been up to 1,000 residents, but others suggest that it contained no more than twenty homes. Although craftsmen (like Joseph) may have commuted to work in neighbouring Sepphoris, many of Nazareth's residents would have been shepherds or workers on the land round about (some down in the Jezreel Valley). The climate was reasonably temperate, as it was spared some of the extremes of both heat and cold found not far away (either down in the Jordan Valley or high up in Upper Galilee).

Some of the farms were owned by larger landlords, who could force the peasant farmers into dire straits. Labourers' earnings were minimal. In addition a range of taxes was imposed upon the population. There was also the 'Temple tax' of two drachmas, which all Jewish families paid annually towards the Jerusalem Temple.

According to Jewish Law, Jewish men over the age of twelve were supposed to go up to Jerusalem each year for all three of the major festivals, but in practice they may only have managed a Passover visit once every few years. It was a major undertaking, which would have taken them away from their work for up to three weeks. No doubt villagers took it in turns to look after each other's property while they were away, and travelled together on the road as much as possible. Luke reports that Joseph and Mary took Jesus up to Jerusalem at the critical age of twelve (Luke 2:41–52), but we have no idea on how many other occasions they had made this excursion as a family.

The wheel below shows the months of the Jewish year and their relation to religious festivals and agricultural seasons.

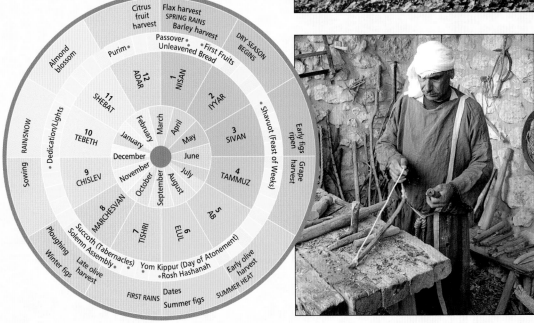

For example, in Nazareth village you can see a reconstruction of a first-century synagogue (built entirely with techniques and material known to have been in use in the first century) or have an authentic 'first-century' meal, seated under a large tent. There are also other features, which give an excellent idea of village life in Jesus' time. The village is located on a line of ancient terraces that would undoubtedly have been in existence in the time of Jesus. Wandering through this area, preserved from modern development, you get a rare glimpse of the landscape and hillsides that Jesus would have known as a boy.

The River Jordan

In the fifteenth year of the reign of Tiberius Caesar… the word of God came to John son of Zechariah in the desert. He went into all the country around the Jordan, preaching a baptism of repentance for the forgiveness of sins. As it is written in the book of the words of Isaiah the prophet:

'A voice of one calling in the desert,
"Prepare the way for the Lord,
make straight paths for him.
Every valley shall be filled in,
every mountain and hill made low.
The crooked roads shall become straight,
the rough ways made smooth.
And the whole human race will see God's salvation."'

John said to the crowds coming out to be baptized by him, 'You brood of vipers! Who warned you to flee from the coming wrath? Produce fruit in keeping with repentance. And do not begin to say to yourselves, "We have Abraham as our father". For I tell you that out of these stones God can raise up children for Abraham. The axe is already at the root of the trees, and every tree that does not produce good fruit will be cut down and thrown into the fire… I baptize you with water. But one more powerful than I will come, the thongs of whose sandals I am not worthy to untie. He will baptize you with the Holy Spirit and with fire. His winnowing fork is in his hand to clear his threshing-floor and to gather the wheat into his barn, but he will burn up the chaff with unquenchable fire.'

Luke 3:1–9

Baptism and renewal

From some of the ways in which people speak of the River Jordan, one might imagine that it was an enormous river like the Nile or the Amazon. Some hymns use it as an image of the river of death, which is impassable unless God leads us through it.

In fact the Jordan is tiny. Rarely is it more than 15 yards (13 metres) wide. Not for nothing did Naaman (an army officer from Assyria in around 730 BC) dismiss it in condescending tones: 'Are not even the Abana and Pharpar, the rivers of Damascus, better than any of the waters of Israel?' (2 Kings 5:12). Once or twice a year it may be affected by a flash flood, but otherwise its path is a slow, endless meander along the floor of the Jordan Valley. Its northern section flows from the foothills of Mount

'When I tread the verge of Jordan,
bid my anxious fears subside.
Death of deaths, and hell's destruction,
land me safe on Canaan's side.'

William Williams, 'Guide me, O Thou Great Jehovah'

Hermon down to Lake Galilee; its main southern section from the Lake to the Dead Sea. The length of this southern section is no more than 66 miles (105 kilometres), but its many bends probably add another 30 per cent to its actual length. It is also scarcely navigable, being punctuated by shallow rocks in many places, and leading nowhere – except the lifeless heat of the Dead Sea.

The River Jordan in the Old Testament

Yet by the time of Jesus this tiny, insignificant river had become associated in biblical thought with some key episodes in Israel's life.

First, this was the eastern border of the 'Promised Land' (see Deuteronomy 3:17): it was the river that Moses himself never crossed, but through which his successor Joshua led the ark of the covenant; it was where the Israelites 'consecrated' themselves afresh to the Lord on their fearful approach to Jericho (Joshua 3–4). Twelve stones, selected from the riverbed, were then placed on the riverbank as a reminder to Israel of God's help at this crucial point in their national life – their moment of entry into the land he had promised them. They remembered it as being similar to the crossing of the Sea of Reeds on their escape from Egypt, a significant 'rite of passage' for their forefathers.

Secondly, it was associated with the great prophets from the eight century BC – Elijah and Elisha (see 2 Kings 2). Before his departure in the 'chariot of fire', Elijah had passed through the River Jordan, using his cloak to strike the waters. When Elisha was then left stranded and alone on its eastern side, he had to exercise faith by using Elijah's cloak in the same way. Those who observed the miracle that followed then declared that Elijah's spirit was now evidently resting on Elisha. It was a sign that he had truly taken up Elijah's 'mantle'. As the Jordan had witnessed Joshua taking over from Moses, so now it witnessed Elisha taking over from Elijah.

The third episode came a few years later in the story of Naaman (mentioned above). Without coming out to meet him, Elisha sent word to this important official that his leprosy would be healed if he washed himself seven times in the Jordan. After scenes of arrogant protest, Naaman was persuaded by his servants to obey the 'man of God' and 'his flesh became clean like that of a young boy'. This Gentile man, working in the army of the enemies of Israel,

then confessed: 'Now I know that there is no God in all the world except in Israel' (2 Kings 5:14–15).

The tiny Jordan thus had some significant biblical resonances: it was a place of new beginnings, both for individuals and for Israel; a place of healing and inclusion for those outside Israel; and a place that revealed God's faithfulness and power.

New beginnings

So it is no coincidence that this is the place associated with the ministry of John the Baptist, the river into which he called the people of Israel to be baptized. For this was the biblical place *par excellence* in which to make a new start.

There was a new start here for *the nation of Israel*. According to the biblical writers, just as God had marked out his people here in the past, so now this was the place where he marked out for himself a new people. In calling them to be baptized, John was giving Israel a new sign to demonstrate their place within God's people. Indeed he was offering them something very similar to 'proselyte baptism', which is what *non*-Jews went through when they wished to 'convert' and to join the people of Israel. So John was giving a startling challenge here to Israel – it was as though their old membership subscriptions had expired and everyone had to subscribe afresh. They could not rely simply on being a descendant of Abraham: '...do not begin to say to yourselves, "We have Abraham as our father". For I tell you that out of these stones God can raise up children for Abraham' (Luke 3:8).

This was also the place where Israel had been called to be 'consecrated' afresh to God in preparation for the new thing that he was about to do in their midst. Many, of course, disliked this challenge

Qumran, the Essenes and John the Baptist

'In the desert prepare the way for the Lord; make straight in the wilderness a highway for our God' (Isaiah 40:3). There is little doubt that these words inspired John the Baptist. He saw himself as the one called into the desert to prepare God's people for the day when God would fulfil his promises to Israel.

Yet these words had also inspired others. Back in the second century BC, a group established itself in a monastic settlement in the desert, close to the shores of the Dead Sea. They had become disillusioned with the Temple hierarchy in Jerusalem and believed they had been called to create an alternative community. Their founding leader was someone whom they referred to as the 'Teacher of Righteousness'. Located in the desert, devoted to the close study of the Scriptures and especially the prophetic books, they may well have seen themselves, through Isaiah's imagery, as a kind of

vanguard – an 'advanced troop' preparing for God's age of fulfilment. Perhaps their commitment to holiness and devotion to Scripture would hasten the day of God's coming to his people.

This group was known as the Essenes. Josephus lists them as one of the main 'philosophies' within first-century Judaism and gives us an idea of their lifestyle. There were Essenes who lived in normal communities throughout the land, but the majority clustered around this Dead Sea settlement, known as Qumran. The small community expanded around 100 BC. It was temporarily disbanded during the years when Herod the Great was fighting in the area to secure his control of the land (40–37 BC); but it regrouped, staying at the site until the Roman armies removed them in AD 68.

The ruined site today gives a strong sense of this community's life. There is a cemetery containing over a thousand graves. Those that have been excavated suggest the community was chiefly (but not exclusively) male; they are likely to have had a rule of celibacy. Clearly visible too are their aqueduct, dining room, council chamber and scriptorium. This 'writing-room' would have been the place where they copied the Scriptures, as well as the other literature for which Qumran has become famous.

In 1947 a Bedouin shepherd boy (called Muhammed ed-Dhib) discovered some scrolls in a cave to the west of the site. In due course a total of eleven caves yielded up these ancient treasures, known as the 'Dead Sea Scrolls'. Presumably these scrolls would have formed part of the community's library but were stored here for safe keeping when the Roman armies approached.

The scrolls have since been a rich quarry for scholarly enquiry and argument. Of particular interest is the complete scroll of the book of Isaiah (now on display in the Israel Museum in Jerusalem). Dating from the first century, this precedes what was previously the earliest copy of the Hebrew text by nearly a thousand years. Yet a comparison of the two manuscripts shows how little the text had been altered during that interval. This provides strong evidence for the thoroughness of those who transmitted the sacred text and gives us greater confidence that the biblical texts we have today are very close to the original.

The Qumran community also gives us a fascinating window into the milieu in which Jesus and his followers were operating. It also helps us understand the New Testament in a new light. For example, the theme of 'light' and 'darkness' is very common in John's Gospel.

that John was making to their ancestral privilege. So they took offence – in a manner not unlike that of Naaman. And, as we saw in Chapter 2, this same violent reaction occurred just a little later when Jesus pointedly cited this same episode of Naaman as an example of God's intention to bless those outside Israel (Luke 4:24–30). Both John and Jesus provoked strong responses – at least when they challenged Israel's presumed status. Meanwhile Luke, himself a Gentile, could not help but notice this theme of God's desire to include Gentiles in his new people. Hence he introduced John's preaching by the Jordan with a quotation from Isaiah 40:3–5, which predicted a time when 'all people' would 'see God's salvation'. God was doing a new thing – for a new people.

Scholars had imagined that this was a sign of Greek influence, but now this can be seen as part of the thought-world of first-century Jews in Palestine. There are also other intriguing parallels between Qumran and the New Testament. In particular, the Essenes longed for the Jerusalem Temple to be replaced – perhaps by a people endowed with God's spirit of holiness, not by a further physical building. The New Testament writers show that Jesus himself thought along these lines – though believing himself, singularly, to be its fulfilment – and that his followers soon saw themselves (through their organic connection to Jesus) as the new Temple community, filled with his Holy Spirit (1 Corinthians 3:16–17; 1 Peter 2:4–10).

It remains unclear, however, whether the New Testament writers would have been consciously familiar, if at all, with any of the Essenes' writings. It is also unclear whether John the Baptist or Jesus himself had any direct contact with the Essenes. There are certainly close parallels between the ascetic style of John's ministry and the disciplined lifestyle of the Qumran community, and John's baptizing ministry (on the southern stretch of the River Jordan) was certainly not so far away. Yet John's message ultimately had a different focus. He was not simply *hoping* for God's promises to be fulfilled; he was acting as a prophet, announcing their *arrival* and pointing to a particular individual who would be the key agent in implementing this promised new age.

Far left Late afternoon view (looking southwards) of the ruined buildings at Qumran.
Left One of the many caves (cave 4), just to the west of the Qumran community, where they hid their valuable scrolls.

There was also a new beginning for *individuals*. Luke describes John being quizzed by individuals in the crowd, by tax collectors, by soldiers. His answers are blunt, giving people practical ways of showing that they have truly repented. But, though forthright and occasionally severe, his words are still described as 'good news' (Luke 3:18); for this call to repentance is accompanied by the promise of the 'forgiveness of sins' (Luke 3:3). Luke loves this theme of God's forgiveness, which the coming of Jesus (heralded by John) now makes possible for individuals. John's strange ministry down by the Jordan is a sign that God is now at work to bring his deep forgiveness to anyone who deeply repents and comes back to him.

Finally the Jordan also marked a new beginning for *Jesus himself*. All the gospel

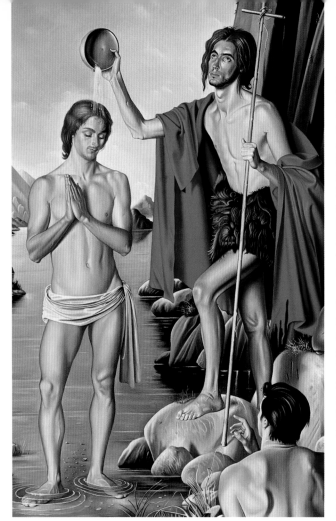

The portrayal of John sprinkling water over Jesus' head (not placing him under the water) goes back to earliest times.

writers see Jesus' coming to be baptized by John as the effective start of his adult ministry. Jesus humbly accepts John's call to a national renewal and restoration; Jesus joins in the hopes of his people, identifying with them in this act of turning to God. So he himself is baptized by John in the Jordan. And, as he does so, God gives him a unique confirmation of his calling: the Holy Spirit descends on him and a voice declares, 'You are my Son, whom I love; with you I am well pleased' (Luke 3:22).

These words mark the start of Jesus' messianic mission. Israel's God is affirming and strengthening his beloved son, expressing the pleasure and delight of a father. No doubt these words could have been said at an earlier point – there is nothing about this episode that *only now* makes these things to be true of Jesus – but they are given as a clear sign that something new is about to take place.

For there is to be a 'handover' of responsibilities. Just as Moses had given way to Joshua and Elijah to Elisha, so now Jesus is given a confirming sign that his ministry will take up from where John's has left off (Jesus in fact compares John to Elijah in Luke 7:27). And in the same way that the River Jordan marked the launch of Joshua's campaign into the Promised Land, so now the same river is marking the launch of the campaign of this latter-day Joshua ('Jesus' is the Greek form for the Hebrew name 'Joshua', meaning 'salvation'). Both would suffer in what followed; it would not be straightforward. But this time the weapons used would not be those of war; and this time the goal would not be the extension of God's rule over just the 'land of promise'. Instead, God would be established as king over 'all the earth'. '*All* people', Luke foresaw, would have the opportunity to 'see God's salvation'.

Key dates: the River Jordan

c. 1400–1200 BC	The Israelites cross the River Jordan on entering the Promised Land (Joshua 1–4). The Psalmist later compares this with Israel crossing the Sea of Reeds (Exodus 14).
c. 870 BC	Elijah departs in a 'chariot of fire' and Elisha tells Naaman to wash in the River Jordan seven times (2 Kings 2–5).
c. AD 27	Jesus baptized in the River Jordan by John the Baptist.
c. AD 240	Origen visits 'Bethany beyond the Jordan' as part of his 'search for the traces' of Jesus and his disciples (*Commentary on John* 6).
c. AD 290	Eusebius refers to the popularity of visiting the River Jordan (*Onomastikon* 58:19).
AD 333	The Bordeaux Pilgrim visits the Jordan, something which Constantine on his deathbed regrets he has not been able to do (Eusebius, *Life of Constantine* 4:62).
1917	The British Army build the Allenby Bridge near Jericho.
1967	With Israeli control over the West Bank, the Jordan becomes the border with the Kingdom of Jordan.

The River Jordan Today

The River Jordan today has changed little since biblical times, but it is now more difficult to access – at least in the areas associated with Jesus and John the Baptist.

This is because for much of its route the river functions as the international border between Israel and the Hashemite Kingdom of Jordan. There is a cordoned-off area along its western banks which is heavily patrolled, and a dusty track that is checked twice a day for any footprints. There are now a couple of crossing points between Israel and Jordan, the chief of which is the **Allenby Bridge** (near Jericho), a temporary pontoon-style bridge built by the British under General Allenby in 1917.

This means that visiting any supposed **site of Jesus' baptism** is difficult. To be honest, there is not much to see. Visitors to this area sometimes content themselves with a visit to the Orthodox monastery of **St Gerasimus** (the silver-domed church visible to the east of Jericho), which is the nearest people can normally get to the river. Only once a year (in January, on the Orthodox feast day for the baptism of Jesus) are

Baptism in the Jordan

Works such as Eusebius' *Onomastikon* give us evidence that Christian visitors in the period of the early church were often very keen to see the River Jordan. The Emperor Constantine, who was baptized just before his death in AD 337, admitted that he had hoped to be baptized in the Jordan. Others no doubt felt the same. And in the fourth century we learn of pilgrims travelling home with bottles of Jordan water for use in baptism back home – a practice that continues to this day.

Those who have been baptized already often still have the desire to be immersed in the same waters in which Jesus was baptized; so this has frequently been combined with a renewal of baptismal vows. For others there has been a symbolic connection between such immersion in the Jordan and preparation for death. The whole imagery of baptism is indeed associated with going down into death and coming up again in resurrection life, as the apostle Paul explains in Romans 6:1–4.

This has been particularly keenly felt in the Orthodox strand of the Christian Church. To this day Greek pilgrims often purchase their own burial 'shroud' in Jerusalem (at the place of Jesus' death and resurrection) and then travel down into the River Jordan, where they are immersed in water while wearing their shrouds. It is a powerful liturgical preparation for that final 'crossing' through death. If the ancient Greeks had their myths concerning Charon (the ferryman who took people across the River Styx from this life to the underworld of Hades), then their modern counterparts have replaced the Styx with the Jordan, and Charon with Jesus Christ. This Orthodox practice was also remarkably popular for the many Russians who visited the Holy Land in the decades prior to the Russian revolution in 1917.

Early icons of Jesus' baptism tend to portray Jesus standing waist-high in the river, with John pouring water over his head. This

may well reflect accurately what John the Baptist did. Equally it may also reflect the baptismal practice of the early church, which suggests that 'total immersion' was not the norm. Instead Byzantine baptisteries tended to allow room for the candidate to walk down into some water; the person baptizing them would then scoop up water and sprinkle it over them as they stood. Often the baptisteries were built so that the candidates would move from west to east, in this way symbolically renouncing the works of darkness and turning towards the light. They would then be given white robes of some kind as a further symbol of forgiveness and new resurrection life.

Above Modern Greek Orthodox pilgrims renewing their baptismal vows by the Jordan (at Yardenit) and wearing their white burial shrouds.

Christian visitors allowed down to the river-site where they remember this event.

Very recently, however, some fascinating archaeological remains have been discovered on the Jordan's east bank (and so not in Israel). This almost certainly marks the site that the Byzantines would have used for their commemoration of Jesus' baptism. John's Gospel expressly states that John was baptizing (at least for some of the time) 'at Bethany on the other side of the Jordan' (John 1:28). This **Bethany** (not to be confused with the Bethany on the Mount of Olives) seems to have been known to the Christian scholar, Origen, in the third century and its site may well have been preserved by these Byzantine ruins.

Later in John's Gospel we learn that John was also baptizing 'at **Aenon** near Salim, because there was plenty of water' (John 3:23). The precise location cannot now be determined, but may well have been some 20 miles (32 kilometres) further north of the Jericho area. Again this is now inaccessible for political reasons; so modern visitors tend to visit **Yardenit**. This is a section of the Jordan, immediately after it leaves Lake Galilee, which is entirely within Israel and is therefore easily accessible. There is no explicit tradition that John baptized as far north as this (his focus was in the Judean Desert to the south), but this is now the most convenient place for anyone wishing to go down into the waters of the Jordan.

There are other opportunities, however, to see the Jordan in its upper section north of Lake Galilee, especially from the bridge on the road between Capernaum and Bethsaida. In Jesus' day this would have been the border between Galilee (the territory of Herod Antipas) and Gaulanitis (the territory of his brother Herod Philip). As a border it may well have been 'patrolled' by tax collectors. 'As Jesus walked along, he saw Levi son of Alphaeus sitting at the tax collector's booth' (Mark 2:14). If not in Capernaum, Levi's booth may well have been somewhere near here, close to the River Jordan.

In Jesus' day the area to the north of this was covered with a small lake (Lake Semechonitis in what is now known as the **Hula Basin**), but this has now been silted up. Finally the Jordan can be seen at various points close to its source in the foothills of Mount Hermon – especially at **Dan** and **Caesarea Philippi**.

Although this river appears to be small and insignificant, it is hard to overestimate its continuous importance. Water is essential for survival, and throughout history the Jordan has been the chief means by which the cool waters from snow-clad Mount Hermon are drawn south into the land. Just west of Capernaum is a major pumping-station which draws off the water and pumps it by underground pipelines to many centres of population. This explains in part why the water levels in Lake Galilee are now often so much lower than they have been, compared both to the biblical era and to quite recent times.

Yet its symbolic significance is also great. Through its occurrence in the biblical drama it has become identified as a key symbol of crossing over from one way of life to another: whether in baptismal imagery (from death to life) or as a metaphor for physical death itself (passing through death to life eternal).

'O, Jordan bank was a great old bank!
Dere ain't but one more river to cross.
We have some valiant soldier here,
Dere ain't but one more river to cross.
O, Jordan stream will never run dry,
Dere ain't but one more river to cross.
Dere's a hill on my leff, and he catch on my right,
Dere ain't but one more river to cross.'

Negro spiritual

The Judean Desert

Jesus, full of the Holy Spirit, returned from the Jordan and was led by the Spirit in the desert, where for forty days he was tempted by the devil. He ate nothing during those days, and at the end of them he was hungry. The devil said to him, 'If you are the Son of God, tell this stone to become bread.' Jesus answered, 'It is written: "People do not live on bread alone."'

The devil led him up to a high place and showed him in an instant all the kingdoms of the world. And he said to him, 'I will give you all their authority and splendour, for it has been given to me, and I can give it to anyone I want to. So if you worship me, it will all be yours.' Jesus answered, 'It is written "Worship the Lord your God and serve him only."'

The devil led him to Jerusalem and had him stand on the highest point of the temple. 'If you are the Son of God,' he said, 'throw yourself down from here. For it is written: "He will command his angels concerning you to guard you carefully; they will lift you up in their hands, so that you will not strike your foot against a stone."' Jesus answered, 'It says: "Do not put the Lord your God to the test."'

When the devil had finished all this tempting, he left him until an opportune time.

Luke 4:1–13

Testing in the wilderness

The Judean Desert is lonely and inhospitable. So it was an odd place for Jesus to go to immediately after his baptism in the River Jordan. Why did he not start his public ministry straightaway? Jesus had a different priority: time alone with his God, and a deliberate resolve to face those temptations that would hover around him in that public ministry. The story may seem strange to our ears, but the secret 'success' and power of his later work, so the gospel writers claim, originated here.

Features of the desert

In geographical terms the ancient land of Israel was in many ways quite remarkable. Unlike its neighbouring countries, which were predominantly made up of arid deserts, Israel was a small, fertile stretch of land that benefited from the rain blown in from the Mediterranean. The Old Testament describes it as a 'land flowing with milk and honey' (Deuteronomy 6:3). Certainly the Israelites, on entering the land, would have noted a sharp contrast with the land of Egypt where they had been slaves: this was a land where water was not only found in rivers (like the Nile and the Jordan) but also fell from the sky.

Yet this is only true for the western side of the land. Running down the centre of the country is a spine of hills that causes the land to the east to fall effectively into a 'rain shadow'. This is the Judean Desert into which Jesus went after his baptism in the Jordan.

It is a place of austere beauty and an almost deafening silence; a place where human beings are acutely conscious of their frailty and utter dependence on water for brute survival. And yet in biblical times it was also a place where people went to find solitude and space, to hear the voice of God addressing them above the cacophony of other competing demands and voices. John the Baptist had begun his ministry here, 'a voice of one calling in the desert' (Isaiah 40:3). It was now the place to which Jesus naturally turned as he sought to forge his own ministry on the words of God.

View westwards across the Judean Desert, looking up the Wadi Qelt towards the outskirts of Jerusalem.

52

The desert in the Old Testament

As Jesus went into the desert he would have been aware of all that the desert had come to signify in the experience of God's people up to that point.

Israel had been forged as a nation by its experience in the 'wilderness': forty years of wandering in the Sinai and Negev Deserts *en route* from Egypt to the Promised Land. This had been the time for receiving God's Law (including the Ten Commandments), a time of testing, preparation and trusting in God's provision (the gift of 'manna' and water from the rocks). Yet it was also the time when the Israelites 'grumbled' against God and which they would later look back on as a period of disobedience to their Redeemer God: 'Today, if you hear his voice', the Psalmist later exhorted them, 'do not harden your hearts as you did... in the desert, where your fathers tested and tried me, though they had seen what I did... They are

'They spoke against God, saying, "Can God spread a table in the desert?"'

Psalm 78:19

Geological features of the Desert

The Holy Land is a land of great variety, ranging from the fertile plains along the Mediterranean coast to the distinctive hill-country running down the centre of the land like a spine from north to south. It also contains two significant deserts: to the south, the Negev Desert which stretches across to the Sinai Desert of Egypt, and to the east, the much smaller Judean Desert (to the north and west of the Dead Sea).

The Judean Desert is effectively in the 'rain shadow' caused by the hill-country – the rain clouds coming in from the Mediterranean are pushed up higher as they pass over the hills and fail to drop much rain. So, as the terrain drops down slowly towards the River Jordan, the annual rainfall also rapidly decreases. Settled human habitation and farming become increasingly difficult.

Unlike some other deserts the Judean Desert is not swept by sand dunes. Instead it is covered with numerous rocky hills, some of them quite rounded. Yet there are also occasional sharp ravines, often marking the line of a dry riverbed (or *wadi* in Arabic), which two or three times a year may become the scene of a 'flash flood'. Water is scarce, but for those with desert experience, it can often be found not so far away, for there are a handful of beautiful springs and a few tiny oases.

Geologically, the higher, western side of the Judean Desert is referred to as 'Syrian Steppe': rough terrain with just enough rainfall to help nomadic people (such as the Bedouin) to eke out an existence. Further to the east we enter a band of rocky desert more like the Sahara. Yet even here, in late spring, the hills can be covered with a sheen of

green as wild grasses and flowers put in a brief appearance before the full heat of summer. Then we come finally to the Jordan Valley, which is effectively the continuation of the East African Rift Valley and is all below sea-level. Thus in the short journey up from Jericho to Jerusalem (a total of only 16 miles or 26 kilometres) Jesus and his disciples would have passed through no less than four major geological areas: from the Rift Valley, through Saharan desert and Syrian Steppe to Jerusalem, which is itself in the hill country and therefore watered by clouds from the Mediterranean. They would also have climbed well over 3,000 feet (914 metres): Jerusalem is at least 2,400 feet (750 metres) above sea level, the Dead Sea 1,350 feet (411 metres) below.

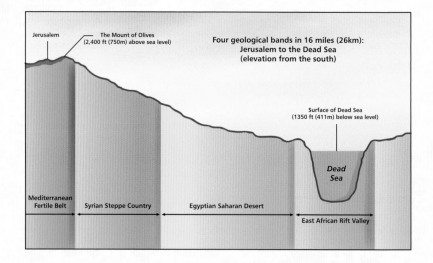

Jerusalem

The Mount of Olives
(2,400 ft (750m) above sea level)

Four geological bands in 16 miles (26km):
Jerusalem to the Dead Sea
(elevation from the south)

Surface of Dead Sea
(1350 ft (411m) below sea level)

Dead Sea

Mediterranean Fertile Belt

Syrian Steppe Country

Egyptian Saharan Desert

East African Rift Valley

a people whose hearts go astray' (Psalm 95:7–10). Later generations were supposed to learn the lessons of the desert: Trust in God, not in yourself, and listen to his Word.

The desert also features quite frequently later in the Old Testament. Sometimes it is the place of escape and refuge, as in the case of the young David on the run from King Saul. Sometimes it is the place of recovery and recuperation, as in the case of the exhausted Elijah. After his encounters with the prophets of Baal, Elijah 'was afraid and ran for his life', going southwards beyond Beersheba into the Negev Desert. Once there

he was reinvigorated by hearing the 'gentle whisper' of God's Word – or, as the older versions say, a 'still, small voice'.

It is also the place of prophecy and expectation, as people looked forward to what God would do for his people after they had gone into exile. When the prophet Isaiah announces his message of 'comfort' in Isaiah 40:1–9, he sees this new work of God as strangely linked to the desert:

Comfort, comfort, my people…
A voice of one calling: 'In the desert prepare the way for the Lord;
make straight in the wilderness a highway for our God…
The rough ground shall become level, the rugged places a plain.
And the glory of the Lord will be revealed…'
'All people are like grass. The grass withers and the flowers fall,
but the word of our God stand for ever.'…
You who bring good tidings to Jerusalem…
say to the towns of Judah, 'Here is your God!'

Just as in the time of the exodus God had used the desert to teach his people, so now, when he moves to restore them from their place of exile, the desert would be involved. There is 'good news'; there are dramatic events as God's people return from exile through the desert; there is a fresh recognition of God's powerful Word; above all, the desert is to be the place of preparation for the arrival of the Lord himself – 'Here is your God!'

The 'Saharan' section of the desert, covered in a sheen of green at the end of March.

'He turned rivers into a desert, flowing springs into thirsty ground, and fruitful land into a salt waste, because of the wickedness of those who lived there. He turned the desert into pools of water and the parched ground into flowing springs.'
Psalm 107:33, 35

Now we begin to sense the rich, biblical resonances 'when the Word of God came to John in the *desert*'. 'He went into all the country around the Jordan,' we read, 'preaching a baptism of repentance for the forgiveness of sins' (Luke 2:3). In other words, just as Isaiah prophesied, the exile caused by God's judgment on sin is now at last coming to an end. And, just as Isaiah had seen this as preparation for the arrival of the Lord himself, so now John warns clearly: 'One more powerful than I will come' (Luke 3:16).

There are similarly powerful resonances when Jesus himself then goes into the desert. Like David, he is a new king in the making, having to face off his enemies. Like Elijah, he is a new prophet at the start of a demanding ministry needing reassurance that he is truly speaking for God. Above all, just as Israel as a nation spent 'forty years' in the desert, so Jesus now spends 'forty days' in the wilderness of Judea – this time not to grumble against God but to trust in his Word, thereby succeeding where Israel had failed.

'But he brought his people out like a flock; he led them like sheep through the desert.'

Psalm 78:52

Luke's account corroborates this parallel between Jesus' story and the ancient story of Israel by reporting that Jesus quoted from the early chapters of Deuteronomy no less than three times (Luke 4:4, 8, 12). These key passages had been given to the Israelites at a critical juncture before they entered the Promised Land: would Israel be a faithful 'son' in the service of God? Now Jesus, in preparing for the 'Promised Land' of his own ministry, is meditating on what it means to be a faithful Israelite, a true Israel. How can he ensure he proves faithful where they proved faithless?

There is also the fascinating possibility that the order of the three temptations mirrors something of Israel's journey into the Promised Land: first the Israelites grumbling in the desert about their food; then Moses climbing Mount Nebo from where he could glimpse the land of promise; and then their eventual establishment of Jerusalem and its Temple as the place for divine worship. In a similar way Jesus is now tempted first by desire for bread, then he is led up to a 'high place' where he is 'shown

all the kingdoms of the world', and finally he is brought to Jerusalem's Temple pinnacle. We are being given clear signals that redemption's story is being repeated, entering its critical moment of fulfilment, and that the outcome of the story rests squarely on the shoulders of this one called Jesus.

Prayer and solitude

So Jesus goes off alone, away from the crowds. Throughout Luke's Gospel Jesus often slips away to escape from the crowds and to get some time alone to pray. Jesus was a man of prayer, someone who sought appropriate solitude so that his relationship with God remained uppermost and his vision of God fresh.

By going out into the desert now, Jesus is underlining the absolute priority of God in his life and ministry. He is acknowledging the true source of his own power and authority. He is going *into* God that he may then go out into his ministry *with* and *for* God. Not surprisingly, we note immediately after this that he 'returned to Galilee in the power of the Spirit' (Luke 4:14). Luke asserts that he had gone into the desert earlier 'full of the Holy Spirit' (Luke 4:1), but now that *fullness* of the Spirit has been transformed into true *power* through the lens of prayer and focused solitude.

There are lessons here that have inspired Jesus' followers ever since: the value of fasting at key junctures in life; the use of Scripture in times of testing; the determination to find appropriate solitude before times of real exertion; the importance of preserving the integrity of one's inner life so that it is of a piece with one's public persona.

'The desert... an opportunity to face our loneliness and turn it into solitude'

Henri Nouwen

Combatting evil

There are lessons too about the reality of spiritual warfare. Although it may sound strange to our ears, the story of Jesus' temptation is portrayed as a battle with a personal source of evil, described by the gospel writers as the 'devil'. This Evil One is threatened by the manifestation of the One who is the 'Son of God'. So he relentlessly challenges this supposed identity ('if you are the Son of God'), perhaps aware that sowing confusion about a person's God-given identity can be one of the most effective means of undermining their subsequent actions for good. He tries to twist the meaning of Scripture. He also falsely claims to be the one with authority over the 'kingdoms of the world', thereby usurping the authority of God himself.

Jesus' answers are blunt and direct, giving no quarter to the devil. He parries the falsehoods with straight quotations from Scripture ('It is written...'). He will not let God's Word be twisted or distorted. If Scripture is being wrongly used, he will not abandon it, but rather will use it more truly and more deeply. If the devil wants to be worshipped, Jesus will offer worship to God alone and preserve his own total obedience to the Lord his God. There is profound irony here. For, although of all human beings Jesus alone would in time be seen as the One who was himself worthy of worship, at this stage Jesus remains resolutely under God's authority – not letting the Evil One come subtly between himself and his Father, not letting his own right to be worshipped be twisted by the devil's false claim to have that right.

We are touching here on things beyond the borders of language. Behind their artful simplicity the gospel writers are hinting at a whole mysterious depth to the ministry of

Jesus that a superficial eye might miss. At this juncture in the story one might even sense that the very nature of God is being put under attack. Certainly the whole success of Jesus' mission seems to hang in the balance.

But the moment passes. Jesus' resolution holds firm. He will not be swayed. He will not abuse the spiritual power and authority that God has truly given him. He will not 'fall' and go over to the 'dark side'. This One, sent by God with his power and authority, will prove true, and will see his vocation through to the bitter end.

The essential battle has been won, and, although the devil leaves him only until another 'opportune time', the outcome of those later skirmishes has already been determined. Even in the agony leading up to the cross, when the temptation to seek an alternative route to glory will be so powerful and when the powers of evil are reaching their fiercest and darkest, this Jesus will prove true.

Life in the place of death

So even in the desert the cross is never far away. In this sense, the desert becomes the unexpected place where the great victory was accomplished. This 'desert campaign' proves decisive in the war. The desert thereby becomes, paradoxically, not a place of death and fatality but rather the place of life and the seedbed of hope. Jesus goes down deep enough to transform the dry and dusty desert into a place of utmost beauty.

And this is something that his followers can treasure when they face their own, smaller but still frightening, deserts. For, following Jesus' lead, they may be able to fulfil the picture in Psalm 84:

'Blessed are those whose strength is in you…
As they pass through the desert valley,
they make it a place of springs.'
Psalm 84:5–6

A small oasis (Ein Farah) in the desert, roughly half way between Jerusalem and Jericho.

Key dates: the Judean Desert

c. 1020 BC	David flees into the desert from King Saul (1 Samuel 24), going to places such as Ein Gedi on the western shore of the Dead Sea.	AD 330	Arrival of Chariton, first based at Ein Farah, then later (AD 340) at Douka (much later identified as the Mount of Temptation), and finally at Souka (*Wadi Khareitun*).	AD 492	Sabas visits Hyrcania (known then as the 'Castellion') and establishes the monastery of the Scholarius.
c. 870 BC	Stories of Elijah being fed by ravens in the Kerith Ravine (to the east of River Jordan) and his fleeing to Mount Horeb (1 Kings 17–18) .	AD 405	Euthymius (AD 377–473) at Ein Farah; later he establishes a *laura* at Khan el-Ahmar, converted into a *coenobium* after his death (478–81).	AD 575–618	Golden age of the monastery of St George of Khoziba (established c. AD 480) overlooking Wadi Qelt; this traditionally became the site where Elijah stopped *en route* to Mount Horeb (1 Kings 19).
c.120 BC	John Hyrcanus builds a fortress (Hyrcania), later used by Herod the Great as a prison and the place of execution, for example, of his son Antipater.	AD 455	Gerasimus (died AD 475) founds a combined *coenobium* and *laura* near the River Jordan (*deir Hajla*).	AD 716	St John of Damascus (AD 675–749) writes in defence of icons while resident in Mar Saba.
AD 67	Simon Bar Giora's use of caves at Ein Farah in rebellion against the Romans, according to Josephus, *War* 4:9.	AD 457	Arrival of Sabas (AD 439–532). He later founds Mar Saba (the 'Great Laura') overlooking the Kidron Valley. By his death over 70 monastic settlements exist in the desert east of Jerusalem.	1100s	Jesus' 'Mount of Temptation' is identified with *Jebel Quruntul* (overlooking Jericho).
AD 68–73	Roman armies pass through (including the destruction of Qumran and the siege of Masada, further south on the west coast of the Dead Sea).	AD 470	Martyrius (AD 457–86), later Patriarch of Jerusalem, establishes his monastery 5 miles (8 kilometres) east of the city (now in the suburb of Maale Adummim).	1875–1895	Greek Orthodox reconstruction of the Monastery of Temptation.
				1930s	Construction of a tarmac road from Amman to Jerusalem by British Mandate, some of it along the route of the ancient Roman road.

The Judean Desert Today

For many westerners, caught up in their hectic, busy schedules, a visit into the desert of the Bible can be a life-changing experience. Suddenly silence replaces noise, stillness replaces bustle, and a developed slow and steady pace takes the place of urban rush and deadlines. Although tourist itineraries themselves can often be marked by a similarly hectic style, wise travellers will at some point insist on tasting the desert for themselves.

There are many ways this can be done and many different aspects of the desert to explore. Here's a list of some feasible options, depending on available time and preferences:

- hiking through bizarre, coloured canyons in the **rock formations** to the south-west of the Dead Sea;
- walking through a *wadi* until you find the spring of water at its source (for example, at **Ein Gedi** or **Ein Farah**);
- approaching **Masada** from its western side (on the tarmac road from Arad);
- visiting the archaeological remains at **Qumran** and then walking up to the cliffs behind to explore the caves where some of the Dead Sea Scrolls were found (see page 46);
- turning off the engine of the car or bus and then asking every passenger to find their own rock for 45 minutes (as long as they do not go out of sight!);

- taking a ride up towards the **Mount of Temptation** monastery and then climbing for another 30 minutes to the promontory's peak for a spectacular view over the Jordan Valley;
- walking the stretch of **ancient Roman road** between Jerusalem and Jericho that follows the ridge overlooking the Wadi Qelt (ideally going downhill!);
- going down into the **Wadi Qelt** itself and walking alongside the water channel until you reach the monastery of **St George of Khoziba**;
- walking further beyond St George's until the *wadi* opens up impressively overlooking Jericho, close by the remains of Herod's Palace;
- going in search of monastic ruins such as **St Euthymius' monastery** (to the south of the main road from Jerusalem to Jericho) or **St Martyrius'** (though less pleasant, now surrounded by the high-rise apartments of the Maale Adummim settlement);
- taking a taxi from Bethlehem out through Beit Sahour to find the famous monastery of **Mar Saba** (St Saba), there to meet some of the Greek Orthodox monks or to wander along the cliffs overlooking the Wadi Kidron.

None of these is especially difficult, though thorough preparation and sensible precautions are clearly necessary: good footwear, adequate protection from the sun, agreed contingency arrangements, a supply of water, some basic foodstuff and a salt-cellar (vital to prevent dehydration!). Such ventures may take up more time than more 'regular' kinds of visit, but that is precisely the point – getting away from schedules for

Modern visitors experiencing the narrow path of the ancient Roman 'road' from Jerusalem to Jericho.

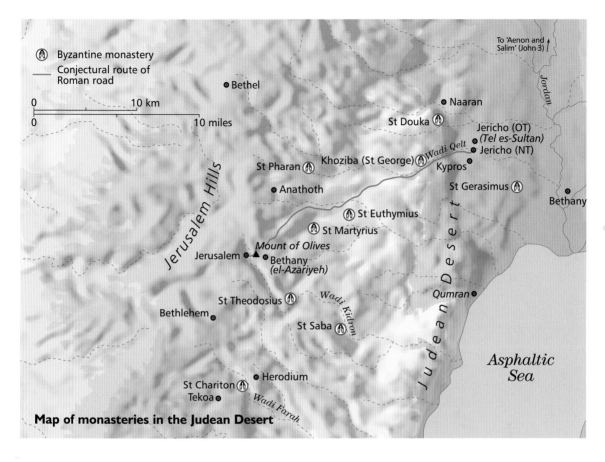

Map of monasteries in the Judean Desert

a place of hushed quiet. The traveller who makes it into the desert rarely comes back untouched in their spirit and without a desire for more.

People are lured into the desert for different reasons: the physical challenge; contending with the heat by day and the cold by night; learning to pace oneself; and becoming more conscious of one's physical strengths and frailties.

Another reason is an interest in Christian history. Five hundred years after the time of Jesus this desert had itself become a veritable 'city', littered with hundreds of monks.

To visit these monasteries is to be struck again with the example of this determined dedication to hear God's call, to imitate Christ, and to hunger after God's Spirit. The precise shape of that calling may be quite different in our modern and busy lives, but its challenge does not go away.

And a brief visit to any monastery that is still operational gives you a further opportunity: to meet people who have embraced that calling in our own day, often having lived very ordinary and 'urban' lives previously. **Mar Saba** (like the monasteries on Mount Athos in Greece) is open only to men, but women are welcome at **St George's** or the **Mount of Temptation**. Even so, most visitors leave intrigued and with questions in their minds: What makes them do it? Could I ever do such a thing, and if not, why not?

For whenever you are alone in the desert, the questions are bound to come. It is in the silence that we become attuned to the nervous inner noise within our own spirits.

The Desert Fathers

The monks of the Judean Desert are known as the 'desert fathers'. They were part of a movement that flourished for around 300 years throughout the Middle East. Monasticism began in Egypt, when a man called Anthony (AD 250–356) first went out to live alone in the desert around AD 280. Soon it spread to Palestine, which had the obvious attraction of being located in the desert where Jesus himself had prayed. However remote their cells, the monks knew that just over the ridge of the western horizon were the 'cities of the Incarnation' (Jerusalem and Bethlehem), which witnessed to the truth of the same Christ whom they now were following. Spirituality was thereby anchored in history, the desert never far removed from the city.

There were two different patterns of monastic life. Some monks lived in solitude in a string of cave-cells, or *lauras* (from the Greek word for 'lane'), spread along a track or lane. They would then come together at weekends in a nearby building. Other monks lived in *coenobia* (from the Greek meaning 'common life'). Here the monks would live together in a shared building, which often looked like a square fort. This pattern was developed by a man called Pachomius (AD 292–346). In Palestine, these two patterns were often combined, with young monks being trained in the *coenobium* before being allowed to live out in the remote cells. The combined pattern was developed by Gerasimus, known as the 'founder and patron of the Jordan wilderness'. In most cases there would normally be a senior monk recognized as the 'Abba' or 'Father' who would be an experienced spiritual master, able to offer wisdom and advice to apprentice monks.

The monks' cells would sometimes have a small plot of cultivated land nearby; they would contain a reed mat, a sheepskin and a vessel for food and water. A monk's daily pattern would consist of meditation on Scripture, reading the Psalms, and also manual work (for example, weaving baskets which could then be sold by the monastery). The staple diet was water and a type of bread (known as *paxamatia*), which could remain edible for several days. Soup, olives, dates and lentils seem to have been quite common; figs, grapes and wine were occasional luxuries.

The Sayings of the Desert Fathers (a collection of stories preserved by later monastic communities as a guide) gives us a good insight into their raw, godly wisdom. Silence and solitude are of course extolled as key virtues: 'A brother went to ask for advice; he was told, "Go and sit in your cell, and your cell will teach you everything." '

The movement effectively came to an end in AD 614, when the Persian armies swept across Palestine; indeed several monasteries have preserved the skulls of the monks killed during that invasion. Some key figures – such as Chariton, Euthymius, Sabas and Theodosius – had founded significant monasteries but only the monastery of Mar Saba survived and has been in use continuously since that period.

The Spiritual Meadow

One special record of monastic life in the Judean Desert comes in a work known as *The Spiritual Meadow*, written around AD 615 by a man called John Moschus. Although born near Damascus he had been a monk for more than ten years in the Judean Desert, first at the large monastery of St Theodosius (near Bethlehem) and then at the more remote monastery founded by Chariton at Paran. He had also spent another ten years as a monk around Mount Sinai.

Aware of the threat posed by the Persians, he and his younger friend Sophronius left the Holy Land, first for Alexandria and then for Rome. After John died Sophronius returned; indeed he was the patriarch of Jerusalem when the Muslim armies arrived in AD 637. Much of John's life had been spent seeking out the best examples of the monastic life, which he sensed was being increasingly compromised, and his writing bears testimony to the last full flowering of the monastic ideal in the Holy Land.

Here is one of his stories, which speaks of a hard-working monk operating in the Judean Desert between Jerusalem and Jericho – the same road used by Jesus as the setting for the parable of the Good Samaritan.

There was a monk living in the cells of Choziba, who was very considerate of those in need. He would travel the road from the holy Jordan to the Holy City carrying bread and water. If he saw a person overcome by fatigue, he would shoulder that person's pack and carry it all the way to the holy Mount of Olives.

He would do the same on the return journey if he found others, carrying their packs as far as Jericho. You would see him, sometimes sweating under a great load, sometimes carrying a youngster on his shoulders. There was even an occasion when he carried two of them at the same time.

Sometimes he would sit down and repair people's footwear, for he carried with him what was needed for that task... If he found anyone naked, he gave them the very garment that he wore.

The Spiritual Meadow, chapter 24

Right The Greek Orthodox monastery of St George of Khoziba, perched on the edge of the Wadi Qelt.

It is in the solitude that we face our own aloneness and confront what it means to be a unique solitary individual, often emerging with a new understanding of ourselves and a new appreciation of our friends and companions.

And in *this* desert especially, perhaps because of its biblical resonances and history, it becomes easier to think of the biblical God – the God who, according to that Bible, called his people through a desert experience, who called prophets out into the desert so they could hear his Word, and who eventually sent Jesus into this desert so that he could win a victory in human history over the forces of darkness.

So, strangely, of all the places in the land of the Bible, the desert can sometimes be the place where it is easiest to get close to the Jesus of the Gospels. He may prove elusive to our imagination in the towns and cities, even in the green hills of Galilee; but something about the hard rocks of the desert brings him closer to our gaze – as one who truly shared our human frailty and can strengthen us in our hours of weakness. In the desert, though we may outwardly be alone, we discover that perhaps we are not so alone after all.

Galilee and its villages

Jesus returned to Galilee in the power of the Spirit, and news about him spread through the whole countryside. He taught in their synagogues, and everyone praised him.
Luke 4:14–15

Scenes of public ministry

From the desert Jesus 'returned to Galilee'. At this point, if not earlier, the centre of his operations shifted from Nazareth, his childhood home, to Capernaum (which means the 'house of Nahum'), a small harbour town on the northern shore of Lake Galilee. 'Leaving Nazareth, he went and lived in Capernaum' (Matthew 4:13), which came in due course to be referred to as 'his own town' (Matthew 9:1). So began Jesus' 'Galilean ministry', which lasted for three years.

Galilee (or '*the* Galilee') probably acquired its names from the Hebrew word *galil* meaning 'circle'. Geographically it was divided into two quite different areas, which Josephus described as 'Upper Galilee' and 'Lower Galilee'. Upper Galilee was the high mountainous region to the north and

Galilee is often envisaged as a haven of peace. It is worth remembering, then, that Josephus' description of the lake and the Plain of Gennesaret come in the section of his *History of the Jewish Wars* that describes Vespasian's ruthless suppression of the First Jewish Revolt in AD 67. The citizens of Tiberias surrendered but there was a fierce battle at Tarichaea (Magdala). There was also a sea-battle on the lake, at the end of which, says Josephus, 'the number of the slain (including those that were killed in the Tarichaea) was 6,500' (*War* 3:10).

So Jesus' ministry on the same shoreline (just 30 years earlier) had been in a Galilee that was on the edge of revolt; it would not take much for his preaching about the 'kingdom of God', if misunderstood, to be the spark that sent the whole region up in flames.

Here is Josephus' description of Lake Galilee and the Plain of Gennesaret:

> Now this lake of Gennesaret is so called from the country adjoining to it. Its breadth is forty furlongs, and its length one hundred and forty; its waters are sweet, and very agreeable for drinking… the lake is also pure, and on every side ends directly at the shores. It is also of a temperate nature when you draw it up, and of a more gentle nature than river or fountain water, and yet always cooler than one could expect in so diffuse a place as this is. Now when this water is kept in the open air, it is as cold as that snow which the country people are accustomed to make by night in summer. There are several kinds of fish in it, different both to the taste and the sight from those elsewhere. It is divided into two parts by the river Jordan…
>
> The country also that lies over against this lake has the same name of Gennesaret. Its nature is wonderful as well as its beauty; its soil is so fruitful that all sorts of trees can grow upon it, and the inhabitants accordingly plant all sorts of trees there… One may call this place the ambition of nature, where it forces those plants that are naturally enemies to one another to agree together. It not only nourishes different sorts of autumnal fruit beyond people's expectation, but preserves them a great while; it supplies people with the principal fruits, with grapes and figs continually during ten months of the year, and the rest of the fruits as they become ripe together through the whole year; for besides the good temperature of the air, it is also watered from a most fertile fountain. The people of the country call it Capharnaum…
>
> **War 3:10**

Elsewhere he paints a picture of Galilee as a populous region that was a hotbed of unrest:

> There are two Galilees, called the Upper Galilee and the Lower… These two Galilees, of so great largeness, and encompassed with so many nations of foreigners, have been always able to make a strong resistance on all occasions of war; for the Galileans are inured to war from their infancy, and have been always very numerous; nor has the country been ever destitute of men of courage, or wanted a numerous set of them… Moreover, the cities lie here very thick, and the very many villages there are everywhere so full of people, by the richness of their soil, that the very least of them contain above fifteen thousand inhabitants.
>
> **War 3:3**

west, which forms a natural boundary with the modern state of Lebanon. Upper Galilee rose in parts to over 3,000 feet (1,000 metres) above sea level; Lower Galilee (around the lake) was 600 feet (180 metres) below and included some fertile areas that produced loaves and grain. Most of Jesus' public ministry, however, would have taken place in 'Lower Galilee'.

Galilee's beautiful lake

Central to this area was Lake Galilee itself. A freshwater lake, replenished by the melting snows of Mount Hermon brought down into it by the River Jordan, this beautiful inland 'sea' was surrounded by numerous harbours and was the centre of a lively fishing industry. From a bird's eye view, it formed the shape of a harp: 16 miles (26 kilometres) from north to south, and 9 miles (14.5 kilometres) at its widest point from west to east. Indeed one of its ancient names – the 'Sea of Kinnereth' – may have been associated with the Hebrew word *kinnor*, which meant 'harp'. Josephus referred to it instead as the Lake of Gennesaret; the gospel writers used this name but also called it the 'Sea of Galilee' or even the 'Sea of Tiberias' (after the new city built recently on its south-western shore). Two miles (3 kilometres) south of Tiberias the waters left the lake along the next section of the River Jordan, on their way to the very different, salt-filled Dead Sea. Lake Galilee, by contrast, was teeming with life.

The lake was surrounded along many of its shores by quite steep hillsides, so it was often well protected from winds and storms. Yet if the wind changed direction, rushing upon the lake through one of the valleys, the lake could suddenly become rough and dangerous. Being some 640 feet (210 metres) below the level of the

Looking through the Arbel Pass towards the Plain of Gennesaret.

Mediterranean, the lake could also become unbearably hot and stifling in summer months. At other times of year, however, it could be a place of welcome warmth for those who had been up in the hills.

Around the lake there was a variety of different landscapes. To the east was the barren stark ridge of the hills of Gaulanitis; to the north, where the waters of the River Jordan passed through a smaller lake (Lake Semechonitis), there was a marshy, inhospitable area, which was gradually being silted up over the years by the Jordan; to the north-west (behind Capernaum) were some low hills, formed from volcanic black basalt rock, and the fertile Plain of Gennesaret; and to the west stood the powerful cliffs of the Arbel Pass, which prevented people travelling by land from the Plain down to Tiberias (approached instead from the south-west, or by boat).

'Galilee of the Gentiles': the Jewish frontier territory

The Old Testament refers to this area on remarkably few occasions. It suddenly comes to the fore in the eighth century BC, when Isaiah prophesies that God will 'honour Galilee of the Gentiles', with people there seeing 'a great light' (Isaiah 9:1–2). Matthew expressly sees Jesus' ministry here as the fulfilment of this prophecy (Matthew 4:13–16).

'In the future he will honour Galilee of the Gentiles, by the way of the sea, along the Jordan. The people walking in darkness have seen a great light; on those living in the land of the shadow of death a light has dawned.'
Isaiah 9:1–2

The locations of Jesus' ministry in Galilee

Jesus' ministry was not confined to his base in Capernaum. Both Luke and Matthew speak of two other towns (Chorazin and Bethsaida), noting that these three towns (together, presumably, with the areas surrounding them) were the places in which, up to that point, 'most of his miracles were performed' (Matthew 11:20). So when we read of Jesus healing a leper, a man with a 'shrivelled hand' or a crippled woman, these miracles may have taken place in or around these other two towns (Mark 1:40–45; 3:1–6; Luke 13:10–17).

Yet Jesus' ministry spread further still. It was, after all, an itinerant ministry. He 'travelled about from one town and village to another' and spoke on one occasion of having 'nowhere to lay his head' (Luke 8:1; 9:58); and he sent his disciples out to 'every town and place where he was about to go' (Luke 10:1). The Gospels indicate that Jesus' itinerant ministry thus took him far and wide. He is described as ministering in the village of Nain (some 20 miles or 32 kilometres to the south-west of the lake), and, on at least one occasion, in the area of 'Tyre and Sidon', known as Syro-Phoenicia (Luke 7:11; Mark 7:24–30). There are further references to places the location of which is now uncertain, such as Magadan and Dalmanutha (see Matthew 15:39; Mark 8:10).

There are also references to less specific locations. Jesus is frequently depicted in people's houses enjoying a meal (Luke 7:36–50; 14:1–24). He walks through a cornfield and is criticized for letting his disciples pluck the grain (Luke 6:1–5). He seeks a 'solitary place' not far from Capernaum where Simon and others find him praying (Mark 1:35–37).

However, the following might act as a useful summary of his ministry around Lake Galilee.

In Capernaum: Jesus teaches and performs an exorcism in the synagogue; many people are healed, including Simon Peter's mother-in-law and a paralytic, who is lowered down to him through a roof; Jesus calls a tax-collector named Levi, and then attends a dinner at Levi's home; a servant in the household of a Roman centurion is healed (Mark 1:21–26, 29–34; 2:1–17; Luke 7:1–10). (Capernaum may also be the location for Jesus' healing of the daughter of the synagogue-ruler called Jairus, and for a pointed discussion, in which Jesus is compared to Beelzebub – see Mark 5:21–43; 3:20–30).

By the lakeside: Jesus calls the first disciples; he commands Simon to put down his nets again; he teaches the crowds from the boat (including the parable of the sower); and the risen Jesus appears to Peter and the other disciples one morning after a night's fishing (Mark 1:14–20; Luke 5:1–11; Mark 3:9–10; Mark 4:1–25; John 21:7–23).

On the lake itself: Jesus calms a violent storm; he walks on the water; and he has a discussion about the 'yeast of the Pharisees' (Mark 4:35–41; 6:47–52; 8:14–21).

On the north-eastern side of the lake: Jesus feeds 5,000 people in a 'solitary place', probably somewhere beyond Bethsaida; in Bethsaida Jesus also heals a blind man (Mark 6:32–46; 8:22–26).

On the south-eastern side of the lake and in the Decapolis: Jesus heals a demon-possessed man known as 'Legion'; he then heals a deaf and mute man; Jesus feeds 4,000 people (Mark 5:1–20; 7:31–37; 8:1–9).

On the Plain of Gennesaret: a time of general healing (Mark 6:53–55).

Mountains, hills and 'level places'

In Matthew's Gospel, there are also frequent references to Jesus being on 'mountains' (Matthew 5:1; 28:16). Matthew is drawing a parallel here between Jesus and the figure of Moses, who was himself associated with Mount Sinai. Yet Matthew and the other gospel writers knew full well that the 'mountains' around Lake Galilee were small when compared with Sinai. It might be better to translate this as Jesus being 'in the hills' or 'on the hillside' (the Greek word can mean either 'hill' or 'mountain'). Matthew is simply helping his Jewish readers to make a useful connection between Jesus and Moses.

Yet Jesus clearly did take advantage of the hills overlooking Lake Galilee when he needed to draw aside from the crowds. Sometimes this may have led him to the lonely heights on the east of the lake. At other times the lower hills behind Capernaum would have sufficed. These lower hills may be where he chose his twelve disciples or preached what we now know as the 'Sermon on the Mount' (Mark 3:13; Matthew 5–7). Yet these extended low-lying hills also have many plateaus within them. So, without any contradiction, Luke may have chosen instead to report that Jesus preached this sermon standing 'on a level place' (Luke 6:17). Matthew is simply emphasizing Jesus' authority, Luke his accessibility.

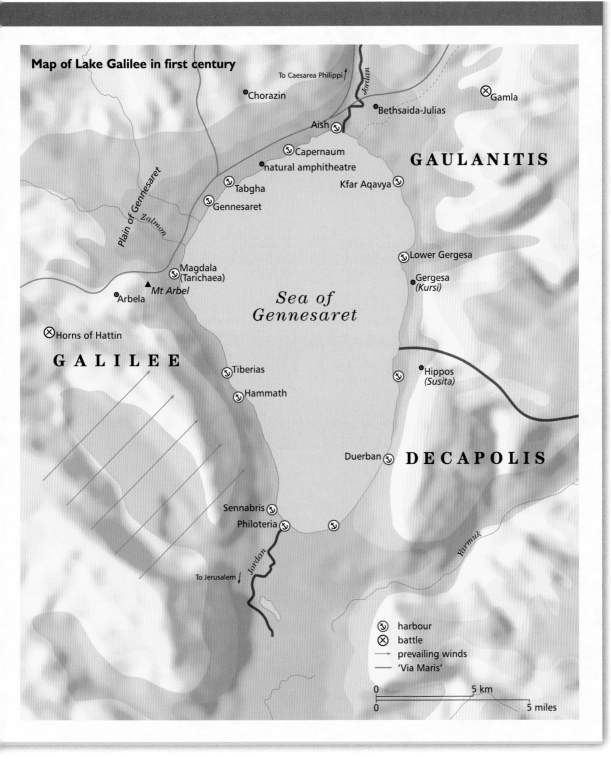

Map of Lake Galilee in first century

To Caesarea Philippi

Chorazin

Gamla

Bethsaida-Julias

Aish

Capernaum

GAULANITIS

natural amphitheatre

Kfar Aqavya

Tabgha

Gennesaret

Plain of Gennesaret

Zalmon

Lower Gergesa

Magdala
(Tarichaea)

Gergesa
(Kursi)

Mt Arbel

Arbela

*Sea of
Gennesaret*

Horns of Hattin

GALILEE

Tiberias

Hippos
(Susita)

Hammath

DECAPOLIS

Duerban

Sennabris

Philoteria

Jordan

Yarmuk

To Jerusalem

⚓ harbour
⊗ battle
→ prevailing winds
— 'Via Maris'

0   5 km
0   5 miles

Aerial view of Capernaum by Lake Galilee. In the Franciscan enclosure the white stones of the large ancient synagogue contrast with the black basalt of the tiny homes nearby. The new red-domed church belongs to the Greek Orthodox.

However, Isaiah's observation that Galilee was 'of the Gentiles' is an important reminder that, ever since the Assyrian invasions of that period (when many of the Israelite population were deported), Galilee's population would always have contained a mixture of Jews and non-Jews. Unlike Samaria to the south, quite a number of the Jewish population returned to the Galilee region from their periods of exile, and by Jesus' day Jews may have been in the majority. Yet it was still very much 'frontier territory'. Compared to Jerusalem in the south this was a place in which Jews were constantly interacting with Gentiles.

In such an environment the Jewish population would constantly be considering how they could keep themselves distinct from their Gentile neighbours. 'Boundary markers' – such as circumcision, observing the Sabbath, rules associated with food and hygiene, and frequent pilgrimages to Jerusalem – would all have had important resonances and significance within such a society. Anyone who challenged these boundaries, for whatever reason, could be seen as undermining the whole strategy of how Jews were to conduct themselves in such an area.

Not surprisingly, then, the Pharisees were a powerful lobby in the region. They had a vision of helping the 'people of the land' to live according to the Jewish Torah, thus hastening the day when God would rescue his people from pagan domination. The Pharisees would let people know when they were unhelpfully 'collapsing the boundaries' and infringing their understanding of these practical laws and rules.

Certain areas were predominantly, if not exclusively, Gentile: the so-called 'Decapolis' (Greek for 'ten towns') to the east and south of the lake; possibly also the new city of Tiberias (built by Herod Antipas in honour of the pagan Roman emperor, and provocatively located on the site of an ancient Jewish cemetery). Elsewhere, however, it was a mixed, polyglot community where Jews and Gentiles lived alongside one another in an uneasy relationship. The local language was Aramaic, but Greek was common too as the *lingua franca* of the eastern half of the empire – the language used between different people groups, for example, in commerce and business transactions. At least two of Jesus' disciples (Andrew and Philip) had Greek names with no Aramaic equivalent and were later found to be Greek speakers.

Capernaum and international trade

All in all, then, Galilee had quite an international feel to it in the first century. Unlike Jerusalem, it lay on a main trading-route – the 'way of the sea' mentioned in Isaiah. This 'Via Maris' connected the markets of Mesopotamia and Damascus with the Mediterranean and Egypt, and it passed through the Plain of Gennesaret, along the northern shore of the lake – right through Capernaum.

Capernaum was also the last town before the new border (established after the death of Herod the Great in 4 BC) between Galilee 'proper' and Gaulanitis to the east. The border was at the crossing of the River Jordan. This meant that Bethsaida – the birthplace of some of Jesus' disciples, Philip, Andrew and Peter – was technically no longer in 'Galilee'. It also meant that Capernaum, as the border town, would be a place of increased revenue and a haven for tax collectors. It probably had both a customs office and a small garrison – hence Luke's reference to a Roman 'centurion' who had helped the poor citizens to build their synagogue (Luke 7:2–5). It is conceivable that the reason why these disciples had moved house to Capernaum was precisely because they could avoid paying repeated taxes as they transported their fresh fish to the places (like Magdala/Tarichaea on the western side of the lake) where their fish could be preserved.

As a result, Jesus' decision to base his ministry in Capernaum can be seen as quite strategic. Nazareth was indeed a by-water, but not so Capernaum. Though small and still fairly poor, it was located in a unique position – just right for a preacher who wished his message to be heard by as many people as possible. From 'Galilee of the nations' there would come in due course a 'light for the world'.

'News about him spread all over Syria... large crowds from Galilee, the Decapolis, Jerusalem, Judea and the region across the Jordan followed him.'
Matthew 4:24–25

Jesus' message and themes

According to the Gospels, Jesus' Galilean ministry was marked by two ingredients which may initially sound contradictory. On the one hand there was the sheer authority with which he taught: 'He taught them as one who had authority, not as the teachers of the law' (Mark 1:27). Jesus spoke directly and clearly about God as one who knew precisely what he was talking about. And this authority was endorsed by his actions: his awesome power over the great enemies of human experience – disease, disasters, demons and even death itself.

On the other hand, the Gospels emphasize the essential simplicity of Jesus' teaching

Galilean imagery in Jesus' teaching

The following list (taken in order from Luke chapters 5–15) gives an overview of the many images Jesus took from everyday life in Galilee to illustrate his teaching about God's kingdom. This list shows the colour and accessibility of Jesus' teaching. Simple, ordinary things could become the vehicle for conveying spiritual realities.

- wedding clothes and traditions
- wineskins
- stolen clothes
- sawdust in the eye
- bad fruit trees
- bad building foundations
- children calling out names in the marketplace
- different types of soil
- house lamps
- funeral practices
- ploughing
- eggs and scorpions
- armed robbery
- dirty dishes
- garden herbs

- unmarked graves
- cheap sparrows
- over-large barns
- ravens and lilies
- good and bad domestic managers
- family disputes
- weather forecasting
- a donkey needing water, or falling into a well
- mustard seeds and dough
- a hen with her chickens
- fields and cows
- military strategy
- useless salt
- lost sheep and coins

style and his accessibility to ordinary people. Jesus' teaching does not deal in abstracts but rather is filled with compelling, everyday examples. From his surroundings in Galilee, Jesus was able to find ample material to draw on.

Yet this very 'earthiness' of Jesus' teaching has sometimes caused people to conclude that his message was gentle. They miss the radical purpose for which Jesus was using such imagery. They conjure up a picture of Jesus as a wandering philosopher, speaking harmless truths in homely imagery, pointing to a divine reality that made few demands.

The truth is quite the reverse. He was proclaiming a radical new message – the kingdom of God. In other words, Israel's God was at last becoming king! Many of Jesus' hearers, of course, were longing for just this; they were ready to take up arms to bring in God's kingdom, if only it would bring about the end of domination by the pagan

Romans. Only thirty years earlier the Galileans had launched a rebellion against Rome (led by Judas the Galilean), but they had failed dismally. Thirty years after Jesus they would try again, and this time, as Josephus makes clear, the slaughter would be terrible.

Into this volatile, electrically charged situation came Jesus. He had the right message – about God's kingdom. No wonder crowds initially followed him, and many, we learn, wanted to make him their king. Yet somehow it was all 'upside down' and the wrong way round.

First, he implied, there was no point in fighting the Romans, for the 'peacemakers' were the ones that God would bless. Instead Gentiles were going to be included in this new kingdom of God. And some of the old ways of being Israel – of keeping themselves apart from Gentiles (like keeping the Sabbath and the food laws) – were going to become obsolete.

Secondly, the king of this kingdom was right there 'in their midst', he claimed; he was the very one who had been teaching them 'in their streets' (Luke 13:26). Jesus himself was the King, the long-awaited Messiah. But if he spoke openly about this, the crowds would almost certainly have misunderstood him. So Jesus spoke in parables and riddles, pointing clearly to the truth and only letting people into the secret gradually. Yet there was no doubting his intention. Jesus was calling his hearers to a radical obedience – to him! He was the one in whom they should put their trust. They were being called on a journey and he was the one they must follow. 'Follow *me*!'

The gathering storm

So, although Luke initially tells us of Jesus' popularity – as people flocked to hear him 'from every village of Galilee and from Judea and Jerusalem' (Luke 5:17) – Jesus' Galilean ministry was not all joy and light. People fell away and lost interest. When the challenge of Jesus' message began to be understood, it alienated as many people as it attracted. And there was a continual note of opposition and controversy throughout, not least from the religious leaders who could detect the radical direction of Jesus' teaching.

So the dark shadows of what would transpire in Jerusalem can be detected in Galilee too. 'The time will come', Jesus expressly teaches near the very outset of his ministry, 'when the bridegroom will be taken from them' (Luke 5:35). Indeed, pursuing Jesus' own marital imagery, we conclude that Jesus' Galilean ministry was no perpetual honeymoon. His message regarding the kingdom of God was radical and demanding from the outset. And, although some of the particular flash points of controversy were different here in this frontier-state compared with those found later in the capital city, we can sense the underlying continuity of his message. Jesus was announcing the dawn of a new age, focused on himself. Galilee was not a place of idyllic calm, but a place of gathering storm.

1350–1150 BC	References to the 'Sea of Kinnereth' at the time of Israel's conquest (Joshua 12:3; 13:27).	c. AD 27–30	Jesus' ministry around the 'Sea of Galilee' (Matthew 4:18; 15:29; Mark 1:16; 7:31), also known as the 'Sea of Tiberias' (John 6:1; 21:1).	c. AD 629	Possible destruction of Jewish synagogue in Capernaum by Christian community, when Byzantine rule is restored under Heraclius.
c. 730 BC	Isaiah prophesies that God will 'honour Galilee of the Gentiles'.	AD 67	The Roman forces under Vespasian besiege Gamla (Josephus, *War* 4:1–83) and destroy Bethsaida-Julias.	AD 700–900	School of Tiberias completes the 'pointing' of the Hebrew text of the Old Testament.
64 BC	Susita (a town on the eastern shore of Lake Galilee) is removed from Jewish control by Pompey and made part of the Decapolis.	c. AD 330	Count Joseph of Tiberias gains permission from Emperor Constantine to build churches in Galilee, possibly including a 'house-church, built over Peter's home in Capernaum' (Epiphanius, *Against Heresies* 30:11).	c. 1033	Destruction of Tiberias by earthquake.
c. 38 BC	Herod the Great 'flushes out' supporters of his rival Antigonus, who are hiding in the caves in Mount Arbel (Josephus, *Antiquities* 14:423–26)			1099	Crusaders under Tancred rebuild Tiberias.
4 BC	Susita reverts to being part of the province of Syria.	c. AD 383	Egeria notes the church built in Capernaum, and identifies the place of the feeding of the 5,000 at Heptapegon (Peter the Deacon 5:2–4).	1187	Saladin defeats the Crusaders at the Horns of Hattin (above Tiberias).
c. AD 20	Herod Antipas founds Tiberias in honour of Emperor Tiberius as the new capital of Galilee (instead of Sepphoris).	c. AD 400	Completion of Jewish *Gemara* in Tiberias.	c. 1894	Franciscans acquire site of *Tel Hum* (Capernaum).
c. AD 20	Herod Philip refounds Bethsaida-Julias (Josephus, *Antiquities* 18:28), probably in honour of Augustus' wife. This was the home of three of Jesus' disciples: Peter, Andrew and Philip (John 1:44).	c. AD 450	Building of new octagonal church over Peter's home in Capernaum.	c. 1933	Chapel built at Heptapegon (*Tabgha*) commemorating the story of John 21.
		c. AD 480	Building of new basilica at Heptapegon to commemorate feeding of the 5,000.	1938	Church built on the Mount of Beatitudes.
		AD 614	Possible destruction of Christian basilica in Capernaum by Jewish community during Persian invasion.	1982	Benedictine basilica built at Tabgha commemorating the loaves and fishes.
				1992	Franciscan construction of modern octagonal structure over Peter's home in Capernaum.

Galilee Today

Those who have never had the opportunity of visiting the Holy Land often imagine that visiting Galilee would be a highlight of any visit. And they would be right. This is not just because of the natural beauty of the lake and its surroundings: here, looking out on the unchanged contours of the land, it is quite easy to imagine scenes from the Gospels, knowing that Jesus looked out on these self-same views. In contrast to Bethlehem and Jerusalem, for example, the lack of noise and buildings can give space for people to gather their thoughts and refuel their imaginations.

The lake is not that large, so although there are many places to see, it is possible to cover these in a comparatively short time. We will be considering the sites in a clockwise direction, following an imaginary group of visitors who, having arrived at the

Visiting Galilee

Modern visitors often only have 24 hours or so in which to visit Lake Galilee. It is worth considering some of these questions before planning an itinerary.

Where to stay
Some prefer – especially during the late summer months, when the lakeside can be sultry and unpleasant – to stay some distance from the lake up in the hills (in Safat or even in Nazareth). Those staying near the lake can consider some of the more 'informal' options (camping or a kibbutz) or the hotels and Christian hostels in Tiberias.

When to visit
Those visiting during the winter, with its shorter hours of daylight, may have to omit some options. There is no doubt that for reasons of climate and colours a visit during April or early May is highly attractive (the lake can be covered in a heat-haze later in the year). However any visitors hoping to swim in the lake should be advised that the water is decidedly icy until well into the summer – much of it is recently melted snow from Mount Hermon!

Taking a boat trip
This can be a special experience, and larger groups are catered for by the boat companies in Tiberias, who sail the 'triangle' of Tiberias-Capernaum-Ein Gev. An early morning trip from Tiberias to Capernaum can work well, as can a late afternoon return from Ein Gev to Tiberias. Lunchtime options, with food on board, should also be considered.

Celebrating communion
Christian visitors may be keen to 'break bread' together at some point during their visit. This can be a powerful experience, providing an opportunity to draw together in a more reflective way the many spiritual insights they have received. Although small groups may be able to find a convenient location 'off the beaten track' or at their overnight accommodation, it is best to gain permission to use one of the designated sites: for example, at the Mount of Beatitudes or Tabgha; or perhaps in the chapel of the YWCA (a little north of Tiberias). The first two of these have great scenic advantages; however, they are run by Catholic communities, so non-Catholic groups will need to pay close attention to what the local communities will allow on their premises.

Visiting the Mount of Beatitudes
The site closes for a couple of hours at 12 noon. However, those who request to celebrate communion here and to have lunch at the hostel can stay on beyond that time. It becomes the perfect place for some quiet reflection in the midst of the day. And after lunch, there is always the possibility of walking down to the lakeside road. This only takes around 20 minutes, but gives visitors a great opportunity to walk quietly 'off the beaten track' in the Galilean hills.

---

southern end of the lake before sunset, then stay somewhere in Tiberias and have the whole of the next day free to explore the area.

Good views of the whole lake can be enjoyed from various places: for example, from the hills above Tiberias or Capernaum. A good first view, however, can be from the **south end of the lake**: for example, on the shore at the outlet into the River Jordan (near the turning to Yardenit), or by driving a little further round to the north-east to one of the viewing stations. On a clear day the snow-peak of Mount Hermon may be visible 60 miles (100 kilometres) to the north.

Modern Tiberias lies 5 miles (8 kilometres) up the western shoreline. As the main town on the lake, it offers visitors many necessary amenities, including a multi-media presentation on the area's geography and history, and even the opportunity to visit some thermal baths. Those with more time can visit the scattered archaeological remains of **ancient Tiberias** (set up in the hills to the south of the modern town): these include a basilica, a bath-house, a theatre and a shopping area. Further up on 'Mount Berenice' is a Byzantine church, later used by the Crusaders. From the second century onwards Tiberias became a flourishing centre for rabbinic Judaism. Here work was done on the *Gemara* (part of the *Palestinian Talmud*), and outside the city are the tombs of some major rabbis: Yohanan ben Zakkai (c. AD 90), Akiva (the rabbi who accepted Bar Kokhba as the Messiah in AD 130) and the great Maimonides (c. AD 1200).

The modern road going north from Tiberias blasts through the previously

'Capernaum, Bethsaida and Chorazin and the other villages in the Gospel are even now to this day pointed out around the lake of Tiberias. This Galilee in which the Christ of God passed most of his life...'

Eusebius, Commentary on Isaiah 9:1

Right: The hull of the so-called 'Jesus Boat', recovered from the bed of Lake Galilee in 1986.

impassable rocks of **Mount Arbel**. On the right there are some enclosed ruins, which probably mark the site of the ancient village of **Magdala** (also known as Tarichaea) – the original home, we presume, of the woman in the Gospels known as Mary Magdalene. A little further on there is a lakeside kibbutz called **Nof Ginnosar** (which houses the famous 'Jesus Boat').

On the left is the fertile **Plain of Gennesaret**, which Josephus described in such glowing terms (see page 66). Then, after passing the modern water-pumping station, visitors gain their first views of the area where Jesus began his adult ministry – in and around **Capernaum**. Much of ancient Capernaum is now owned by the Franciscans; the red-domed white church in the enclosure beyond belongs instead to the Greek Orthodox.

Here we gain a good idea of the town chosen by Jesus as a base for his ministry. Of particular note is the small size of most of the dwellings. Almost all are built out of black basalt rock. Perhaps it was in one of these houses that Jesus' preaching was interrupted by a paralyzed man being lowered down on a mat by his friends (Luke 5:17–26). The walls of these poor houses would not have coped either with windows or with a heavy roof, so the roof was probably made of branches covered with mud and straw. Their cobbled black floors would also be an easy place to lose things – like the precious coin lost by a woman in one of Jesus' stories (Luke 15:8–10).

From around the middle of the first century AD one of these rooms seems to have been set aside for public, rather than private, use (judging from the kind of artefacts found). Indeed its walls were plastered around that time, and some of them were marked with graffiti that referred to Jesus as Lord and Messiah. This provides strong evidence that the room was used as a place of Christian worship – almost certainly because it was believed to be the room used by Jesus, perhaps in the home of Simon Peter (Luke 4:38). In the fourth century Christians built a 'house-church' over this room, and in the fifth century it became the centre of a larger, octagonal church containing elaborate mosaics (later destroyed in the seventh century). Although it has recently been covered by a modern octagonal structure (often closed except for Catholic groups celebrating Mass), the original room is still visible, as are the later church walls. Given that the early tradition goes back to the first century, this is almost certainly the very place where Jesus stayed – the home of his chief apostle, Peter.

Just 40 yards (35 metres) to the north are the impressive ruins of a synagogue. We know that Jesus taught in Capernaum's synagogue and it may have been on this site. But the first-century synagogue, paid for by a Roman centurion (Luke 7:2–5), would have been a modest affair. This impressive edifice, with its imported white

Key

First-century AD housing complex

Fourth-century AD redevelopment

Fifth-century AD octagonal church

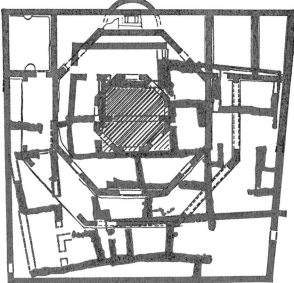

Plan showing the churches built over Peter's home.

0   10 metres

0   10 yards

limestone, dates to either the third or fourth century AD. Its proximity to the church built over Peter's home may suggest the uneasy coexistence and rivalry of the Jewish and Christian communities during this time (Galilee was a predominantly Jewish area, but the Byzantine imperial authorities were Christian). One alternative suggestion remains intriguing: might this impressive 'synagogue' have been built not by Jews, but rather by Christians – to help pilgrims visualize the synagogue mentioned in the gospels?

Leaving Capernaum and backtracking slightly with the lake now on the left, there is a small bay that has been demonstrated to function as a natural amphitheatre. Mark tells us that, on at least one occasion, the crowd gathered round Jesus was 'so large that he got into a boat and sat in it out on the lake, while all the people were along the shore at the water's edge' (Mark 4:1). This small bay, the acoustic 'centre' of which is under 10 yards (9 metres) from the shore, could have been the ideal spot. It is not hard to imagine people hanging on Jesus' every word as the quiet waters lapped the boat. Those who had

Peter's home in Capernaum. The concentric octagonal walls (dating to the fifth century) show how the original home was converted for church use. The central room of the home is in the shade and can now best be viewed by looking down through the glass floor of the Catholic church recently built above it.

Modern statue of Jesus with Simon Peter at Tabgha.

'Break thou the bread of life, dear Lord to me, as thou didst break the bread by Galilee.'

Mary Lathbury, 'Break thou the bread of life'

'ears to hear', as Jesus would have said, 'let them hear!' (Mark 4:9)

Just over a mile to the west of Capernaum there are two lakeside sites in an area now known as **Tabgha** – an Arabic corruption of a Greek word (*Heptapegon*) that refers to the 'seven springs' found in this area. This was the area conveniently selected by Byzantine Christians to commemorate a string of gospel episodes.

The first of these sites is now called the **Church of Peter's Primacy**, where people remember a story found only in John 21. After his resurrection Jesus stands on the lakeside, preparing breakfast for his tired disciples who have been fishing. He then speaks to Peter (who had recently denied him three times) and asks him, 'Do you love me?' A modern statue depicts an encounter between Peter and Jesus. Presumably it was designed to illustrate this encounter from John's Gospel, but it may also depict another episode from the start of Jesus' ministry, when a large haul of fish caused Peter to ask Jesus to leave him: 'Go away from me, Lord, for I am a sinful man!' (Luke 5:1–8). These powerful gospel stories, together with the ambience of the whole site, cause many people to pause here. If Jesus met here with his followers and fed them, might he somehow do the same today? So, not surprisingly, some people will arrange to take communion together here, sometimes returning at the end of the day for this more reflective experience.

In fact, several features of this place probably date back to the centuries *after* the time of Jesus: the six heart-shaped stones set in the sand, which were later associated with 'twelve thrones' promised by Jesus to his twelve disciples in Luke 22:30 (each half representing a disciple); and the rock-cut steps below the church, which Egeria thought had been used by Jesus. The natural flat rock to the east of the present small chapel may have been what she refers to as 'the stone on which the Lord placed the bread'. If so, her diary indicates that this had been made into an 'altar' and incorporated into a small church (built just before her visit in the 380s AD). This may suggest that this site was also remembered as the place where Jesus fed the 5,000.

It was not long, however, before a separate, larger church was constructed nearby to commemorate this other 'feeding miracle'. This second site at Tabgha (known as the **Church of the Loaves and Fishes**) is about 200 yards (180 metres) to the west. Visitors find themselves in the courtyard of a modern Benedictine building, completed in 1982, which is designed to replicate as much as possible the atrium and basilica which was built on exactly this spot around AD 480.

The interior of this church gives a great idea of the 'open plan' style of Byzantine churches throughout this period (fourth to seventh centuries AD): a nave and two side aisles would focus towards a rounded 'apse' at the east end for the clergy; and the communion table would be visible to all, with only a low partition wall (if anything at all) separating the 'chancel' from the 'nave'. In this case, some of the original floor mosaics are visible, including the famous mosaic of the loaves and fishes, and others brilliantly depicting birds and plants from around the lake, as well as from the Nile region. There is also evidence of the much smaller church built here during the fourth century.

In this beautiful, prayerful place, it seems almost churlish to ask the awkward questions about historical authenticity. The gospel accounts, however, almost certainly suggest that the feeding of the 5,000 took place on the other side of the lake: they speak of a 'solitary place', far removed from any villages, and suggest that, if anywhere, Bethsaida was the nearest town. Meanwhile those concerned to locate the repeated feeding of the 4,000 should focus on the Gentile territory to the south-east of the lake (the 'Decapolis'), since there are fairly clear hints that this took place amongst Gentiles (see Mark 7:31–8:10; Matthew 15:29–39).

If so, the Byzantines were incorrect in their identification of the place. Yet this should not be too surprising or bothersome. By its very nature, the precise location of such an event is hardly likely to have survived. And, given the transport difficulties of ancient pilgrims, it was almost inevitable that a place would be selected that was conveniently *en route* towards Capernaum and which could double up neatly with the other famous feeding story from the Gospels in John 21.

The Church of the Loaves and Fishes, showing its reuse of the ancient Byzantine pattern: a triapsidal basilica under a cross-shaped roof, with an atrium (courtyard) to the west.

The church on the Mount of Beatitudes. Its octagonal shape reflects Jesus' eight 'blessings'.

This desire for overlap and convenience can be seen as well in the way the Byzantines also associated this area with the Sermon on the Mount. Hence the few remains of a small fourth-century church and monastery on the far (inland) side of the road. In 1938 a new church was built much further up the hill to commemorate Jesus' sermon. To reach this by road requires quite a detour. Yet it is worth the effort. For from the so-called **Mount of Beatitudes** there are great views over the whole lake and over many of the sites associated with Jesus' ministry. For those who enjoy walking, there is also a comparatively easy walk back down to the lakeside through some Galilean fields.

Visitors to the Mount of Beatitudes should not look for strict authenticity: Jesus used many different locations to speak his message, and Matthew's account is a short selection and summary of Jesus' teaching, perhaps repeated on many other occasions and in other places. But going to see the site can help visitors to imagine this in its context.

The serenity of this beautiful place, however, may be slightly unhelpful here, suggesting that Jesus' words were calm and soothing when in fact they were radical, demanding, authoritative, revolutionary and countercultural. Jesus was calling Israel to a new way of life; his kingdom was surprising. 'Only a few' would find the 'road that leads to life' and those who disobeyed would find their houses falling 'with a great crash' (Matthew 7:14, 26–27). The Sermon on the Mount remains the most powerful of discourses, and some use their visit to read it through from beginning to end in the hope of hearing and heeding its message afresh.

Travelling eastwards across the **River Jordan** visitors come to **Bethsaida**. The site has only recently been excavated and there is comparatively little to see. Some have even disputed whether this is truly Bethsaida. It is over a mile from the current shore of the lake and is at an altitude that could never have been accessible by water, even if the lake's water level was slightly higher in antiquity. Yet one room, with various fishing artefacts, has come to light; so Bethsaida may have been a town in which fishermen lived but which had no direct access to the water. For Christian visitors it remains significant as the original hometown of Peter, Andrew and Philip before they moved to Capernaum. The distance between the town and the lake may have been one of several factors that influenced their decision to move – in Capernaum they could have lived much nearer the water.

A few miles down the eastern side of the lake lie the ruins of a Byzantine church and monastery at **Kursi**. This name may be a corruption of 'Gergesa', a name which itself reflects some confusion in the biblical manuscripts concerning the site of one of Jesus' most unusual miracles: the healing of a demoniac called Legion and the casting of the demons into some nearby pigs, who stampeded into the lake and were drowned. The gospel manuscripts give the name variously as 'Gadara', 'Gerasa' or 'Gergesa' (Matthew 8:28; Mark 5:1; Luke 8:26), and various solutions have been proposed, which need not detain us here. What is certain is that the site of this miracle must be a steep bank not too far from the lake (though not a cliff) and in Gentile territory – no Jew would have been rearing pigs!

Kursi is not an improbable location, being not far from the Gentile town of Susita/Hippos. The Byzantines seem to have identified a place on a hill a little further to the south of the monastery as the actual site (marked by a huge boulder). However, there are perhaps even more likely places further to the south. Once again the ruins give a good idea of Byzantine church architecture, and of a place that has been used for prayer in ancient times.

A further 3 miles (5 kilometres) south is the distinctive hill of ancient **Susita** (also known as **Hippos**, presumably because it reminded someone of a horse). Those with more time might like to visit this city with its Roman and Byzantine ruins (including a fine fifth-century church). It was once part of the Decapolis but by Jesus' day it had been brought into the province of Syria – a reminder of how close 'Syria' was to 'Palestina' at this point. Intriguingly, Matthew's very first comment about Jesus' popularity states that 'news about him spread all over Syria' (Matthew 4:24); only in the next verse does he talk about crowds coming from 'Galilee, the Decapolis, Jerusalem, Judea and across the Jordan'. Again we sense something of Galilee's 'international' location as an outpost of Judaism set in the midst of the nations.

On the lakeside (in front of Hippos) is the **kibbutz Ein Gev**. From here visitors can take a **boat trip** back across the lake towards Tiberias. Often, once the boat is out on the middle of the lake, the engines are turned off so that people can sense the calm of the lake. The stories about Jesus walking on the water and calming the storm make for powerful reading at such a moment. 'The storm subsided and all was calm' (Luke 8:24). People have an opportunity to sense the sheer awe of those events; to see themselves in the disciples' place; and, with them, to ask that age-old question: 'Who is this? Even the wind and the waves obey him!' (Mark 4:41). The questions raised by the 'solitary life' of the man from Galilee continue to ring down the centuries.

'Vicisti, O Galilæe' ('You have conquered, Galilean').

The dying words of the pagan emperor, Julian the Apostate (AD 332–63)

Samaria

Now he had to go through Samaria. So he came to a town in Samaria called Sychar, near the plot of ground Jacob had given to his son Joseph. Jacob's well was there, and Jesus, tired as he was from the journey, sat down by the well. It was about the sixth hour. When a Samaritan woman came to draw water, Jesus said to her, 'Will you give me a drink?'… The Samaritan woman said to him, 'You are a Jew and I am a Samaritan woman. How can you ask me for a drink?' (For Jews do not associate with Samaritans.) Jesus answered her, 'If you knew the gift of God and who it is that asks you for a drink, you would have asked him and he would have given you living water.'… 'Sir,' the woman said, 'I can see that you are a prophet. Our fathers worshipped on this mountain, but you Jews claim that the place where we must worship is in Jerusalem.' Jesus declared, 'Believe me, woman, a time is coming when you will worship the Father neither on this mountain nor in Jerusalem. You Samaritans worship what you do not know; we worship what we do know, for salvation is from the Jews. Yet a time is coming and has now come when the true worshippers will worship the Father in spirit and truth, for they are the kind of worshippers the Father seeks. God is spirit, and his worshippers must worship in spirit and in truth.'

John 4:4–24

Samaria in the fourth century

Here is Mount Gerizim. Here the Samaritans say that Abraham offered sacrifice (Mount Moriah), and one reaches the top of the mountain by steps, three hundred in number. Beyond this, at the foot of the mountain itself, is a place called Sichem. Here is a tomb in which Joseph is laid, in the 'parcel of ground' (villa) which Jacob his father gave to him (Joshua 24:32). From there Dinah, the daughter of Jacob, was carried off by the children of the Amorites (Genesis 34:2). A mile from there is a place named Sichar, from which the woman of Samaria came down to the same place in which Jacob dug the well, to draw water from it, and our Lord Jesus Christ talked with her (John 4:5–30); here there are plane-trees, which Jacob planted, and a bath (balneus) which is supplied with water from the well.

Bordeaux Pilgrim, 587–88 (visiting in AD 333)

The enemy within

It is hard for us to imagine, but right in the middle of Palestine in Jesus' day there was a 'no-go area' – the territory of the Samaritans. Galileans, if travelling to Jerusalem, would tend to bypass this whole area on their way southward, going instead down the Jordan Valley and then making their way up to Jerusalem from Jericho. It added about another 25 miles (40 kilometres) to the journey, but it was worth it, if only to avoid the hazards of passing through Samaria.

After at least 400 years of being sworn enemies, the situation could be described bluntly in John's Gospel: 'Jews do not associate with Samaritans' (John 4:9). So, despite this long-standing animosity, would Jesus himself ever visit Samaria? And what attitude towards the Samaritans would he encourage in his followers?

The evidence is clear. On at least one occasion Jesus *did* chose to travel right through the heart of Samaria:

it would be the scene of a significant encounter between Jesus and a Samaritan woman (John 4:1–42). On another occasion his disciples, James and John, asked if they should 'call down fire' upon an unwelcoming Samaritan village (Luke 9:54). Jesus rebuked them. It was not his way.

Instead he ensured that the Samaritans were included in some of his healings. On one occasion, recorded only by Luke, he healed ten lepers, but the only one who returned to thank him was a Samaritan (Luke 17:16). 'Was no one found to return and give praise to God', Jesus pointedly asked, 'except this foreigner?' And Jesus famously forced his audience to rethink their whole idea of 'foreigners' and 'others' by telling his parable about a good Samaritan (Luke 10:25–37). By making the hero of the story a Samaritan, Jesus was stretching people's sympathies way beyond their comfort zone: acting in a 'neighbourly' way to their fellow Jews was one thing, but not to the Samaritans – their political 'neighbour' right next door. That was too much to ask.

Geography and History

The territory occupied by the Samaritans in Jesus' day was quite large, in square area almost the equivalent of the whole of Galilee. It was in the central hill-country, which was covered with characteristic

'...he sent messengers on ahead, who went into a Samaritan village to get things ready for him; but the people there did not welcome him, because he was heading for Jerusalem. When the disciples James and John saw this, they asked, "Lord, do you want us to call fire down from heaven to destroy them?" But Jesus turned and rebuked them...'

Luke 9:52–55

Aerial view of Sebaste, showing an ancient Israelite tower near to the much later Christian Basilica of St John the Baptist.

terraced farming, and it focused around some key sites that had ancient biblical pedigree.

Shechem, for example, was the ancient town visited by Abraham and associated with his grandson Jacob, who purchased a well here. Joshua also summoned the early Israelites here when he called them to 'chose this day which god you will serve' (Joshua 24:15). It was a natural place for a significant town: it was surrounded by springs and lay at the centre of an ancient road-system, as it was located at the entrance to the only east-west pass within the hill-country. That pass lay between two important hills that faced each other: Mount Ebal and Mount Gerizim.

Another example was the ancient city of Samaria itself (renamed 'Sebaste' by Herod the Great), which in ancient times had been chosen as the capital of the northern kingdom of Israel for over 200 years during the reigns of kings such as Omri, Ahab and Jeroboam.

The animosity between the Jewish people and the Samaritans went back a long way. The potential for a rift between north and south was clearly there ever since the tenth century BC, when the ten tribes of 'Israel' split off from the two tribes of 'Judah' after the unifying era of David and Solomon. Not surprisingly, a prophet from the south, like Amos, would in due course have much to say about the decadence he noted in the rulers of the northern kingdom.

It was the northern kingdom of Israel that later suffered at the hands of the Assyrian empire when, in 722 BC, many were deported and the area of Samaria was largely repopulated by foreigners. One hundred and fifty years later Judah suffered a parallel fate under the Babylonians; but when the Jewish exiles returned to rebuild Jerusalem, they experienced significant opposition from the Samaritans. To the Jews this may have felt like treachery from supposed cousins. From then on they saw the

The Samaritans according to Josephus

Josephus refers to Samaria and its inhabitants in several places. At one point he summarizes the reasons why the Jewish people saw the Samaritans as their enemies (some from way back in history, some from recent events):

Shalmanezer [the Assyrian] exiled the Israelites and replaced them with the nation of the Cutheans; they had formerly belonged to the inner parts of Persia and Media, but came to be called Samaritans, by taking the name of the country to which they were removed... [Two hundred years later] the Samaritans persuaded the nations of Syria... to put a stop to the building of the temple, and endeavoured to delay and protract the Jews in their zeal about it .
Antiquities 10:9; 11:4

When Coponius was procurator of Judea, the following incident occurred [c. AD 10]. The Jews were celebrating the Feast of Unleavened Bread (which we call Passover). It was customary during that season for the priests to open the temple-gates just after midnight. But on this occasion when the gates were first opened, some Samaritans came privately into Jerusalem and threw some human corpses into the temple cloisters. As a result

the Jews then banned Samaritans from the temple, even though they had not previously done this at such festivals.
Antiquities 18:2

Eventually in AD 36 (only a few years after Jesus' visit to the area of Mount Gerizim) the Samaritans rose up against Rome. Pontius Pilate's brutal response was sufficient for him to be recalled by the emperor to Rome. Here is Josephus' account:

The nation of the Samaritans was involved in a revolt. The man who excited them to it bid them to get together upon Mount Gerizim, which is by them looked upon as the most holy of all mountains. He assured people that he would show them those sacred vessels which were buried there, because Moses had put them there. So his hearers armed themselves... and tried to go up the mountain in a great multitude together. Pilate, however, prevented their going up, ordering a great band of cavalry and infantry to fall upon those who had gathered in the village. When it came to an action, they killed many of them; others fled, but most of them were captured and put to death at Pilate's order.
Antiquities 18:4

Samaritans as consisting largely of foreigners and viewed their religion as compromised and impure. Meanwhile the Samaritans themselves claimed to follow a purer form of Judaism, focused exclusively on the first five books of Moses (Genesis to Deuteronomy). So Nehemiah declined their offers of help and in due course he persuaded the Persian authorities to set Jerusalem free from Samaritan control. In retaliation the Samaritans then built their own Temple on Mount Gerizim. Matters came to a head when John Hyrcanus, one of the Hasmonean rulers in Jerusalem, sent in troops to destroy the Samaritans' Temple. In response, when the Roman general Pompey set the Samaritans free from Jerusalem's rule 50 years later, the Samaritans refused to have any further dealings with the Jews. Ancient Judaism had effectively been split in two.

Jesus and the Samaritan woman

It was into this irreconcilable 'stand-off' that Jesus came. Many of his fellow-Jews were longing to shake off the burden of Roman rule, but for the Samaritans the arrival of the Romans had had a beneficial effect – they were no longer under Jewish rule. So there were contrasting political agendas between the two races as well as deep religious disagreements. The question posed to Jesus by the Samaritan woman was therefore not some vague, innocuous spiritual quest, but was highly charged; it represented centuries of dispute and was fuelled by mutual recriminations and atrocities: 'Our fathers worshipped on this mountain [Mount Gerizim], but you Jews claim that the place where we must worship is in Jerusalem' (John 4:20). Put on the spot like this, how would Jesus answer?

Jesus cuts the 'Gordian knot' with an answer marked by astonishing authority. Already recognized by the woman as a 'prophet' because of his awareness of her secret marital history, he answers by predicting a time when her question will simply no longer be relevant. God's agenda will have moved beyond the impasse of this 'either/or' situation. Implicitly he is foreseeing the imminent demise of Jerusalem's treasured Temple: just as the Samaritans' temple had been destroyed by Hyrcanus, so Jerusalem's Temple would soon be no more.

Yet Jesus is not speaking here out of some self-critical apology for Jewish beliefs and practice. On the contrary, he makes it quite clear that in his view Samaritan worship is based on ignorance, not on revelation, and that the true vehicle for God's saving purposes in the world has been Jerusalem-based Judaism (John 4:22). No, his reason for this outrageous prophecy against his own Jerusalem is the new thing that God is doing. God is launching a new era when people throughout the world will be able to access God directly: not through physical locations such as Jerusalem or Gerizim, but through the availability of God's own Spirit. 'God is spirit, and his worshippers [can and] must worship in spirit and in truth' (John 4:24). How can he be so confident of these new requirements and possibilities for true worship? And how will they be introduced? The dialogue moves towards its climax and closure. The woman raises the issue of the 'Messiah' – the unique prophet that Samaritans too were expecting. 'I who speak to you', replied Jesus, 'am he' (John 4:26).

For John this episode with the Samaritan woman is deeply significant. It shows Jesus' involvement with all types of people, whether the religious Jewish man, Nicodemus (John 3:1–21), or the irreligious Samaritan woman (here in chapter 4). It

'A time is coming, when you will worship the Father neither on this mountain nor in Jerusalem.'
John 4:21

conjures up ancient biblical stories, like that of Isaac talking to Rebecca by the well (Genesis 24:10–27). It shows Jesus being willing to break through a range of taboos – be they religious, racial, sexual or social – in order to reach out to someone in need. And it shows his masterly way of handling conversations that took people on a journey of discovery into hidden and unacknowledged areas of their lives.

But for John it showed above all the new reality that had become available through the coming of Jesus: the reality of God's Spirit, which Jesus refers to here as the 'living water' welling up within a person like 'a spring' (John 4:10, 14). So this ancient well, fixed in its location since the time of Jacob, takes on a whole new meaning: it is a foretaste of the water of God's Spirit pouring out into the world. The water of God's Spirit could heal the deep rifts that had kept Samaritan and Jew apart for centuries, filling the 'cracks' between these people with new life and hope.

Healing for the world

Luke, from a different perspective, says much the same in his references to Samaria. In his Gospel, the coming of Jesus melts the animosity between these long-standing enemies (see page 82). Then in the book of Acts Luke describes how the message about Jesus, ushered in by his Spirit, goes out from Jerusalem through 'Judea and Samaria' and then 'to the ends of the earth' (Acts 1:8). The message about Jesus, who had himself been rejected by a Samaritan village because he was 'heading for Jerusalem' (Luke 9:53), now comes out from Jerusalem through Jesus' followers – in this case through Philip (Acts 8:5–25). Knowing so well the ancient tensions between Jews and Samaritans, the apostles in Jerusalem were presumably both surprised and delighted when they 'heard that Samaria had accepted the word of God' (Acts 8:14). So they sent a top delegation (Peter and John) to confirm that the Samaritans were now fully included in Jesus' kingdom by bringing them the gift of the Holy Spirit.

So once again, as in John 4, there is a link between Samaria and the Spirit of God: the Spirit is the sign of God's new age dawning in the world and breaking down the ancient barriers between people.

Finally, in all this there is also the intriguing role of Jesus' disciple, John. He and his brother James had wished to call down fire on the Samaritan village; but now we see him going into Samaria, not with fire, but with a new message about Jesus and the fire of his Spirit. Peter and John preached 'the gospel in many Samaritan villages'. What a contrast, we may note, with what they had been tempted to do just a year or two earlier! John's attitude towards Samaria has been transformed by his response to the message of Jesus.

'But you will receive power when the Holy Spirit comes on you; and you will be my witnesses in Jerusalem, and in all Judea and Samaria, and to the ends of the earth.'

Acts 1:8

Samaria Today

Because of recent political troubles this part of the Holy Land is often overlooked by visitors. This is hardly surprising, as the modern city of **Nablus**, which lies directly between Mount Gerizim and Mount Ebal, has been marked by significant unrest for many years. On the positive side, it means that any intrepid visitors to sites in this area can often have the place to themselves.

Key dates: Samaria

Within the territory of 'Samaria' there are several sites: ancient Shechem, the neighbouring hills of Gerizim and Ebal, the village of Sychar, and some miles to the west, the city of Samaria itself (founded by Omri in c. 880 BC). Dates associated with all of these are listed below.

c. 1850 BC	Shechem visited by Abraham and then Jacob (Genesis 12:1–7; 33:18–20); burial place of Joseph (Joshua 24:32).
1300–1700 BC	'Golden age' of Shechem (rival to Megiddo).
1400–1200 BC	Assembly of Israelite tribes under Joshua (Joshua 24).
1300–1100 BC	Abortive attempt of Abimelech to become king (Judges 9).
930 BC	Northern kingdom (Israel) splits off from southern kingdom (Judah) after the death of Solomon (1 Kings 12–13) with Shechem as its first capital.
c. 880 BC	Founding of the city of Samaria by King Omri.
c. 870 BC	Reign of King Ahab (married to Jezebel); ministries of Elijah and Elisha (1 Kings 16–2 Kings 10).
780–30 BC	Reign of King Jeroboam II; ministries of Amos and Hosea.

722 BC	Invasion of Samaria and the northern kingdom of Israel by Assyrians; deportation of 30,000 citizens and repopulation with non-Israelites (2 Kings 17:24).
500s BC	City of Samaria as capital of a province within the Persian empire.
c. 450 BC	Samaritan opposition to the rebuilding of Jerusalem Temple (Nehemiah 4); end of Samaritan rule over Judah.
333 BC	Alexander the Great installs veteran Macedonians in city of Samaria; residents move to a new city on Mount Gerizim; some rebuilding of Shechem.
c. 190 BC	Building of an alternative temple on Mount Gerizim (2 Maccabees 6:2; Josephus, *Antiquities* 11:8)
108 BC	City of Samaria destroyed by John Hyrcanus; area brought under Jerusalem's rule.
107 BC	John Hyrcanus destroys Samaritan temple and Shechem (Josephus, *War* 1:2).
64 BC	Territory of Samaria brought under Roman rule by Pompey.
57 BC	City of Samaria rebuilt by General Gabinius.
30 BC	City of Samaria given by Augustus to Herod the Great, who rebuilds much of the city (now renamed Sebaste, Greek for 'Augustus').

AD 36	Pontius Pilate removed from office following his massacre of Samaritan crowds near Mount Gerizim.
AD 72	Founding of Flavia Neapolis (just to west of Shechem) by Titus.
c. AD 100	Justin Martyr born in Neapolis.
AD 200	Septimius Severus makes the city of Samaria a Roman colony.
AD 300s	Samaritan 'golden age' under the rule of Baba Rabba.
c. AD 380	Construction of the cruciform church over Jacob's Well.
AD 484	Samaritans revolt in Neapolis against Byzantine Christians; Emperor Zeno builds the church of Theotokos on Mount Gerizim.
AD 529	Samaritans revolt again, attacking churches and monasteries through a wide area; Emperor Justinian's savage response leads to the virtual extinction of the Samaritans.
AD 700s	Muslims destroy the Byzantine church on Mount Gerizim.
1800s	Samaritans allowed back to Mount Gerizim for annual 6-week celebration of Passover.
1893	Greek Orthodox crypt built over Jacob's Well.
1927	Major earthquake in Nablus.

Yet a journey into ancient Samaria well repays the effort. For example, this particular section of the West Bank (where not covered by recent settlements) gives perhaps the clearest example of what the **hill-country** of the Promised Land looked like in ancient times. Rounded hills are marked by terracing that is thousands of years old and may have changed little since the patriarchs walked along the hill-tops nearly 3,000 years ago.

Jacob's Well too is quietly impressive. For it offers one of the most assuredly authentic sites in the country. Wells do not move, so we can be fairly confident that this well marks the precise spot where Jesus sat talking to the Samaritan woman. As she rightly said, 'the well is deep' (John 4:11) – indeed it goes down over 70 feet (20 metres)! And it still provides chill, clear water for drinking. Nowadays it is surrounded by the crypt of a half-built Orthodox church (never completed because of the First World War).

But the general location gives a good opportunity to imagine Jesus resting here from his journey, while the disciples and the Samaritans were walking to and fro between the well and the town of Sychar – a ten-minute walk to the north-west.

Going over to the ancient *tel* of **Shechem** (*Tel Balata*), visitors can still pick up pot-shards from ancient times and sense the antiquity of this city, whose heyday was way back at the start of the second millennium BC. There are a couple of ancient temples here, but perhaps the most impressive site is the city gate, which gives visitors a good opportunity to imagine this key social institution from biblical times.

For there are several references in the Old Testament to the social function of the **city gate** – the place were a town's leaders would gather to conduct any necessary business. For example, it was 'in the city gate' that Abraham bought the area for his wife's tomb (Genesis 23:8–10); Boaz agreed to act as Ruth's kinsman-redeemer while sitting in the town gate (Ruth 4:1); and a man with a good wife or several sons is said to have a good reputation and will not be ashamed when he is 'in the gate' (Psalm 127:5; Proverbs 31:23). Such ancient, everyday scenes come vividly to mind here, as do the stories associated with Abraham.

Mount Gerizim, aerial view of excavations from the north-east.

Breathtaking views over central Samaria can be seen from **the summit of Mount Gerizim** (best approached now not via Nablus but from the south). Visitors can clearly sense why the Samaritans view the slightly higher Mount Ebal (to the north) as accursed – nothing much grows on its barren grey rocks – and also why this pass between Ebal and Gerizim was so important as a trade route, linking up the central hill-country with the Mediterranean coast. From the summit it is easy to see the plateau area where the small surviving Samaritan community come to celebrate the six weeks of their Passover season. The summit itself is marked by the **octagonal church**, built in the late fifth century and destroyed by the Muslims in the eighth century, and also by the site of the **ancient Samaritan temple** (immediately to its east), which was destroyed in the late second century BC.

Fine views are also possible from amidst the ruins of the **ancient city of Samaria**. On a clear day visitors can see the coastline from its acropolis – a significant point because this new capital built for the northern kingdom of Israel was thereby signalling its intended contact with the wider world of the Mediterranean.

The ruins prove to be quite extensive: city gates, the line of a colonnaded street, a marketplace and a Roman theatre. Evidence of Herod's builders refounding the city as **Sebaste** can be seen throughout, but especially in the temple he dedicated to Augustus ('the venerable or worshipful One') on the summit of the acropolis.

In the Byzantine and Crusader era, the city of Samaria was associated by Christians with the **burial place of John the Baptist**. According to the Gospels (for example, Mark 6:17–29), John was executed on the orders of Herod Antipas as part of Herod's birthday celebrations (see page 13). We do not know where this took place, but Herod is more likely to have been in his new capital of Sepphoris (see page 33). Even so, there is a **small sixth-century church** here, said to mark the site of the discovery of his head; and the adjacent town of Sebastiya is the site of a large **Crusader cathedral**, which supposedly contains his tomb.

Finally, however, visitors to **Samaria** cannot come away without being made more aware of the religious and political tensions that have beset this area throughout much of its history – and especially in the present. There is profound irony in the fact that the hill-country that the ancient Israelites defended against the Philistines to the west is the same country that the Palestinians now seek to maintain as their home against the incoming settlements of Israelis (as it were, from the west). Somehow some roles and situations have been reversed, bringing great struggles in their wake.

Yet maybe the words Jesus spoke in Samaria, when faced with the acute and critical religious tensions of his own day, still have something to teach us. He foresaw a day when Jewish–Samaritan tensions would become irrelevant because of the new era that he himself was bringing into the world: a day when bitter fighting over precise locations would be unnecessary because God would be available to all people everywhere, regardless of their culture or geography. It is a vision still worth pursuing, as we seek to be true bridges for peace and reconciliation.

'The time has now come when the true worshippers will worship the Father in spirit and in truth.'
John 4:23

The great cathedral in the middle of the modern village of Sebastiya dates from the twelfth century and is a powerful witness to an important era in the life of the Holy Land: the Crusades.

The Crusaders were in the land from 1099 (capturing Jerusalem on 15 July) through to 1291, when the coastal city of Akko fell to the Mamluks. The 'Latin Kingdom' was at its most powerful in the middle of the twelfth century. Two powerful military orders were established during this period: the Hospitallers and the Templars – so-called because of their headquarters on Jerusalem's Temple Mount in the El-Aksa mosque, which the Crusaders thought was the 'Temple of Solomon'.

The Latin Kingdom then suffered an almost irreversible defeat at the Horns of Hattin above Tiberias on 4 July 1187. Saladin lured the Crusader knights into a confrontation in the full heat of the sun when the Crusaders were cut off from their water supplies. Some territory in Galilee was regained after the Third Crusade (1189–92), but the Crusaders were gradually pushed back to the sea.

The Crusaders have left numerous buildings that have stood the test of time: impressive castles such as Belvoir (overlooking the Jordan Valley and Samaria); and some distinctive churches, like those at Latrun, Abu Ghosh and Qubeiba (see page 205). In Jerusalem itself their influence can be seen in their renovations to the church of the Holy Sepulchre (see page 190) and the church of St Anne, by the pool of Bethesda (see page 170).

Aerial view over the ruins of Belvoir Castle on one of the hills of ancient Gilboa, looking down over the Jordan Valley beyond.

This last church has been virtually unaltered since the twelfth century and gives a good idea of the simple strength of Crusader design and architecture. After years of disuse it was given by the Turks to the French as a sign of gratitude for assistance in the Crimean War in 1856.

Reflecting on the Crusades

The era of the Crusades, however, has left its mark on the Holy Land in other, more painful ways. Western interest in the Holy Land today is often interpreted as a modern form of this Crusading instinct – a desire for control. The butchery associated with the storming of Jerusalem in 1099 brought to an end the established *modus vivendi* between Eastern Christians and Muslims (who had coexisted in the city for over 500 years); no doubt there was savagery on both sides, but this slaughter is still remembered today and plays its part in stirring contemporary grievances.

So images of the Crusaders entering the Holy Sepulchre carrying blood-stained swords and singing the *Te Deum* linger long in people's minds. And the sight of a Crusader cross conjures up very different images from the ones it would originally have invoked when Christians first developed it as the symbol of their faith in Christ crucified. Moves by Christians in recent years to apologize for the Crusades have been appreciated, but in some ways only reveal that this is still an open wound.

There are many lessons to learn from the Crusades. Perhaps one of the most important concerns how Christians should approach the Holy Land. Indeed is it a 'holy land' at all? Some prefer to call it the 'land of the Holy One' – as a sign that this land should not point to itself, but to the God who has revealed himself here. Certainly the belief that the land itself is somehow 'holy' has led paradoxically to some most *un*holy behaviour. The same dynamic occurs today when people are convinced in the name of *their* God that the land must belong to *them*.

The Crusades then warn of the dangers of going beyond what the New Testament teaches. It is one thing to believe that Jesus was God incarnate, that this was the land truly visited by 'those feet in ancient time'. It is quite another to deduce from this that Jerusalem is therefore still a 'holy city', that the land is still somehow inherently special, or that the Bible gives one group of people a right of ownership over it. For there is a strong strand within the New Testament that suggests that, with the coming of Jesus, both Jerusalem and the land lost some of the significance they had previously enjoyed. Perhaps with Jesus' departure the 'glory has departed'. This would mean that neither the city nor the land is worth fighting over.

In light of this, Jesus' words spoken to the Samaritan woman can take on a whole new force. Previous concern with physical places, Jesus warns, must now be eclipsed by a focus on God's universal presence by his Spirit: '...a time is coming when you will worship the Father neither on this mountain nor in Jerusalem... true worshippers will worship the Father in spirit and in truth, for they are the kind of worshippers the Father seeks' (John 4:21, 23).

St Anne's Church in Jerusalem's Old City.

7 Caesarea Philippi

Once when Jesus was praying in private and his disciples were with him, he asked them, 'Who do the crowds say I am?' They replied, 'Some say John the Baptist; others say Elijah; and still others, that one of the prophets of long ago has come back to life.' 'But what about you?' he asked. 'Who do you say I am?' Peter answered, 'The Messiah of God.' Jesus strictly warned them not to tell this to anyone. And he said, 'The Son of Man must suffer many things and be rejected... and he must be killed and on the third day be raised to life.'

[Jesus] took Peter, John and James with him and went up onto a mountain to pray. As he was praying, the appearance of his face changed, and his clothes became as bright as a flash of lightning. Two men, Moses and Elijah, appeared in glorious splendour, talking with Jesus. They spoke about his departure, which he was about to bring to fulfilment at Jerusalem. Peter and his companions were very sleepy, but when they became fully awake, they saw his glory and the two men standing with him... a cloud appeared and enveloped them... A voice came from the cloud, saying, 'This is my Son, whom I have chosen; listen to him.' When the voice had spoken, they found that Jesus was alone. The disciples... told no one at that time what they had seen.

The next day, when they came down from the mountain, a large crowd met him. A man in the crowd called out, 'Teacher, I beg you to look at my son... A spirit seizes him and he suddenly screams; it throws him into convulsions so that he foams at the mouth... I begged your disciples to drive it out, but they could not.' 'O unbelieving and perverse generation,' Jesus replied, 'how long shall I stay with you and put up with you? Bring your son here.' Even while the boy was coming, the demon threw him to the ground in a convulsion. But Jesus rebuked the evil spirit, healed the boy and gave him back to his father. And they were all amazed at the greatness of God.

Luke 9:18–22, 28–43

Time for a decision

On a clear spring day you can see the snow-covered peak of Mount Hermon from about 70 miles (110 kilometres) away. Rising to 9,000 feet (2,750 metres), it formed a natural boundary in ancient times for the land of Israel. The Old Testament writers had often spoken of the land stretching from 'Dan to Beersheba', and Dan was one of the towns in the foothills of Mount Hermon. Near to Dan was the town of Paneas – itself on a plateau about 1,150 feet (350 metres) above sea level. Paneas's chief natural feature was a spring, located in a large cave (one of the sources for the River Jordan); so it was a natural place for the veneration of Pan, a 'nature god'. However it had recently been renamed by Herod the Great's son, Philip. The name 'Caesarea Philippi' was chosen in honour both of Philip himself and of the Roman emperor, Augustus. It was somewhere around here 'in the region of Caesarea Philippi' (Matthew 16:13) that Jesus came with his disciples at a pivotal period in his ministry.

Far from the Jewish heartland

There were other times when Jesus left behind the shores of Lake Galilee and ventured north. He had earlier travelled up to the coastal area of Tyre and Sidon (or 'Syro-Phoenicia'). But this visit to Caesarea Philippi was the furthest north he would go within the ancient borders of biblical Israel. In this more secluded part of the land, which was scarcely populated, he could ponder and perhaps get some perspective on the dramatic events that would unfold once he turned his face southwards again. So not surprisingly this would be the place where he announced his intention to go up to Jerusalem. It was also the place where he hoped his disciples would gain a new perspective on his identity.

Intriguingly we do not know if Jesus ever ventured into the city of Caesarea Philippi itself. Quite probably he and his followers stayed somewhere more remote. Mark speaks of him being 'in the villages around' it (Mark 8:27). This may have had something to do with the city's past. Although the whole area was notionally within the ancient borders of Israel, its history and now its population were almost totally Gentile. Close to the Roman province of Syria, this region was known as 'Gaulanitis' (like the modern 'Golan Heights'), and its sparse population would have owed little allegiance to Jerusalem. And the new capital, as its various names would suggest, had long been associated with paganism. In fact the name that would stick was Caesarea Paneas. But this only made plain that this was a very non-Jewish place, dedicated to pagan worship and honouring the Roman empire.

Even in late summer the snows of Mount Hermon stand out above the villages of northern Israel.

No wonder, perhaps, that Jesus kept away. At the same time, it would also be a fitting general location for him to begin to reveal to his disciples the truth about his own identity. Augustus Caesar might claim to rule the world, perhaps even to be acclaimed by some as divine, a 'son of god'. But what if Israel's long-expected royal ruler (the anointed 'Messiah') had now appeared on the scene? Was he not the world's true ruler? Would he not be a better candidate for receiving divine honours?

At this point in their account of Jesus' ministry, the gospel writers cluster together three particular episodes: Peter's confession of Jesus as the Messiah, the transfiguration, and the healing of the demon-possessed boy.

Peter's confession

'In a location which was newly proclaiming that the Roman Emperor (Caesar) was the lord of the inhabited world, Jesus advanced his own claim to be the Messiah of Israel, the rightful and true lord of the world.'

C.P. Thiede

The first of these episodes marks a clear watershed in the whole story of Jesus. The crowds have seen Jesus do some remarkable things and have listened to his authoritative teaching, but they have been struggling to work out who he is. The best category they can come up with is that of a 'prophet'. Given that there had been no authentic 'prophecy' since the days of Malachi 400 years earlier, this in itself was no small claim. By listening to Jesus, so people sensed, they were hearing the authoritative voice of Israel's God. They had said similar things about John the Baptist, and Jesus had agreed with them – up to a point. Yes, John was a prophet, Jesus said, but 'more than a prophet' (Luke 7:26).

But then what did that make Jesus himself? He described himself as the 'Son of Man', but what did that mean? It was all too puzzling. Moreover, the final verses of Malachi's prophecy contained a divine promise to 'send the prophet Elijah before that great and dreadful day of the Lord' (Malachi 4:5). What did that mean? Was either John or Jesus to be identified with this 'returned Elijah'?

So, in private, on this memorable, quiet 'retreat' far away from their homes in Galilee and away from all the crowds, Jesus eventually drops them the direct question: 'Who do *you* say I am?' The time for hiding behind other people's answers is over. The moment for vague mutterings is past. Their embarrassed confusion is revealed. And in the midst of that stunned silence Peter finds himself putting into words what had never quite been said before: 'You are the Messiah of God' (Luke 9:20).

And Jesus does not rebuke him. The truth is out.

Note, however, that in calling Jesus 'Messiah', Peter was *not* at this stage automatically thinking that Jesus was in some sense 'divine'. 'Messiah' was a title for a human being who would rule God's people, representing them before God and bringing them to victory over the pagans. And Peter may well have been using it with some of these more 'political' connotations in mind. If their Master was the true Messiah–King, then it was time to march on Jerusalem and start the armed revolution against God's enemies. Jesus' political career had now begun and Peter would be his campaign manager or his second-in-command!

That's why Jesus' next words (about the necessity of his suffering in Jerusalem) hit Peter so hard. Jesus was making it immediately clear that, if he was the Messiah, then his kind of Messiahship was totally at odds with people's current expectations. He *would* rule God's people and free them from their enemies, but in a quite different way. He would not be taking up arms against the Romans; instead his own arms would in due course be stretched out on a Roman cross. And those who wanted to follow Jesus would have to be ready to 'take up their cross daily' too.

With these words Jesus is pouring cold water on a misplaced messianic enthusiasm. Indeed Peter's reaction only makes it clear why Jesus would always have to be so careful in public contexts when hinting at his Messiahship – his so-called 'messianic secret'. For it was almost impossible for this title not to be misunderstood. Jesus was doing something unheard of. He was putting together two Old Testament themes that had never been linked before: on the one hand, the royal, ruling Messiah and, on the other, the 'Suffering Servant' spoken of by the prophet Isaiah (Isaiah 52–53). It seemed a contradiction in terms. Yet this was the messianic vocation that Jesus had discovered. This was his distinctive manifesto. This was his unique identity and destiny. It was very different to anything expected within Judaism. And, of course, it stood even more at odds with anything within paganism. This was not the way Caesar – nor indeed puppet-kings like Philip – ruled the world.

Glory on the mountain

'About eight days later' Peter was in for another shock: a revelation of Jesus' true identity that went even beyond that of 'Messiah'. This time the group of disciples has been whittled down to just three: Peter, together with the brothers, James and John. Jesus takes them 'up onto a mountain' – almost certainly the slopes of Mount Hermon.

'Mountains' in biblical usage can mean what we might refer to simply as 'hills'; so we should probably be thinking of a hillside somewhere (there is also, by the way, no necessity for the episode to have taken place on a mountain-top or peak). Even so, in this region, where much of the area is marked by the flat volcanic rock of Gaulanitis, the most obvious location is somewhere on the lower slopes of Mount Hermon. Jesus is taking them to a place that is far removed from others, out of sight and hearing. It is a place for a private revelation of God. And its location on a 'mountain-side' may have been deliberately chosen by Jesus to conjure up memories of another mountain where God had revealed himself to Moses and later to Elijah – namely Mount Sinai.

Suddenly, as Jesus was praying, 'the appearance of his face changed, and his clothes became as bright as a flash of lightening' (Luke 9:29). This is the so-called transfiguration of Jesus, a unique moment when something of his unique inner identity was unveiled.

For Jesus himself, this strange event acts as a timely encouragement as he sets out on the lonely road towards his 'departure' (literally 'exodus') in Jerusalem. In a similar way to what happened at his baptism in the River Jordan, he now receives from God a father's affirmation: 'This is my Son, whom I have chosen' (Luke 9:35).

For the disciples, however, it is a powerful challenge. Their view of Jesus' identity must yet again be stretched beyond their wildest dreams. They see Jesus with Moses and Elijah, the two greatest figures of the Old Testament (representing the Law and the Prophets), but evidently Jesus is not just on a par with them. No, he is somehow more important still. Jesus is indeed a lawgiver and a prophet, but he is so much more. Like Moses he will be involved in bringing about another 'exodus', but unlike Moses this exodus will be for the benefit of *all* people – not just Israel. Indeed the disciples see his 'glory', a word closely associated with *God himself* in biblical thought. Moreover, they are enveloped by a cloud (clouds too in the Bible are associated with God, as the sign of his real presence). These are all hints at Jesus' divine identity. The voice that they hear then confirms this explicitly. And they are

'We have seen his glory, the glory of the One and Only, who came from the Father, full of grace and truth.'

John 1:14

The scene of the transfiguration: Tabor or Hermon?

'He was transfigured on Mount Tabor.'

Cyril, *Catechetical Lectures* 12:16

The precise identification of this important event must remain a mystery. However, since the middle of the fourth century Christians have traditionally identified this event with Mount Tabor – a distinctive, small mountain rising up from the Jezreel Valley, located some distance to the south-west of Lake Galilee.

There were aesthetic reasons for this identification. Tabor's well-rounded appearance gives it a natural aura of distinction, making it an easy place to identify with a sacred mountain; and, unlike many mountains, it has an accessible peak on which it is easy to imagine a mysterious event like the transfiguration taking place.

There were also practical reasons. As Christian tourism increased throughout the fourth century, visitors would have increasingly demanded a precise site for this event. And, given that visitors would be chiefly concerned to visit Nazareth and Lake Galilee, it made sense to select a location conveniently *en route* to these other sites. There was no point in selecting a site many miles to the north of Lake Galilee, since most visitors would never go that far. So we find Bishop Cyril of Jerusalem confidently asserting in AD 348 that the transfiguration took place 'on Mount Tabor' (*Catechetical Lectures* 12:16).

In reality the event is more likely to have occurred on the lower slopes of Mount Hermon, 50 miles (80 kilometres) to the north of Lake Galilee, or in the

adjacent hills of Gaulanitis. There is nothing in the biblical accounts to suggest that Jesus was on the peak of a mountain; they speak only of Jesus going up a 'high mountain' (Mark 9:2). And the word 'mountain' in our translations is also a little misleading, since the same word covers what we would refer to as a 'hill'. All that the biblical text requires is a remote hillside at some altitude. There are many such sites in the foothills of Mount Hermon. And the gospel reader is led naturally to this area through noting how the event comes a few days after Peter's confession in the area 'around Caesarea Philippi' (Mark 8:27). It is most unlikely that Jesus would have travelled to the diametrically opposite area beyond the lake in such a short space of time.

This preference for Mount Hermon was sensed before the time of Cyril by Christians such as Eusebius. Writing in the generation before Cyril, he seems to have known of the developing Tabor tradition, but still expresses a preference for Mount Hermon. In his *Commentary on the Psalms* he suggests that Psalm 89:12 (which refers to both Tabor and Hermon) could be a prophecy of Christ's 'marvellous transfigurations' on both these mountains. As a historian he may also have known from reading Josephus that in the first century there had been a village on the top of Mount Tabor: indeed Josephus himself built a wall around it to defend the site in the Jewish Revolt of AD 67 (*War* 2:20; 4:1). From a historian's perspective this was hardly a likely place for the transfiguration.

This is a good example of the tension that can sometimes exist between historical enquiry and the spiritual needs of visitors to identify an accessible and appropriate site. This happens elsewhere in the Holy Land where the less historically feasible site turns out to be more conducive to prayer and reflection. It forces upon us a realization that ultimately the event may be more important than the exact place, that theological truth may be more important than geographical exactitude.

The rounded hill of Mount Tabor standing out above the Plain of Jezreel. The village Deburriyah at its foot takes its name from Deborah, the Old Testament leader involved in the battles against Sisera in this Jezreel Valley (Judges 4–5).

Of all the events in the gospel accounts, the transfiguration is itself perhaps the best one to endorse this approach. It counters Peter's instinct to try to capture the event with physical markings (the building of three tents for Jesus, Elijah and Moses). It also forces the disciples to pay greater attention not to physical places but to God's word – 'Listen to him!'

Even so, this upward focus must never become merely spiritual, forgetting that, according to the Gospels, this and other events occurred in real historical time and place. In this sense the Christian faith is neither *mere history*, nor *mere spirituality*, but a delicate combination of the two. The transfiguration is an event rooted in the historical episode of Christ's incarnation, yet it points to the eternal realm of Christ's exaltation.

The transfiguration has continued to fire the imaginations of people down the centuries, as seen both in art and literature. It has become a major theme in Eastern Orthodox theology, being seen as a revelation of God's pattern that all believers should increasingly share in the 'divine nature' (known as *theiosis*). This language of 'participating in the divine nature' is derived from 2 Peter 1:4. In this short letter Peter reflects on this transfiguration event – it clearly marked him profoundly for the rest of his life – and wants the reader to sense its significance too:

We were eyewitnesses of his Majesty. For he received honour and glory from God the Father when the voice came to him from the Majestic Glory, saying 'This is my Son, whom I love; with him I am well pleased'. We ourselves heard this voice that came from heaven when we were with him on the sacred mountain.
2 Peter 1:16–18

left with a solemn command to obey: 'Listen to him'. If this is who Jesus truly is, his words must be heeded as God's words, and his commands obeyed as the commands of God.

And then suddenly, eerily, things return to normal: 'they found that Jesus was alone' (Luke 9:36). Not surprisingly, they keep quiet about what they have seen. Yet it will have made a profound and lasting impression.

And some weeks later, when in Jerusalem, Jesus will take the same three disciples with him to another hillside at the foot of the Mount of Olives – Gethsemane. This time, however, they will see a man in tears and deep distress. They will spend the rest of their lives putting these two powerful pictures together: the suffering of Gethsemane with the glory of the transfiguration.

The transfigured Jesus surrounded by Moses and Elijah (representing the Law and the Prophets).

Down from the mountain-top

Peter was on a steep learning curve. And it wasn't over yet. On the mountain he had blurted out the first thing that came into his head – 'Let's put up three shelters!' (Luke 9:33) – and had been politely interrupted by the divine voice, commanding him to stop talking and to listen. He had wanted to hold onto this precious experience, perhaps even to contain it or control it; but it had been snatched away as quickly as it had arrived. And then, as they leave the mountain, he and the other two disciples hit cold reality.

'Tabor has the aura of a sacred mountain.'

J. Murphy O'Connor

While they have been away, the remaining disciples have signally failed to heal a demon-possessed boy brought to them by a desperate father. Just as Moses, coming down from Mount Sinai, had encountered Israel's faithlessness in the episode of the golden calf (Exodus 32), so now Jesus runs straight into his disciples' lack of faith: 'O unbelieving and perverse generation; how long shall I stay with you?' (Luke 9:41). Jesus heals the boy. The result is that everyone – not just those who had been on the hillside with Jesus – is now 'amazed at the greatness of God'.

These episodes in the region of Caesarea Philippi prove to be central to the story of Jesus. Far removed from both Galilee and Jerusalem, they point to the deeper meaning of what is going on beneath the surface in those places. The disciples (and therefore the gospel readers too) are being ushered into a whole new way of seeing Jesus. Challenged by his questions and rebuked by his exasperation, their faith in him is being tested. And a new vision is being offered to those who have 'ears to hear'.

Meanwhile for Jesus, the die has been cast. The preliminary phase of his ministry has ended. Coming down from the mountain, he now 'resolutely sets out for Jerusalem' (Luke 9:51), and tells his disciples plainly what really lies in store for him in the capital city: 'The Son of Man must suffer many things and be rejected... and he must be killed...' (Luke 9:22). So Luke begins a long section of ten chapters (sometimes known as the 'Travel Narrative') in which we see Jesus pressing on towards his goal of Jerusalem. At one point in the middle of this narrative Jesus summarizes his journey and its destination. 'I must keep going today and tomorrow and the next day – for surely no prophet can die outside Jerusalem!' (Luke 13:33). Jesus knows where and how it will all end. From the mountain-top experience of the transfiguration, there is a sense in which it is now down hill all the way.

Key dates: Caesarea Philippi

c. 198 BC	The Seleucids of Syria conquer the Ptolemies of Egypt near Paneas, bringing the area under Syrian control.	2 BC	Herod's son Philip makes Caesarea Philippi the capital of his 'tetrarchy', renaming it after himself and the emperor.	AD 300	Christian church now well established, with some continuing Jewish presence. Eusebius mentions a statue preserved here of the woman whom Jesus healed of the issue of blood (*Ecclesiastical History* 7:18).
20 BC	Area given by Emperor Augustus to Herod the Great, who builds a temple of white marble near Pan spring.	AD 55	Herod Agrippa attempts to rename the city 'Neronias' after Emperor Nero.	1100–1300	Various conquests by the Crusaders and later by the Mamluks.
		AD 70	Titus spends some time in the area after his capture of Jerusalem. Many of his Jewish prisoners died here.	1967	The tiny Syrian village on the site (now known as Banyas) is brought within Israel.

Caesarea Philippi Today

Ancient Caesarea Philippi can be identified with confidence because of its proximity to the **great cave** at the foot of Mount Hermon. The headwaters of the River Jordan used to flow out directly from a spring within this cave, though now, because of an earthquake, they come through a crack beneath the cave. In many ways this natural feature remains the most significant site to visit in the area. Nearby (slightly over to the right) are some remains from the second and third centuries AD – an open air shrine and a temple. The cave itself, however, was brought within Herod the Great's temple to be its inner sanctuary. Meanwhile, further to the left, there is a natural terrace that may possibly have been the site of Philip's palace.

Across the road are the remains of the **medieval town**, with some clear evidence of Crusader walls and towers. The best evidence of the first-century town are the remains of **twelve parallel vaults**, which are thought to have been warehouses close to the city's forum or marketplace.

The site serves as a clear reminder of the non-Jewish nature of the area in the time of Jesus. Since the Gospels suggest that Jesus may not have visited the city itself, visitors may prefer to focus on the general surroundings. One can sense the close proximity of Mount Hermon and the importance of this fresh water for all the land to

Canaanite and Israelite remains on the site of ancient Hazor, with views across the Hula Valley.

the south – supplied by the melting snows of this massive mountain.

Some may then choose to visit nearby **Dan**, another area marked by fresh water springs that feed into the Jordan. Others will go up the winding road to visit **Nimrod Castle**, an impressive Muslim castle built in the era of the Crusades. From its battlements there are fine views back across the Hula Valley. Nowadays this area is marked by well-organized agriculture. But until the nineteenth century the area was covered with malarial swamps (partly overcome by the many eucalyptus trees imported to help drain the area). It seems likely that in the time of Jesus much of the area along the upper stretches of the River Jordan would have been marshy and inhospitable. This may only strengthen the case for suggesting that Jesus was quite deliberate in bringing his disciples this far north, away from their normal comfort zones. The site of Caesarea Philippi is just over 30 miles (48 kilometres) to the north of Lake Galilee.

Jericho

*As Jesus approached Jericho, a blind man was sitting by the roadside begging.
When he heard the crowd going by, he asked what was happening. They told
him, 'Jesus of Nazareth is passing by.' He called out, 'Jesus, Son of David, have
mercy on me!'... Jesus stopped and ordered the man to be brought to him... [He]
asked him, 'What do you want me to do for you?' 'Lord, I want to see,' he
replied. Jesus said to him, 'Receive your sight; your faith has healed you.'
Immediately he received his sight and followed Jesus, praising God. When all
the people saw it, they also praised God.*

*Jesus entered Jericho and was passing through. A man was there by the name of
Zacchaeus; he was a chief tax collector and was wealthy. He wanted to see who
Jesus was, but being a short man he could not, because of the crowd. So he ran
ahead and climbed a sycamore-fig tree to see him, since Jesus was coming that way.*

*When Jesus reached the spot, he looked up and said to him, 'Zacchaeus, come
down immediately. I must stay at your house today.' So he came down at once and
welcomed him gladly. All the people saw this and began to mutter, 'He has gone to
be the guest of a "sinner".' But Zacchaeus stood up and said to the Lord, 'Look,
Lord! Here and now I give half of my possessions to the poor, and if I have cheated
anybody out of anything, I will pay back four times the amount.' Jesus said to him,
'Today salvation has come to this house, because this man, too, is a son of
Abraham. For the Son of Man came to seek and to save what was lost.'*

Luke 18:35–19:10

The lowest city in the world

In order to avoid travelling through Samaria, Galilean pilgrims on their way to
Jerusalem normally travelled down the Jordan Valley and then approached Jerusalem
from the east. So when Jesus set out on his final journey to Jerusalem, we can imagine
him travelling with his followers along this valley with the hills of Samaria and Gilboa
on their right (to the west) and the hills of Gilead on their left.

Because it was below sea level, the Jordan Valley would have been quite hot and
sultry – even in March. At this time of year the hills may well have been covered with
a feather-light greenness, and there may have been some vegetation close by the banks
of the River Jordan, but the chief oasis in this otherwise barren terrain would have
been Jericho – some 55 miles (90 kilometres) south of Lake Galilee and just 7 miles (11
kilometres) north of the Dead Sea. Almost everyone travelling from Galilee to
Jerusalem would inevitably pass through Jericho, a vital refreshment point before
making the ascent up to Jerusalem.

The mound of Old Testament Jericho (*Tel es-Sultan*), showing the large excavation trenches, with the greenery of the oasis beyond.

It was indeed a beautiful oasis in the middle of the desert, filled with date palms, bougainvilleas and fruit trees. Although stiflingly hot and humid in high summer, in wintertime it came into its own as a balmy tonic for those who came down from the chill winds in Jerusalem. Not surprisingly some of Jerusalem's aristocracy had 'second homes' here, such as King Herod's winter palace.

By the time of Jesus there had been people living in this oasis for nearly 8 millennia. Jericho is the oldest continually inhabited town in the world, with settlements going back to nearly 8000 BC. In the last 100 years a 'new' Jericho had grown up, located over half a mile to the south of the old town. The old town was now abandoned – an ancient mound that bore ample testimony to Jericho's antiquity.

Jericho: Old and new

As Jesus passed ancient Jericho and approached the modern town, he would have been aware of just how significant Jericho had been in the past. For this was the place where the Israelites had first entered the Promised Land. Crossing over the River Jordan from the east under their new leader, Joshua, their first task was the capture of this strategic town. Their victory here was a sign that God was at work for his people and a 'first-fruit' or 'pledge' of what they would then take many years to achieve – the full possession of the land.

Visitors to Jericho, both ancient and modern, have often visited the Dead Sea as well, just 7 miles (11 kilometres) to the south of Jericho. The Bordeaux Pilgrim, for example, when visiting in the fourth century, made a detour here and commented: 'its water is extremely bitter, fish are nowhere to be found in it, and no ships sail there. If anyone goes to swim in it, the water turns him upside down' (*Bordeaux Pilgrim* 597). Similarly the Roman general Vespasian, when in the area in AD 68, could not resist forcing some people who could not swim into the Dead Sea to see if they could float – even with their arms tied (Josephus, *War* 4:9). More amusingly, the Byzantine designer of the Madaba Map mosaic (see page 199) inserted a delightful depiction of fish coming down the River Jordan and then trying to swim back. There is a stark contrast between this 'sea of death' and Lake Galilee in the north, brimming with life.

The unique nature of the Dead Sea has attracted comment throughout history. Associated with the biblical stories of Sodom and Gomorrah that were in the 'land of the plain' (Genesis 19), it was also mentioned by classical writers such as Aristotle and Strabo, who refer to it as 'Lake of Asphalt'. Its distinctive character is a result of there being no exit at the southern end for the water that has entered it (either from the Jordan or from the *wadis* that bring flash floods down from the surrounding hills); this in turn is caused by the fact that it is the lowest place on the planet. Its surface lies at 1,350 feet (411 metres) below sea level.

Because of the amount of water taken from Lake Galilee for modern consumption, the water levels of the Dead Sea are continuing to drop yet further. The only escape for water is therefore by evaporation. The result is that the remaining water is a concentration of such minerals as magnesium, calcium and potassium. From ancient times to the present, these minerals have been collected and used for industrial purposes. More recently its waters have become attractive to tourists, with several spas being built along its shores.

There are several historical sites along the shorelines of the Dead Sea and in the hills beyond. In the hills of Jordan (to the east) can be seen both Mount Nebo, the traditional site from which Moses viewed the Promised Land before his death (Deuteronomy 34:1), and the fortress of Machaerus, where Herod Antipas had John the Baptist executed according to Josephus (*Antiquities*, 18.5). Down the western shore lie Qumran (see page 46), the springs of Ein Gedi (where David hid from Saul according to 1 Samuel 24), and the famous outcrop of Masada (see page 105).

It is a famous story, which the people of Jesus' day would have remembered for various reasons.

- ◆ The importance of Israel being 'consecrated to the Lord' and obeying his commands, not departing 'to the right or to the left' (Joshua 1:7);
- ◆ The mysterious appearance of the 'Commander of the Lord's army' (Joshua 5:13–15). Was this the Lord himself?
- ◆ The judgment of Achan, but the rescue of Rahab – the latter being an example of God rescuing people of faith (even those outside the people of Israel);
- ◆ God's provision to Israel of a successor to Moses: Joshua, a man whose name fittingly meant 'God saves' or 'salvation'.

Now another person with that powerful name was approaching Jericho – not Joshua, son of Nun, but Jesus of Nazareth. And in his wake are his twelve disciples. Symbolically they are a miniature version of the twelve tribes of Israel, Jesus' new people. Like Israel of old who grumbled in the desert, they have been arguing along the road, trying to work out which of them is the greatest. For they sense that Jesus' journey is going to lead to the establishment of God's kingdom, and they want to have prime seats at the royal party.

Indeed, to them it seems that history is repeating itself: just as Joshua went into the long-awaited 'Promised Land', so now Jesus is going to establish the long-awaited 'kingdom' and overthrow God's enemies. And Jesus indeed seems to have a sense that judgment is looming. His parable about the stern king who came back from a long journey expecting to receive appropriate fruit from his servants concludes with the killing of the king's enemies: 'Those enemies of mine who did not want me to be a king over them – bring them here and kill them in front of me' (Luke 19:27).

So what will Jesus do when he approaches this new Jericho? In fact Jesus does not speak out against God's enemies here; he keeps that stored up for Jerusalem. Instead he highlights God's concern to rescue those who call out to him. There is the healing of the blind man, whom Mark names as Bartimaeus. Bartimaeus calls out to Jesus, calling him 'Son of David' (that is, the one many believed would be the next king). Because of his faith in Jesus, he is healed.

And, above all, there is the famous story of the man who climbed up a fruit tree to catch a glimpse of Jesus: Zacchaeus. This wealthy Jewish tax-collector, hated by his own people for being on the side of the Romans, was the one whom Jesus insisted on visiting.

For Luke this episode takes us to the heart of what Jesus was about: his lack of concern for his own reputation; his concern for specific individuals; his challenge to financial corruption; and his welcome to 'outsiders' (even the wealthy, even those who 'collaborated' with the Romans). Jesus was the one who had come actively seeking 'to save what was lost' (Luke 19:10).

A few chapters earlier Jesus had told some parables explaining his own actions, all of which highlighted how God seeks out the lost: the shepherd who lost his sheep; the woman who lost a coin; and the father of the Prodigal Son (Luke 15). All of these went seeking for what was lost and were delighted when they found it. So now Jesus does exactly this for a lost individual named Zacchaeus. He is doing God's work.

Finally, there is something about the way Jesus focuses exclusively on this one person, Zacchaeus, which is strangely reminiscent of what had happened here so many centuries before to Rahab. Alone among all the inhabitants of Jericho, it was this Gentile prostitute who was rescued by Joshua. And just as Joshua (the man of

'On the seventh day, they got up at daybreak and marched around the city seven times…
The seventh time around, when the priests sounded the trumpet blast, Joshua commanded the people, "Shout! For the Lord has given you the city!"'

Joshua 6:15–16

The siege of Masada

Masada came to prominence in the years after the destruction of Jerusalem, when it became the last ditch stand-off for the Zealots (AD 73–74). Josephus describes the Romans' siege of Masada in graphic detail, including a speech (extracts below) given by Eliezer, a Zealot leader, in which he encourages all the besieged to commit suicide rather than be found alive by the Romans. The next day, says Josephus, the Romans were greeted by an eerie silence and just seven survivors (two women and five children).

It seems likely that Josephus embellished the story quite considerably; there seem to be some parallels, for example, with Josephus' own claim to have survived a mutual suicide pact at Jotopata. The length of the speech he gives to Eliezer is comparable to other such dramatic speeches in ancient authors, but it sounds very much like Josephus writing in his own style. Yet his account still makes for powerful reading.

Masada marks the tragic endpoint of the nationalistic zeal which was growing apace throughout the previous generations and set the backdrop for Jesus' ministry. And with its fall, we come to the close of the first-century world that he would have known and recognized. Jesus had warned what might happen in one brief sentence: '…all who draw the sword will die by the sword' (Matthew 26:52).

Since we long ago, my generous friends, resolved never to be servants to the Romans, nor to any other than to God himself, who alone is the true and just Lord of mankind, the time is now come that obliges us to make that resolution true in practice… We were the very first that revolted from them, and we are the last that fight against them;… it is still in our power to die bravely, and in a state of freedom, which has not been the case of others…

It is very plain that we shall be taken within a day's time; but it is still an eligible thing to die after a glorious manner, together with our dearest friends… It had been proper indeed for us to have conjectured at the purpose of God much sooner… and to have been sensible that the same God, who had of old taken the Jewish nation into his favour, had now condemned them to destruction; for had he continued favourable, he would not have overlooked the destruction of so many men, or delivered his most holy city to be burnt and demolished by our enemies… So consider how God has convinced us that our hopes were in vain, by bringing such distress upon us in the desperate state we are now in…

These punishments let us not receive from the Romans, but from God himself, as executed by our own hands; for these will be more moderate than the other. Let our wives die before they are abused, and our children before they have tasted of slavery; and after we have killed them, let us bestow that glorious benefit upon one another mutually, and preserve ourselves in freedom, as an excellent funeral monument for us. But first let us destroy our money and the fortress by fire; … and let us spare nothing

but our provisions; for they will be a witness when we are dead that we were not subdued for want of necessities, but that, according to our original resolution, we have preferred death before slavery.'

Josephus, *War* 7:8

Herod's palace on the extreme promontory of Masada, with store houses and bath complex (above and to the south).

Key dates: Jericho

7800 BC	Mesolithic villagers in the area.	30 BC	Gardens returned to King Herod by Octavian/Augustus; development of 'Cyprus' (a stronghold to the west overlooking the town), and the Roman road up to Jerusalem.	AD 400s	New Byzantine town (Ericha) built a mile to the east of Roman Jericho.
6850 BC	Building of walls (6.5 feet/2 metres thick): settlement for 200 people (covering over 8 acres/3 hectares).			c. 1850	Greek Orthodox monastery built on side of the Mount of Temptation ('Quarantal').
1400–1200 BC	Era of Joshua and the Israelite conquest.	4 BC	Herod the Great dies in his palace in Jericho.	1930s	Excavations of *Tel es-Sultan* by James Garstang.
c. 870 BC	Jericho resettled in the time of King Ahab and visited by the prophets Elijah and Elisha (2 Kings 2).	AD 69	Jericho's inhabitants are expelled by Titus (Josephus, *War* 4.8).	1950s	Continued excavations by Kathleen Kenyon.
37 BC	Mark Anthony gives to Cleopatra the date-orchards and balsam gardens in Jericho.	AD 200	Some scrolls of the Bible are discovered near the town (according to Origen).	1967	Jericho comes under Israeli rule.
36 BC	Seventeen-year-old High Priest Aristobulus (the last of the Hasmonean dynasty) is drowned at a garden party in Herod's Palace (Josephus, *War* 1:2).	c. AD 333	The Bordeaux Pilgrim visits the area and records its chief sites (see page 107).	1994	Jericho is one of the first areas to be brought under Palestinian control (as a result of the Oslo accord).

'salvation') had entered Jericho, so now Jesus hints at his own role as the unique Saviour who has been sent both to this town and to the world. Truly, in several senses of the word, '*Salvation* has come to this house today!' (Luke 19:9).

Jericho Today

Modern Jericho has expanded considerably in recent years. It was one of the first areas to be ceded back to Palestinian control in the early 1990s. From a distance, it can appear at first to be a mirage on the horizon, but gradually it is revealed as a stunning oasis in the desert. At the heart of this oasis there still remains the ancient spring which, it is estimated, produces over 1,000 gallons (3,800 litres) a minute. This is still a vital meeting place for many as they collect water for the coming day.

As one approaches it from the north, some of the area to the right shows signs of the mud-hut camps where Palestinian refugees lived for several decades after 1948. Then the high mound of the **ancient city** (known as *Tel es-Sultan*) comes clearly into view, standing up from the plain as a discrete entity, covering an area of 8 acres (3 hectares). By the time of the Israelites' entrance into the Promised Land (there remains considerable controversy as to whether this was in the fourteenth or twelfth century BC), this mound had already played host to at least *twenty* different settlements. Today, helped by some archaeological surgical sections, one can see evidence of some of the ancient walls and a great circular stone tower (30 feet or

On the right-hand side, as one descends from the mount, behind a tomb, is the sycamore tree into which Zacchaeus climbed… A mile and a half from the town is the fountain of Elisha… Above the same fountain is the house of the harlot Rahab… Here stood the city of Jericho, round whose walls the children of Israel circled with the Ark of the Covenant… Nothing is to be seen of it except the place where the Ark stood, and the twelve stones which the children of Israel brought out of Jordan.

These are the notes of a visit to the Jericho area made by someone travelling from Gaul (modern France) to the Holy Land in the year AD 333, known to us as the Bordeaux Pilgrim. His style is brief but this log book of his journey gives us an insight into the very earliest days of 'pilgrimage' to the Holy Land. Constantine had come to power in the eastern half of the empire only nine years previously at the Battle of Adrianople. The fact that the Pilgrim made the journey at all is a witness to how Constantine's reign was opening up new travel opportunities. His record is also a fascinating window into what the local guides were pointing out to their new visitors!

Generally he comes across as a little gullible. He makes some evident mistakes (for example, thinking the Mount of Olives was the scene of the transfiguration, not the ascension) and many of the things pointed out to him could hardly be authentic: had Rahab's house really survived for 1500 years? Had Zacchaeus' sycamore tree been identified and preserved for 300 years? By and large, one senses that local guides are quick and resourceful, pandering to visitors' desires for biblical stories to be anchored in assured locations. Not surprisingly then, scholars tend to view with some scepticism 'traditions' which only appear for the first time in the fourth century.

The Bordeaux Pilgrim visited Bethlehem and ancient Samaria (see page 82), but his most copious notes were made when visiting Jerusalem and the Mount of Olives. Here are a few more extracts as we approach Jerusalem:

There are in Jerusalem two large pools at the side of the temple… which were made by Solomon; and further in the city are twin pools, with five porticoes, which are called Bethsaida…

Here is also the corner of an exceeding high tower, where our Lord ascended and the tempter [tempted] him… And in the building itself, where stood the temple which Solomon built, they say that the blood of Zacharias… remains to this day… There are two statues of Hadrian, and not far from the statues there is a perforated stone, to which the Jews come every year and anoint it, bewail themselves with groans, rend their garments, and so depart.

Also as you come out of Jerusalem to go up Mount Sion, on the left hand, below in the valley, beside the wall, is a pool which is called Siloe and has four porticoes; and there is another large pool outside it. … On this side one goes up Sion, and sees where the house of Caiaphas the priest was, and there still stands a column against which Christ was beaten with rods…

From thence as you go out of the wall of Sion, as you walk towards the gate of Neapolis, towards the right, below in the valley, are walls, where was the house or praetorium of Pontius Pilate. Here our Lord was tried before his passion. On the left hand is the little hill of Golgotha where the Lord was crucified. About a stone's throw from thence is a vault (crypta) wherein his body was laid, and rose again on the third day. There, at present, by the command of the Emperor Constantine, has been built a basilica, that is to say, a church of wondrous beauty, having at the side reservoirs from which water is raised, and a bath behind in which infants are washed.

Also as one goes from Jerusalem to the gate which is to the eastward, in order to ascend the Mount of Olives, is the valley called that of Josaphat. Towards the left, where are vineyards, is a stone at the place where Judas Iscariot betrayed Christ; on the right is a palm-tree, branches of which the children carried off and strewed in the way when Christ came…

From there you ascend to the Mount of Olives, where before the Passion, the Lord taught his disciples. There by the orders of Constantine a basilica of great beauty has been built. Not far from thence is the little hill which the Lord ascended to pray, when he took Peter and John with Him, and Moses and Elias were seen.

9 metres high), with 22 steps down its centre – dated by carbon dating to 6850 BC (plus or minus 210 years).

Standing on top of the mound and looking up and down the Rift Valley, one is conscious of being in a place of vast antiquity. This was where our predecessors nearly 10,000 years ago eked out an existence in this harsh landscape and first built walls around themselves for protection. There is no denying that it stood at a critical location – the meeting-point of the valley (north and south) and the roads across the Jordan to the hill-country (east and west). The nearby Allenby Bridge crossing is now the main way to Amman, another 25 miles (40 kilometres) beyond, its lights visible in the evening from the top of the TransJordan hills.

Although there is an Orthodox Church dedicated to Saint Zacchaeus and various trees may be pointed out as the supposed 'sycamore tree' of the Gospels, the other major site to focus on is **Herod's Palace**. This is 1.5 miles (2.5 kilometres) to the south of the ancient *tel* and was adjacent to the area where New Jericho was being built in the days of Jesus. The remains of the palace, with its two swimming pools, give a clear indication of Herodian luxury. From here there is a clear view up to Herod's fortress (named 'Cyprus' after his mother); evidently, even when relaxing, Herod always had the issue of security clearly on his mind. Right by the ruins is the track that goes west up into the Wadi Qelt towards Jerusalem. Jericho, then as now, is the necessary crossroads for those travelling both north and south, east and west.

Sunrise over the hills of TransJordan from the western side of the Dead Sea.

Bethany

While he was in Bethany, reclining at the table in the home of a man known as Simon the Leper, a woman came with an alabaster jar of very expensive perfume, made of pure nard. She broke the jar and poured the perfume on his head. Some of those present were saying indignantly to one another, 'Why this waste of perfume? It could have been sold for more than a year's wages and the money given to the poor'... 'Leave her alone,' said Jesus. 'Why are you bothering her? She has done a beautiful thing to me. The poor you will always have with you, and you can help them any time you want. But you will not always have me. She did what she could. She poured perfume on my body beforehand to prepare for my burial. I tell you the truth, wherever the gospel is preached throughout the world, what she has done will also be told, in memory of her.'

Mark 14:3–9

A quiet haven

Bethany was a tiny hamlet, consisting of perhaps just twenty homes. It was perched on the south-eastern slopes of the Mount of Olives. If you lived in the first century and wanted a place of quiet retreat, this was the ideal location. If you looked out from your doorway to the east and to the south, you could look over the dry expanses of the Judean Desert. Apart from a few nomadic tents, there would be no signs of human habitation in your view, because Bethany was the last outpost before the desert.

So you could wake in Bethany and see the sun rise over the hills of Trans-Jordan from the western side of the Dead Sea, then watch as its light gradually flooded the Jordan Valley some 3,000 feet (900 metres) below you and began glinting on the surface of the Dead Sea 12 miles (20 kilometres) to your east. Turning a little to the south you would also be able to make out the distinct conical shape of the Herodium, the hill-fort bunker not far from Bethlehem, which Herod the Great had used as his last bastion and hideout just over 30 years before.

When the wind was in the east, the dry heat of the desert would waft over you oppressively; but mercifully the wind normally came from the other direction, sometimes bringing fresh breezes up from the Mediterranean. So you could look over the desert at one remove from some of its heat. And you were sheltered too from something else: the bustle of Jerusalem, just 2 miles (3 kilometres) behind you, out of sight on the far side of the Mount of Olives. It was the ideal location if you wanted to get away from it all – just 45 minutes' walk from the busy city, but a different world breathing a different air.

The Greek Orthodox church (top) and the Franciscan church (bottom) in Bethany. Between them (near the mosque's minaret) is the traditional tomb of Lazarus. In Jesus' day this tomb would have been outside the village, itself lying further up the hill to the west.

Jesus' 'home from home'

We learn from all the Gospels that this was a favoured haunt of Jesus in the days leading up to his death. He had been here before and established a loyal friendship with at least one family – that of Lazarus and his two sisters, Mary and Martha. Although Luke only speaks of a 'certain village', the famous story of Martha's complaints amid her domestic chores is almost certainly to be located here in Bethany. (If so, it is evidence that Jesus had been up to Jerusalem on other, earlier occasions, not only for this last visit emphasized by the three Synoptic Gospels.) One senses that the home of Mary and Martha was a place where Jesus felt welcome, comfortable and relaxed – a 'home from home'. For one who had an itinerant lifestyle and who had once commented that he had 'no place to lay his head' (Luke 9:58), such places were no doubt doubly welcome.

So as Jesus came up the Roman road from Jericho wanting to make some distinctive preparations for his entrance into Jerusalem, he sent his disciples on a slight detour south to the neighbouring hamlets of Bethphage and Bethany. Perhaps in keeping with a previous arrangement, they would find a donkey there, ready for their master's use (Luke 19:28–32). Because Jesus had friends in Bethany, the antics of his disciples would not be questioned.

'Bethany – the "home of Jesus".'

Origen, Commentary on Matthew 26:26

And from then on, as the storm clouds gathered over his public ministry, Bethany would become for Jesus a vital safe haven. In the days leading up to Passover, Luke talks of Jesus leaving Jerusalem each night for the 'Mount of Olives'. Almost certainly this refers to Bethany (Matthew 21:17). Lazarus' home was a place of retreat and refreshment, from which Jesus went out revitalized to face the heat of Jerusalem, its leaders and its crowds.

We sense an implicit contrast here between the big city of Jerusalem and the tiny hamlet of Bethany – one a place of controversy and ultimate rejection, the other a place of peace and safety. So it would be no coincidence that, when the time came for Jesus to bid his disciples a final farewell (at his ascension), this too would take place near Bethany. For this, not Jerusalem, had been his true home.

Place of escape

Lazarus' home in Bethany was also, in all probability, the place to which most of the male disciples would flee on the night of Jesus' arrest. The Gospels simply state that 'they deserted him and fled' (Mark 14:50). But where would they have fled to? Jesus was being led back *westwards* into the city from Gethsemane, itself located at the foot of the Mount of Olives. The logical path of escape was therefore *eastwards*, beyond the tents of the Passover pilgrims sleeping out on the hillside, and over the crest of the hill to Bethany. Here they could regroup.

But if so, then they probably kept themselves out of Jerusalem for the rest of that fateful weekend – they would not have seen Jesus die. Mary would sneak into the city on the Friday, but quite probably the disciples who remained in Bethany would not have been brought up to date with the awful news of Jesus' death until after the Sabbath ended on the Saturday evening. Bethany was indeed a safe place, but it was also too far away for news to travel quickly, and it would therefore have been a place of anxious waiting. They probably did not dare go back into Jerusalem until some time on the Sunday.

If correct, this gives another reason why it was fitting for Jesus' final departure to take place near Bethany. For this place had proved to be a vital home, not just for Jesus himself, but also for his band of friends. Jerusalem was potentially a dangerous place, but this was the place – as it were 'under the nose' of Jerusalem – from which Jesus could effectively launch his alternative community into the world. And in this way the place of their earlier anxious waiting would also become the place of confident expectation. Jesus would return.

Yet Bethany stands out in the other Gospels for two other remarkable episodes: one poignant and sombre, marked by death; the other quite the reverse, speaking powerfully of victory and life beyond the grave.

The intuitive anointing

For whatever reason, the woman who anointed Jesus at the house of Simon the Leper is not named by Mark, but John states that it was Mary (John 12:3). The woman who had chosen earlier to sit at Jesus' feet and listen to his words now approached him with an alabaster jar of expensive perfume and began to pour its contents over his feet. It was so embarrassing.

Those gathered there, including Judas Iscariot, rebuked her, focusing on the issue of sheer extravagance – the perfume could have been sold for 'a year's wages' (John 12:5). But Jesus saw it as an intuitive and symbolic act. Mary had sensed what others had not: that Jesus would soon be dead. This was her way of anointing his body in advance; it was her way of showing that she knew and that she cared; it was her way of doing what she might not be able to do later; indeed her way of giving her most precious thing as a gift to the one she loved. And Jesus did not rebuke her.

With hindsight we can note the bitter irony that for Jesus (whom his followers would soon be proclaiming as the true king of the world and indeed as the heavenly 'bridegroom') this anointing in Bethany would be the closest he ever came in his human life to a coronation or a wedding. But this anointing was simultaneously a prophetic symbol of his own funeral. Jesus indicated that this strange, silent act at this meal in backwater Bethany would be told 'throughout the world… in memory of her' (Mark 14:9). And it has been.

Power and emotion at the tomb: the raising of Lazarus

Yet Bethany stands out in the gospel tradition most famously because it is the scene of Jesus' most powerful miracle – the raising of Lazarus. The last word in Bethany is not death, but life.

Now a man named Lazarus was sick. He was from Bethany, the village of Mary and her sister Martha… So the sisters sent word to Jesus, 'Lord, the one you love is sick.'… On his arrival, Jesus found that Lazarus had already been in the tomb for four days… Now Jesus had not yet entered the village, but was still at the place where Martha had met him. When the Jews who had been with Mary in the house, comforting her, noticed how quickly she got up and went out, they followed her, supposing she was going to the tomb to mourn there. When Mary reached the place where Jesus was and saw him, she fell at his feet and said, 'Lord, if you had been here, my brother would not have died.' When Jesus saw her weeping, and the Jews who had come along with her also weeping, he was deeply moved in spirit and troubled. 'Where have you laid him?' he asked. 'Come and see, Lord,' they replied. Jesus wept. Then the Jews said, "See how he loved him!"… Jesus, once more deeply moved, came to the tomb. It was a cave with a stone laid across the entrance. 'Take away the stone,' he said. … Then Jesus said, 'Did I not tell you that if you believed, you would see the glory of God?'

When he had said this, Jesus called in a loud voice, 'Lazarus, come out!' The dead man came out, his hands and feet wrapped with strips of linen, and a cloth around his face. Jesus said to them, 'Take off the grave clothes and let him go.'

John 11:1–42

This is a story filled with grief and human emotion. Jesus is seen weeping. Yet the ultimate message of Bethany for John is clear: Jesus is the one with unique power over the grave; he is himself the 'resurrection and the life' (John 11:25).

Yet this climax to the first half of John's Gospel ends on an ironic note. This miracle causes some people to go back from Bethany to the religious leaders in Jerusalem who in turn begin to plot Jesus' death. The questions for those reading the Gospel become: Why is this Jesus, who evidently has power over death, himself going to die? And what will happen after he has died? Will death really be the final word?

In this way Bethany sends an advance signal back to Jerusalem – a signal of God's resurrection power in Jesus. Bethany is thus not just a safe haven, a home for Jesus and the disciples; it is not just a place where we see Jesus deeply involved in the life of a human family; it is not just a place of preparation – for the events of Palm Sunday or for the crucifixion. It is also the place of new life, a tiny hamlet with a tomb outside it that has witnessed the life-giving power of Jesus the Messiah.

> *'Jesus said to her, "I am the resurrection and the life. Anyone who believes in me will live, even though they die…"'*
>
> **John 11:25**

Key dates: Bethany

c. 530 BC	Exiles from the tribe of Benjamin inhabit the village of Bet Ananiah further up hill (Nehemiah 11:32).	c. AD 350–80	Building of the 'Lazarium' church, with the atrium and entrance to the tomb lying to the west of the church.
c. AD 290	Eusebius refers to Lazarus' tomb as a 'vault' (*Onomastikon* 58:15–17).	AD 381–84	Egeria visits on 'Lazarus Saturday', eight days before Easter.
AD 333	The Bordeaux Pilgrim speaks of 'the vault (*crypta*) in which was laid Lazarus, whom the Lord raised' (*BP* 596:1).	AD 500s	Expansion of 'Lazarium' church (apse moved further to the east)
		c. 1138–44	Queen Melisende builds a convent and Crusader church over the tomb.
1300s	Churches in ruins; tomb-entrance now a mosque.		
1566–75	Franciscans cut a new tomb-entrance (from northern side).		
1954	Franciscan church built (over the site of the fourth-century church), including excavations by the Franciscan archaeologist, Saller.		
1965	Greek Orthodox church built on a new site to the west of the tomb.		

Bethany Today

There is no doubting the general location of Bethany. The Arabic village of El-Azarieh preserves in its name the way the Byzantines referred to it – as the 'Lazarium', that is, 'the place of Lazarus'. Until recently this was a tiny village. If you were able to walk there directly from the peak of the Mount of Olives it would only be 20 minutes away, going in a south-easterly direction. This is clearly the area of Jesus' Bethany. And, although there has been much building and expansion in the last 70 years, one can still sense that this is the last place of habitation before the Judean Desert to the east.

However, we do not know the exact location of the home of Simon the Leper or of Lazarus and his sisters. The homes of first-century Bethany may have been a little further up the hill, in an area now inaccessible to visitors. This has come about because the prime focus in the early church was not on these homes but on the location of Lazarus' tomb, which by the nature of things would have been *outside* the village (and normally to the east). In the writings of Origen (c. AD 240) we see some early Christian reflection on Bethany being the place where Jesus felt at home, but there is no evidence that Origen went in search of the ancient village. In the writings of Eusebius and Cyril (50 to 100 years later) the focus has shifted to the miracle of Lazarus being raised from the dead.

There is a strong likelihood that **Lazarus' tomb** has been correctly identified and preserved. Certainly the traditional tomb that is now known as his tomb was in a

Egeria's visit to Bethany

Below is Egeria's description of prayers at the Lazarium in Bethany on the Saturday before Palm Sunday:

At one o'clock all go to the Lazarium – that is, Bethany… And as they go from Jerusalem to the Lazarium, there is… a church in the street on that spot where Mary the sister of Lazarus met with the Lord. Here, when the bishop arrives, all the monks meet him, and the people enter the church… and that passage is read in the Gospel where the sister of Lazarus meets the Lord…

Then they go thence with hymns to the Lazarium. And on arriving at the Lazarium, so great a multitude assembles that not only the place itself, but also the fields around, are full of people. Hymns and antiphons suitable to the day and to the place are said, and likewise all the lessons are read. Then… the priest ascends to a higher place and reads the passage that is written in the Gospel ('when Jesus six days before the Passover had come to Bethany' etc)… This is done on that day because… these events took place in Bethany 'six days before the Passover'.

Egeria 29:3–6

As we journey closer to Jerusalem we will refer to Egeria more often. Already we have noticed some of her comments from her visit to Galilee (see page 78). Who was she? And why is her diary so important?

Egeria seems to have been a Spanish nun. She made an extended visit to the eastern half of the Roman empire between AD 381 and 384. Travelling from Constantinople she arrived in Jerusalem in time to celebrate Easter in AD 381. She then stayed in the Holy Land for three years, making excursions to Egypt, the Sinai Desert, Mount Nebo and Galilee. She left after Easter in AD 384, returning to Constantinople via Antioch and Edessa. She seems to have had an indomitable spirit and a hardy constitution, travelling all these distances by mule or on foot.

Writing for her community of nuns back home, she kept a detailed record of her travels. The one surviving manuscript was discovered in Arezzo in 1884 and since then has been recognized as a key text giving insight into how much Christian pilgrimage had developed within just two generations of Constantine. Almost every site mentioned in the New Testament (and several in the Old) had now been identified, and many had been marked by a church building. Numerous pilgrims travelled to the Holy Land from all parts of the empire and beyond. A good number of monks and nuns came not just to visit, but to stay in Jerusalem and Bethlehem.

Most importantly, a whole calendar had been developed for the celebrating of particular gospel events at their appropriate time. This 'liturgical year' (probably designed by Bishop Cyril of Jerusalem) proved to have a lasting influence on the worldwide church for generations to come (see page 198). Some of these celebrations would have taken place on the Mount of Olives – in Gethsemane or in the *Eleona* church near its peak. The majority, however, took place in the complex of buildings over Golgotha and the site of Jesus' tomb. Egeria refers to

these as the 'great church' or *Martyrium* (which means 'witness'), the area 'Before the Cross', and the *Anastasis* (which means 'resurrection'). She also frequently comments on her delight in finding that the Scripture readings have been so carefully chosen to fit the exact time and place in which the services were being held.

Here are some extracts showing how Egeria experienced the remembrance of Jesus' entry into Jerusalem on Palm Sunday in AD 384. Although not explicit, it appears that Bishop Cyril effectively took Jesus' place on the donkey!

On the Lord's Day (which begins the Paschal week)… everyone hastens home to eat, so as to be ready at 1 o'clock in the Eleona on the Mount of Olives (where is the cave in which the Lord used to teach). … At 3 o'clock they go up with hymns to the Imbomon (from where the Lord ascended into heaven), and there they sit down (for all the people are always told to sit when the bishop is present)…

Around 5 o'clock the Gospel is read (where the children, carrying branches met the Lord)… The bishop immediately rises, and all the people with him, and they all go on foot… going before him with hymns and antiphons, saying to each other: 'Blessed is he that comes in the name of the Lord'. And all the children in the neighbourhood, even those who are too young to walk, are carried by their parents on their shoulders, all of them bearing branches, some of palms and some of olives, and thus the bishop is escorted in the same manner as the Lord was of old. For all, even those of rank, both old men and women, accompany the bishop all the way on foot from the top of the mount to the city.

Egeria 30–31

The Greek Orthodox Patriarch and his clergy in Bethany on 'Lazarus Saturday' (the day before Palm Sunday).

Interior of the
traditional tomb
of Lazarus.

cemetery in the first century (other first-century tombs have been found just to the
north). And there are references to the tomb going back to the third century AD (in
Eusebius' *Onomastikon*). By the time of Egeria's visit in the early 380s AD, a church
had been built to the east of the tomb, with a courtyard and a passageway leading
westwards from the church to the tomb. It was used for pilgrim services, especially
during Holy Week, but it was already too small. Two centuries later it was duly
expanded.

Evidence for these two different churches on the same site can be clearly seen
when visiting the **modern Franciscan church,** which contains some pleasant wall
paintings of the various scenes associated with Bethany. The tomb, however, now needs
to be visited separately because of various subsequent buildings, including a small
mosque. Although this might well be the authentic site, much of the original rock
within the tomb is now obscured by masonry – probably inserted by the Crusaders
when building their church above the tomb.

El-Azarieh is not used by the western churches in *their* Palm Sunday procession.
This starts from the neighbouring hamlet of **Bethphage**. Instead Bethany comes to
life on the Saturday one week before Orthodox Easter, when there are colourful
processions to the tomb from the parish church approximately 500 yards (450 metres)
to the east. Visitors to the tomb on that particular morning are advised to get out of
the tomb before the clergy arrive and start to read the gospel passage from John 11. It
has been known for unwitting tourists to emerge from the tomb into the sunlight just
as Jesus' powerful words are recited: 'Lazarus, come out!'

*'Every home is a
Bethany, if Christ
lives there.'*

Patience Strong

The Mount of Olives

Each evening he went out to spend the night on the hill called the Mount of Olives.
Luke 21:37

Jesus went out as usual to the Mount of Olives, and his disciples followed him.
Luke 22:39

Then they returned to Jerusalem from the hill called the Mount of Olives,
a Sabbath day's walk from the city.
Acts 1:12

Jesus' favoured location

In the time of Jesus, the Mount of Olives (sometimes known more poetically as 'Olivet') was, as its name implies, a hill covered with olive groves. From Bethany it would take about 20 minutes to walk up to the crest of the Mount of Olives, and from there another 20 minutes or so to walk down its western slopes into the city of Jerusalem. It was really the southernmost of a string of hills (including, for example, Mount Scopus) that came southwards, forming a protective barrier between Jerusalem and the Judean Desert to the east.

The Mount of Olives in the Old Testament

In the Old Testament the writers of the Psalms had spoken appreciatively of the various hills that encompassed Jerusalem: 'As the mountains surround Jerusalem, so the Lord surrounds his people' (Psalm 125:2). Of these the Mount of Olives was the highest, its peak being some 300 feet (90 metres) above the city. Watchmen on the city's walls would have 'lifted their eyes to the hills' for any first sight of the enemy; and any 'watchmen waiting for the morning' would have particularly looked eastwards to see the first streaks of dawn lighting up the crest of the Mount of Olives (Psalm 121:1; 130:6).

During the Old Testament period, the Mount of Olives is mentioned explicitly on just five occasions:

- When confronted with Absalom's treachery, King David had fled the city, going 'up the Mount of Olives, weeping as he went' (2 Samuel 15:30).
- Over 300 years later, according to 2 Kings 23:13, the reforming King Josiah had torn down some 'high places' (or small temples) that were 'east of Jerusalem on

the south of the Hill of Corruption' – built there by King Solomon for the gods of his foreign wives (Ashtoreth, Chemosh and Molech).

- More positively, the Mount of Olives had been included in the rituals of the Temple for the purification ceremonies associated with the sacrificing of a red heifer. Israel had been commanded to make this unusual sacrifice 'outside the camp' (Numbers 19:1–10); so according to the *Mishnah* the high priest would process out from the Temple to perform the sacrifice on the summit of the Mount of Olives.

Looking westwards over the summit of the Mount of Olives towards Jerusalem's Temple Mount. The tower belongs to the Russian Church of the Ascension.

- In a different vein, when Ezekiel was given a vision of the 'glory of the Lord' departing from the Temple, he had seen it go 'up from within the city and stop above the mountain east of it' (Ezekiel 11:23). Within this dramatic vision of God's judgment the Mount of Olives was, as it were, the 'last port of call' for God's presence before it left his people, seemingly never to return.
- Finally some of the later prophets had portrayed God rising up to judge the nations in the valleys and hills around Jerusalem. Joel 3:2 depicts this taking place in the 'Valley of Jehoshaphat' (later identified with the 'Kidron Valley'), while Zechariah chooses the Mount of Olives: 'The Lord will go out and fight those nations; on that day his feet will stand on the Mount of Olives, east of Jerusalem, and the Mount of Olives will be split in two from east to west' (Zechariah 14:4). These powerful visions of divine judgment may have contributed to the practice of Jewish burial on the slopes of the Mount (and in the Kidron Valley), in the belief that the dead buried there would be the first to be blessed by God on the day of judgment.

A place of protection, a place of escape and departure, a place of idolatry, a place of sacrifice, a place of judgment and burial: these were some of the images conjured up by the Mount of Olives in the minds of Jesus' Jewish contemporaries.

The pilgrims' rest

More practically, it was the place from which the tired pilgrim, coming up from Jericho through the desert, could at long last see the Temple for the first time. It was also the place where many pilgrims would end up sleeping. Especially during Passover season, when the population of Jerusalem more than tripled, most pilgrims would be found sleeping out under the trees on the Mount of Olives. For, apart from Bethany and Bethphage, very few villages seem to have been built anywhere on the Mount.

So the Mount of Olives features quite frequently in the account of Jesus' last visit to Jerusalem. When he is not within the actual walls of the city (or relaxing in Bethany), this is where he is to be found. In the words of Eusebius 300 years later, this is the 'mountain he frequented' (Eusebius, *Life of Constantine* 3:43). Three particular gospel episodes are remembered here: his 'triumphal entry' into the city; his private conversation with some disciples about the future of the Temple; and his final time of prayer before his arrest in Gethsemane, the olive grove at the foot of the Mount.

The triumphal entry

When he came near the place where the road goes down the Mount of Olives, the whole crowd of disciples began joyfully to praise God in loud voices for all the miracles they had seen: 'Blessed is the king who comes in the name of the Lord!'
Luke 19:37–38

The 'triumphal entry' is a strange name for a strange event. It was clearly intended as a dramatic moment, carefully planned in Jesus' mind, but the symbolism was anything but 'triumphal'. After all, Jesus chose to enter not on a horse, but on a donkey! And in the midst of the celebration Jesus himself wept – evidently not the actions normally associated with a victor entering a city in triumph.

Luke's account, which speaks of the disciples bursting into spontaneous praise as they started to go down the Mount, gives a good sense of the excitement the pilgrims must have felt as they finally saw the panorama of the city. On any visit to Jerusalem, this was the moment the pilgrims had been waiting for. This time, however, the weary Galileans had something unusual to bring to the attention of those living in Jerusalem: the arrival of this powerful Galilean preacher, a worker of 'miracles', and one whom they thought would now be ushering in the long-awaited 'kingdom of God'.

Not surprisingly some Pharisees, looking on, did not like it; but Jesus did not try to silence the crowds. The disciples were on to something. Indeed this was a key moment in the history of Jerusalem – perhaps the moment of its greatest destiny, the time for which its stones were created. So Jesus replied enigmatically: 'If they keep quiet, the stones will cry out' (Luke 19:40).

Yet this 'king' was no straightforward king. His deliberate choice of a donkey signalled that he had come in peace, not with a desire for war; although he *would* pose a distinct challenge to Jerusalem's authorities, they did not need to fear a *military* confrontation. So, even though some of his followers might have wished otherwise, he had not come to start a fight – either with the pagan Romans or with the Jewish Temple aristocracy. Instead, when he had made his dramatic 'entrance', he would go back quietly to Bethany for the night (Mark 11:11). Any hotheads would be cruelly disappointed. Jesus deliberately did not 'seize his moment'.

But, for those well tuned to Old Testament prophecy, the donkey signified something else. Zechariah had foreseen Jerusalem's joy at the arrival of her king.

'Ride on, ride on in Majesty, in lowly pomp ride on to die.'
Henry Milman, 'Ride on, ride on in Majesty'

Rejoice greatly, O Daughter of Zion! Shout, Daughter of Jerusalem! See, your king comes to you, gentle and riding on a donkey... He will proclaim peace to the nations. His rule will extend from sea to sea and from the River to the ends of the earth.
Zechariah 9:9–10.

In deliberately evoking this prophecy by his choice of a donkey, Jesus wanted people to see not only the 'gentleness' of his reign, but also that he was both the true king over Jerusalem and the true ruler of the world. If the mode of his ruling was not by military might, yet the extent of his rule was vast. This was truly a messianic act – a claim to be Israel's long awaited 'Anointed One', the one who would rule both Israel and the world.

And yet there is also a deeper, more mysterious, layer to this event. For in biblical thought there was a particular sense in which the true 'king of Zion' was none other than *God himself*. Jerusalem was, as Jesus himself had called it, the 'city of the Great King' (Matthew 5:35), the city over which Israel's God alone was truly king. It was celebrated in the Psalms as the 'city of God' (Psalm 46:4; 48:1). And in Isaiah's famous vision, the time when Zion/Jerusalem could shout 'our God reigns!' was precisely the moment when the Lord was 'returning to Zion' (Isaiah 52:7–8). Could it be that Jesus was hinting – simply through sitting on a donkey as 'Zion's king' – that this was the moment when the *Lord himself* was returning to Zion?

As we saw earlier, the prophet Ezekiel claimed to have seen the Lord's presence depart from Zion going eastwards over the Mount of Olives. There is therefore something strangely powerful about now seeing Jesus making his entrance back westwards from the Mount into the city. Was he somehow the embodiment of God's presence, in human form, returning after all these centuries to the city? If so, we should not be too surprised that, in due course, there was some controversy in the Temple. This is a spine-chilling moment for the Temple and for Jerusalem – the arrival, it seems, of her true king, none other than the Lord himself.

It is this deeper meaning, lying just beneath the surface and currently 'hidden from people's eyes', that may explain something of Jesus' tears at this critical moment: 'As Jesus approached Jerusalem and saw the city, he wept over it' (Luke 19:41). Jesus could see what neither his critics nor supporters could see. This, he said, was truly the 'time of God's coming to you' (or, more literally, the time of a divine 'visitation'). This was Jerusalem's 'hour' of destiny. The *city* of God in this moment was witnessing the arrival of the *Son* of God, her true ruler.

But she did not 'recognize' it, and her blindness would have tragic consequences: 'your enemies will... encircle you; ... they will not leave one stone upon another' (Luke 19:43). With prophetic insight Jesus could foresee how this same panorama would look within a generation – with the Roman legions camped around the city, having destroyed the Temple.

It was an awful prospect. It would be brought about partly by political mistakes and by people failing to find the right peace terms ('what would bring you peace'); and partly because of Jewish nationalism, the longing for independence from pagan control and domination. Yet it would also come about because people in Jerusalem failed to see their Jewish, biblical aspirations for the kingdom being genuinely fulfilled in a quite different way through this non-fighting Messiah from Nazareth. If they had seen what Jesus was offering, they would not have fought. There was a different way of being Israel – of being God's people in and for the world – but they did not want this alternative fulfilment of their hopes. And the result, for anyone with a heart for God's people, was enough to make one weep. Not for nothing did this so-called 'triumphal entry' end in tears.

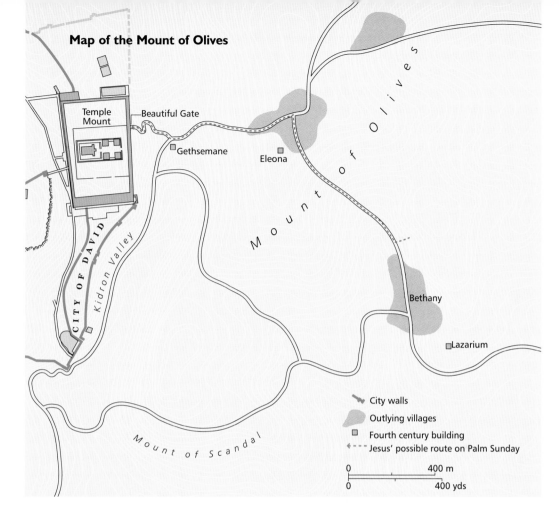

Map of the Mount of Olives

Temple Mount

Beautiful Gate

Gethsemane

Eleona

Bethany

Lazarium

CITY OF DAVID

Kidron Valley

Mount of Olives

Mount of Scandal

City walls

Outlying villages

Fourth century building

Jesus' possible route on Palm Sunday

0   400 m

0   400 yds

Secret revelations on the Mount

Some of his disciples were remarking about how the temple was adorned with beautiful stones and with gifts dedicated to God. But Jesus said, 'As for what you see here, the time will come when not one stone will be left on another; every one of them will be thrown down.'
Luke 21:5–6

A few days later Jesus spoke again of the imminent destruction of the Temple. Understandably his disciples asked when this ghastly event was going to happen. And Jesus responded with an extended discourse, seated with four of his disciples somewhere 'on the Mount of Olives opposite the Temple' (Mark 13:3). This is known as the 'Apocalyptic Discourse' (a discourse that 'unveils' divine secrets about the present and the future). This is because Jesus took the disciples' question about the Temple's destruction (which might have seemed to them like the 'end' of the Jewish world as they knew it) as his cue to unveil some further things relating also to the *ultimate end* of all things.

In this discourse Jesus spoke both about the destruction of Jerusalem *and* about the 'coming of the Son of Man'. These two levels of meaning have, needless to say, caused untold confusion at both scholarly and popular levels ever since. Yet there was something very appropriate about Jesus talking in this mysterious way on the Mount of Olives.

' ...authentic history informs us that in this very cave the Saviour imparted his secret revelations to his disciples.'
Eusebius, *Life of Constantine* 3:43

For not only had Zechariah associated this hill with *his* apocalyptic visions of the future; it was also (as the only place from which one can get an overall view of Jerusalem) the natural place for Jesus to offer *his own* reflection on the city's destiny and to force his disciples to look up from the city to see God's wider purposes for the world. Moreover, as the place which stood 'opposite' the Temple, it was also the obvious place for Jesus to question the long-term uniqueness of the Temple, showing instead how God's purposes were now gathering around a different centre – namely himself as the 'Son of Man'. In this way the *physical* contrast between the Temple and the Mount reinforced symbolically the *spiritual* contrast between the Temple and Jesus; it signalled the transference of God's focus from the one to the other. In this way Jesus could begin to wean his disciples away from their longings for the Temple by replacing it with a new vision of their prime commitment to him. Sitting on the Mount of Olives, their allegiance was to shift from Jerusalem to Jesus.

There was also, of course, the practical point that the Mount of Olives provided the only possible place for some peace and quiet in an otherwise festival-packed city. It was the only place for any 'calm before the storm'. Something of this can be sensed in the third and final gospel episode on the Mount prior to Jesus' death: Jesus praying in Gethsemane. This was Jesus' last moment for any quiet before his arrest and execution.

Gethsemane: Jesus' final place of quiet

Jesus went out as usual to the Mount of Olives, and his disciples followed him. On reaching the place, he said to them, 'Pray that you will not fall into temptation.' He withdrew about a stone's throw beyond them, knelt down and prayed, 'Father, if you are willing, take this cup from me; yet not my will, but yours be done.'
Luke 22:39–42

'Gethsemane' means 'oil press'. We are probably to imagine a walled area, owned perhaps by an acquaintance of Jesus and his disciples, containing an olive grove and some olive presses. They may have slept there on previous nights, slightly separated from the many other Galilean pilgrims bivouacked on the hillside. The gospel writers speak at this point of Jesus going out *'as usual* to the Mount of

Olives' (Luke 22:39) and of Judas knowing the place well 'because Jesus had often met there with his disciples' (John 18:2). So Jesus' chosen place for his final place of prayer was a familiar one. Under the light of the full Passover moon, singing a few hymns or psalms interspersed with gloomy silence, they would have walked from the Last Supper in the Upper City down into the Kidron Valley and then up towards Gethsemane. 'They crossed the Kidron Valley; on the other side there was an olive grove, and he and his disciples went into it' (John 18:1).

Here we see Jesus in 'anguish', a figure on his own, some distance from his sleeping disciples, crying out in agonizing prayer to his Father. The same three disciples who earlier had seen Jesus transfigured in glory, now (when they are not falling asleep) see him in the depths of sorrow. Here we also see something of the inner questioning that assaulted Jesus, and the grim reality of the necessity of the cross; for if there had been some other way to fulfil his task, surely it would have been found. The 'cup' was an Old Testament picture for the 'wrath of the Lord', which God required his enemies to drink (Jeremiah 25:15–16). Now Jesus was to drink from this cup of judgment, so that his followers would never need to.

A key point to learn from Gethsemane, however, is that Jesus actively chose the path to the cross. It was no accident. For, if he had wished to escape, he could have been

'Going a little farther, he fell with his face to the ground and prayed, "My Father, if it is possible, may this cup be taken from me. Yet not as I will, but as you will."'

Matthew 26:39

safely in Bethany (or in hiding in the desert) within 40 minutes. Instead he waited here in Gethsemane, possibly for up to two or three hours (being fishermen the disciples were used to keeping awake at night, but they fell asleep *three* times). So the location of Gethsemane speaks volumes about the nature of Jesus' mission. If he had wished to *fight*, he could have entered the city to the west; if his preference was for *flight* and quietism, he could have gone over the Mount of Olives to the east. But instead he stayed resolutely in the middle ground, the most extreme and painful place of all – seemingly passive and at the mercy of others, but, according to the Gospels, actually the one who was truly in control.

So Judas, after urgent conversations and strategizing in the city, eventually arrives with some soldiers. They fall back when they see Jesus, but Judas kisses Jesus as a signal for his arrest, and Jesus is taken, bound, back into the city. Two disciples follow him at a discreet distance, but the others flee in the only possible direction – up the Mount of Olives towards Bethany.

After the resurrection: from Jerusalem to the Mount of Olives

Yet that is not the end of the story. For the Mount of Olives features again, we must note, in that unique period that follows Jesus' resurrection.

First, there are some appearances of the risen Jesus which, though not expressly located by the gospel writers, may well have occurred somewhere on the Mount of Olives – as a discreet place away from the city's crowds. For example, this may have been where Simon Peter had his significant one-to-one encounter with Jesus (mentioned in Luke 24:34). Some have suggested that Peter, full of remorse for having so recently denied Jesus, could have taken himself off to Gethsemane again, to think and to pray alone – there to be met by Jesus.

And what about Jesus' meeting with the two women (as mentioned in Matthew 28:9–10)? If most of the disciples were in Bethany, the women may well have been on their way there to break the surprising news of the empty tomb when suddenly they were met by Jesus, again somewhere on the Mount of Olives. It was, after all, the place he had frequented most often during the previous week.

And finally the Mount proves to be the place for Jesus' final departure – what is known as his ascension (Acts 1:1–12). We saw (page 111) how Luke describes this as taking place 'near Bethany' (Luke 24:50). Yet in his second volume Luke simply refers to 'the hill called the Mount of Olives' (Acts 1:12). Therefore the precise location for this event must remain unclear (there is nothing to suggest, after all, that it had to take place at the *highest* point on the Mount). Yet its location somewhere on the Mount of Olives is fitting and appropriate.

For not only was this where Jesus had spent so many of his last days with his disciples. It was notionally within the Jerusalem area – 'a Sabbath day's walk from the city' (Acts 1:12); yet at the same time it stood symbolically 'opposite' Jerusalem. In other words it was the perfect place for the establishment of a new, alternative focal point at the heart of God's purposes. Jesus had indicated that the days of Jerusalem's unique status at the centre of God's purposes were fast drawing to an end. Something new had passed through the city, which meant it would never be the same again. That

Key dates: The Mount of Olives

c. 980 BC	David flees over the Mount of Olives (2 Samuel 15:30); later the Mount is used by Solomon as a 'high place' for shrines for foreign gods (1 Kings 11:7–8).	
c. 622 BC	King Josiah's reforms lead to the removal of these shrines (2 Kings 23:13).	
c. 592 BC	Ezekiel in exile has a vision of the Lord's glory leaving the Temple (Ezekiel 11:23).	
c. AD 30	Jesus' activity on the Mount.	
c. AD 55	Governor Felix puts down the attempted storming of Jerusalem by a Jewish prophet from Egypt, gathered with forces on the Mount of Olives (Josephus, *War* 2:13.5).	

c. AD 200	The apocryphal *Apocalypse of John* (chapter 97) refers to Jesus appearing to John in a cave on the Mount of Olives (supposedly during the time of his crucifixion).	
c. AD 290	Eusebius describes many Christian visitors to the Mount.	
AD 333	The Bordeaux Pilgrim visits the Mount.	
c. AD 335	Completion of the *Eleona* church over a cave on the Mount of Olives (Eusebius, *Life of Constantine* 3:43).	
AD 381–84	Egeria records her visit to the Mount of Olives, including services at *Eleona* and on the summit.	
AD 392	Poemenia funds the *Imbomon* to mark the site of the ascension.	

AD 400–600	Development of many monasteries and churches on the Mount.
c. 1198	Saladin gives control of the ascension site to local Muslims.
1857	Development of *Pater Noster* site as a French convent for Carmelite sisters.
1883	Franciscans build a church at Bethphage.
1924	Church of All Nations built by Benedictines at Gethsemane.
1955	Franciscans build 'Dominus Flevit'.

'something' was Jesus himself; and from now on he, not Jerusalem, would be the focus of their attention and worship. The Temple had stood on the 'mountain of the Lord' (Isaiah 2:2). There was a real sense now that the Mount of Olives was peculiarly the preferred and chosen 'mountain of the Lord'.

So Jesus took them somewhere over the crest of the Mount of Olives. Perhaps there were echoes here, once again, of Ezekiel's vision of the 'glory of the Lord' resting over the Mount of Olives as it left behind the city of Jerusalem. Or perhaps Zechariah's strange prophecy that 'the Lord's feet will stand on the Mount of Olives' (Zechariah 4:14) was finding an unexpected level of fulfilment. In any event, it was here that he was 'taken up before their eyes, and a cloud hid him from their sight' (Acts 1:9) – with due warning given that one day he would return.

The Mount of Olives Today

As we approach Jerusalem, the visitor's itinerary inevitably becomes more complex. Gospel sites are not laid out in any convenient geographical order that matches their sequence in the life of Jesus; and we are often forced to consider several different episodes in one place (for a suggested itinerary for visiting the Jerusalem area, see page 130). This becomes apparent immediately as we come to the Mount of Olives: one moment, for example, we are thinking of Palm Sunday; the next of Jesus' ascension. It is also a great place for viewing the surrounding area and sensing the topography of Jerusalem. Many visitors will come here right at the start of their visit to Jerusalem, not to see the sites on the Mount, but to get its view over the city (see page 117).

The best way to enjoy the Mount of Olives is on foot. Within a morning it is quite possible to walk from Bethphage over the crest of the Mount, down past Gethsemane and into Jerusalem's Old City in time for lunch. So in this section we follow some imaginary visitors who have been dropped quite early in the morning at Bethphage (the starting point of Jesus' 'triumphal entry').

Bethphage (which probably means 'house of unripe figs') can be approached from various directions. There is no road linking Bethany to Bethphage (it is now obstructed by a security wall) but there is a road that comes up to it from the south. Most, however, will drive up the wide road from the north-east corner of the Old City, turning right at the junction on the crest of the Mount and then, having passed through the village of Et Tur, turn left towards Bethphage round a tight, narrow bend. It is worth noting that the earlier junction (on first reaching the crest of the Mount) forms a 'saddle' in the ridge of the Mount and was the place where the **Roman road** crossed the Mount on its way down to Jericho. Alternatively this road junction can be approached from the north – there are good views of the desert to be had from behind the Hebrew University campus on Mount Scopus and from the grounds of the Augusta Victoria Hospital – or from the east coming up from the desert on the line of the ancient Roman road (but this ascent is quite steep and not easy for some vehicles).

Bethphage is found nestling in the curves of the Mount and is now marked by a church, built in 1883 on the ruins of a medieval church. In fact the exact location of Bethphage must remain uncertain, but this area has a reasonable chance of being in the correct general vicinity. It seems to have been selected in the fourth century as the location for a small church commemorating Jesus' meeting with Mary and Martha (outside Bethany). Meanwhile the Crusaders were interested in it because of a large stone, now found inside the church, from which they imagined Jesus might have mounted his donkey (forgetting that, with a small donkey rather than a large horse, this would hardly have been necessary!).

Yet this peaceful sanctuary can be the ideal place to begin a quiet, more reflective meditation on the events of Palm Sunday. Some people walk from here up to the crest of the Mount in silence. On Palm Sunday itself, the church is the starting point for an

The Mount of Olives from the Old City walls (near St Stephen's gate). The area of Gethsemane is marked by two churches: the Russian church of St Mary Magdalene (with golden domes) and the Church of All Nations near the main road. In Jesus' day the whole Mount would have been covered with olive trees, but these were destroyed by the Roman forces besieging Jerusalem in AD 70.

incredibly long procession (the front of which arrives in the Old City before the clergy at the rear have even started!); the road is filled with banners and people singing hymns (such as 'Ride On in Majesty', or 'Hosanna to the Son of David'). It is good, in these various ways, to try and imagine the excitement of the crowds as this 'prophet from Galilee' made his strange, dramatic entrance into the nation's capital.

Once up on the crest of the Mount, the focus on Palm Sunday has to be interrupted. Thirty yards to the right is a small mosque and its enclosure: these mark the traditional **site of Jesus' ascension**. This is in fact the highest peak of the Mount of Olives. For this aesthetic reason it was selected by Byzantine Christians in the fourth century as the most appropriate place to celebrate Jesus' ascension (though, of course, there is nothing in the Bible which requires the ascension to have been on a mountain peak).

However, the first Byzantine church on the Mount was not this one but the church 50 yards (45 metres) to the south – built over a cave and known as the *Eleona*. Initial attempts to use this building to commemorate the ascension, however, were thwarted by the natural desire of pilgrims for the ascension to be remembered in a place open to the sky. Already, by the time of Egeria's visit in the early 380s AD, celebrations were taking place outside the church on the nearby hillock, and a decade later a woman called Poemenia had funded the construction of a suitable structure (known as the *Imbomon*). It was not strictly a church, but rather a round courtyard, surrounded by a circular colonnade and focused at its centre on some natural rock and dust in which pilgrims thought they could see sure signs of Jesus' footprints.

Today the site is marked instead by Crusader buildings, which the Muslims then took over, putting a roof over the central structure and inserting within it a *mihrab* – a prayer niche pointing in the direction of Mecca. The supposed mark of Jesus' right foot is still preserved. Although the Orthodox churches are able to use the octagonal courtyard on their Ascension Day, it is hard (if not prohibited) to pray in this location. For this reason, and given the many subsequent historical layers that have intervened, many find it a hard place to focus on the original account of the ascension. This is a pity – given that the ascension is a key and vital part of the Christian Creed – but the ascension's theological meaning remains in tact regardless of geographical uncertainties and the oddities of subsequent history.

Visitors retrace their tracks, and soon enter the so-called '**Pater Noster' Church**. This is in fact a half-reconstructed version of the chief Byzantine church on the Mount known in its day simply as the *Eleona* (literally 'of olives'). After their excavations at the site of the crucifixion, Constantine's architects set to work on two further buildings: here on the Mount of Olives and in Bethlehem. In the thinking of Archbishop Eusebius, each of these three sites was associated with a 'cave' and also with a key part of the Creed (Jesus' birth, death/resurrection and ascension). This tidy thinking was a bit contrived and failed to convince others for long. In particular, Eusebius' promotion of a 'cave of the ascension' was unlikely to be successful. So, as we have seen, the ascension was soon commemorated further up the hill.

You can now step down into this cave, located under the raised sanctuary of the Byzantine church. Constantine's excavators seem to have uncovered a first-century *kokh* tomb in the course of their work. They blocked this up with masonry, but it is now easily visible. It is worth noting too that some bishops of Jerusalem (including Bishop Cyril) were buried on the Mount, possibly in or near this cave. For all its strangeness, this cave clearly meant a great deal to early Christians (see page 129) and it is not

'Yonder stands even to this day Mt Olivet, all but showing even now to the eyes of the faithful him who ascended, and the heavenly gate of the Ascension.'

Cyril, *Catechetical Lectures* 14:23

impossible that Jesus himself used it at some point. Of this we can be sure: it was there in his day.

Returning to ground level, visitors gain a good sense of the proportions of the *Eleona* – both its nave and the courtyard to the west. They are also confronted with no less than 62 versions of the Lord's Prayer in different languages! The identification of this site as the place where Jesus also taught the Lord's Prayer came only later – some time before the arrival of the Crusaders – but it has been a dominant tradition ever since.

Leaving the premises and turning left, visitors walk southwards, not aware of what is about to hit them. Suddenly, after walking past some buildings on the right, the panorama of Jerusalem comes into view. This is a good time for orientation (see page 130). Yet, picking up the Palm Sunday theme once more, it is also the moment to remember Luke's graphic words: 'When he came near the place where the road goes down the Mount of Olives, the whole crowd of disciples began joyfully to praise God in loud voices' (Luke 19:37). Luke has captured brilliantly the joy of that electric moment, when pilgrims see Jerusalem at last.

Walking down some steps, visitors begin the steep descent down the Mount. Facing them is the golden dome of the Muslim 'Dome of the Rock'; to the left are some first-century tombs (wrongly identified with some of the Old Testament prophets); and on the right, in due course, a tiny church with a distinctive roof, built in the shape of a teardrop. This is '**Dominus Flevit'** (Latin for 'the Lord wept'). Built by the

Jerusalem as seen through the window of 'Dominus Flevit': the cross and chalice deliberately focus, not on the golden Dome of the Rock, but on the church of the Holy Sepulchre.

Franciscans in 1955 over a Byzantine monastery and some oft-used cemeteries, it is a modern church that powerfully evokes that moment on Palm Sunday when Jesus began to weep for Jerusalem (Luke 19:41–44).

Looking through the arched window with its central motif of a chalice orientated powerfully towards the traditional site of Golgotha, visitors gain a nuanced view of Jerusalem. They are viewing it, as it were, through the lens of the gospel narrative, seeing the city as the place where Jesus was rejected and put to death – the place that 'did not recognize the hour of God's coming'. Sitting outside on the garden walls, listening to the noise of the city across the valley, it is good to continue trying to see modern Jerusalem from Jesus' perspective – through his eyes, which wept. Paradoxically, one probable meaning for the name 'Jerusalem' is 'city of peace'. Given the troubles experienced by this city through the centuries, it is hard not to leave the compound without thinking of Jesus' powerful words: 'If only you, even you, had known on this day *the things that would bring you peace!*' (Luke 19:42).

Continuing down the slope, surrounded in the main by high walls, visitors eventually pass some gates into the Russian Orthodox **Church of St Mary Magdalene**. The gates are open for only a few hours each week, so a return visit may be necessary at some point – ideally to join in some of the beautiful liturgy sung by a small group of nuns. Celebrating some of the services here on Good Friday or at midnight on Easter Sunday morning can be a powerful experience – an entrée into a quite different world.

Before AD 300 the Mount of Olives was the easiest place where visitors to Jerusalem could reflect on the gospel story. For, in contrast to the city itself, which had twice been destroyed by enemy action, little had altered on the Mount.

We learn as much from Eusebius, the Christian scholar who worked in Caesarea Maritima (see page 14). Commenting on Zechariah 14:4 ('On that day his feet shall stand on the Mount of Olives') he wrote the following about the Mount of Olives in his day (c. AD 315):

Believers in Christ gather from all parts of the world… in order to learn about the city being taken and devastated as the prophets foretold, and to worship at the Mount of Olives opposite to the city…

[Also this was where] the glory of the Lord had migrated when it left the former city [Ezekiel 11:23]… There stood in truth, according to the common and received account, the feet of our Lord and Saviour, Himself the Word of God, through that tabernacle of humanity he had borne up the Mount of Olives to the cave that is shown there; there he prayed and delivered to his disciples on the summit of the Mount of Olives the mysteries of his end, and thence he made his Ascension into heaven.

> **The Proof of the Gospel 6:18**

Early Christian pilgrimage

Although Eusebius may have been exaggerating, he gives the impression that quite a few Christians travelled to Jerusalem before the era of Constantine. We know the names of only a few: Melito from Sardis; Alexander (who during his visit was asked to become bishop of Jerusalem); Origen (the biblical scholar from Alexandria who settled in Caesarea to continue his biblical research) and a man called Pionius (later martyred for his faith in Smyrna). Elsewhere Eusebius suggests that such visitors also visited Gethsemane and the River Jordan (*Onomastikon* 74:16–18; 58:19). Here he says that the Mount of Olives was a key place for their 'worship'. Yet this is not the fully-fledged desire for searching out 'holy places' that will emerge in the fourth century. Instead we are dealing with what might be called 'informed Christian tourism'.

The significance of Jerusalem's fall (AD 70)

Secondly, we see in these quotations something of the early Christian approach to the fall of Jerusalem. It was seen as a powerful confirmation of the gospel – a fulfilment of predictions made both by Old Testament prophets and by Jesus. The Temple's destruction concluded that era of biblical history when God's purposes were focused on a particular land. Now, as predicted in Isaiah 2:2, the 'word of the Lord was going out' from Jerusalem to the 'ends of the earth'.

This meant that Jerusalem itself, though still historically interesting, had lost its theological status. Quoting verses such as Galatians 4:26 and Hebrews 12:22, Eusebius argued that Christians were not to focus on the physical Jerusalem but on the 'heavenly' or 'spiritual' city. So, if any Christians *did* visit Jerusalem, one of their chief goals (he suggests) should be to focus on the implications of its dramatic ruin. Eusebius' highly 'spiritualized' emphasis would naturally lose some of its appeal when Christians under Constantine began to renew their interest in the physical Jerusalem.

The mysterious cave

Finally, Eusebius mentioned 'the cave that is shown there'. Evidently this cave near the summit of the Mount had become associated by Christians with events in the life of Jesus. Originally perhaps it had simply been a convenient place for small groups to pray – undisturbed by weather or people. Gradually, however, it had become associated with Jesus' 'Apocalyptic Discourse' (Luke 21:5–36) and also with other conversations with his disciples prior to his ascension (Acts 1:3–8).

Today we probably imagine these taking place in the 'open air', with Jesus and his followers looking out over the panorama of the Temple. The suggestion of a cave, however, sat naturally with the idea of Jesus imparting secret truths about the future (and 'the mysteries of his end'). It also caught the imagination of more heretical groups – hence its appearance in the *Apocalypse of John*.

At the end of his life Eusebius tried to develop his 'cave theology': Constantine's three new churches in the Jerusalem area promoted a triad of such mysterious caves. It was a neat idea, but it did not really catch on. The theme of mystery, however, comes through clearly in Eusebius' colourful words about the building of the *Eleona* church, which resulted from the visit to Jerusalem of the emperor's mother, Queen Helena:

The emperor's mother erected on the Mount of Olives the monument to the journey into heaven of the Saviour of the Universe in lofty buildings; up by the ridges at the peak of the whole mountain she raised the sacred house of the church, and constructed just there a shrine for prayer to the Saviour who chose to spend his time on that spot; since just there a true report maintains that in that cave the Saviour of the Universe initiated the members of his guild in ineffable mysteries. There also the emperor bestowed all kinds of offerings and ornaments on the great King.

> **Life of Constantine 3:43**

Below: View from the south of the Old City walls looking towards the Jewish quarter (left) and the Temple Mount platform (right).

Visitors need to arrive in the **Garden of Gethsemane** before it is closed at noon for lunch. The exact location of where Jesus prayed cannot now be determined, but this is certainly in the right area. From before the time of Constantine, Christians have identified a large natural rock here as the place of Jesus' agony. This became the centrepiece of an 'elegant church' built here just before Egeria's visit in the AD 380s; and it is now likewise the key feature inside the deliberately dark **Church of All**

A weekend in modern Jerusalem

Like any city, there is more to Jerusalem than can be discovered in a few days. Yet a few days in the city may be sufficient to give the modern visitor a good idea of its main features. The following is a suggested outline for those who have the opportunity to visit for a long weekend, and who are particularly interested in its New Testament sites.

Friday

Early departure for a full day visit to Masada, the Dead Sea and Qumran. Return late afternoon, stopping in the Judean Desert for a view over the Wadi Qelt. Then come back up to the Mount of Olives to stop at the 'panorama' viewpoint (in front of the Seven Arches Hotel) just before sunset. This is a great way to see Jerusalem for the first time, approaching it as Jesus did through the desert, and then getting a general 'orientation' over the city.

Saturday

Visit to Bethlehem (Shepherds' Fields, then Manger Square and Church of the Nativity); lunch in Bethlehem (perhaps at one of the local Christian institutions in the town). Back to Jerusalem for an afternoon visit to Mount Sion (Cenacle, St Peter in Gallicantu, Dormition Abbey); sunset visit on foot to the Western Wall to observe the end of *Shabbat.*

Sunday

Early morning services in the church of the Holy Sepulchre and/or other churches in the Old City (Christ Church; Lutheran church) with breakfast nearby. Lunch in the area of the Cardo Maximus, followed by a visit to Herodian Mansions or Burnt House in the Jewish Quarter.
Late afternoon visit to Yad Vashem in West Jerusalem.

Monday

Early morning departure for Bethphage. Walking tour back over the Mount of Olives, arriving at the Pool of Bethesda or the *Ecce Homo* excavations before lunch. Lunch at the start or end of the *Via Dolorosa*. Early afternoon visit to the church of the Holy Sepulchre. Last visit to the Garden Tomb (and its bookshop).

Those departing the next day for Galilee sometimes benefit from a silent morning walk in the Judean Desert (following the line of the ancient Roman road towards the monastery of St George's Khoziba), followed by lunch in Jericho – an opportunity to reflect on the many things seen and learnt in Jerusalem.

Visitors may also wish to make contact with people living in Jerusalem to learn about life in the city from their perspective. Those in groups can often have special meetings set up for them, so that they can hear local speakers. Evenings can be a good opportunity for this: for example, meeting Palestinian Christians on the Friday, taking a guided tour round the Orthodox Jewish area of Mea Shearim on the Saturday (after *Shabbat* has ended), and then hearing from some Jewish Christians on the Sunday. Other speakers (for example, Muslim, Jewish, or Armenian Christian) can also be arranged. A wide variety of religious and political views will be heard, but this may be necessary to help visitors come to terms with the complexity and stresses of modern Jerusalem.

There is a wide choice of places to stay, ranging from smart hotels in West Jerusalem to smaller Christian hostels in and around the Old City. Even if not staying within the Old City, many like to be within walking distance of it (so they can explore it on their own) and so chose a place to stay somewhere to the north of the Damascus Gate.

Nations. The church is designed for private prayer, an opportunity to respond to Jesus' words to his disciples in the garden: 'Could you not watch with me for one hour? Watch and pray so that you will not fall into temptation' (Matthew 26:40–41).

Outside there are ancient olive trees which, even if they do not themselves go back to the first century, take visitors back in their mind's eye to that first-century olive grove. With the busy modern road nearby, it can be hard to imagine it as it was. But visitors can come back for a more leisurely visit in the afternoon, or wander back up the hillside a little way to find other olive trees. It can be powerful to come back after dark, ideally under the light of a full moon, and consider again what Jesus went through in this place.

Gethsemane is a fitting place to conclude any visit to the Mount of Olives. It is where Jesus had the choice of whether to flee back up the Mount or to wait for his arresting party from the city. As visitors make their way towards lunch (possibly inside the Old City), it is worth remembering that, when Jesus left Gethsemane, he too re-entered the city – but under arrest.

The Temple

Then he entered the temple area and began driving out those who were selling. 'It is written,' he said to them, "My house will be called a house of prayer"; but you have made it "a den of robbers".'

Every day he was teaching at the temple... The chief priests and the teachers of the law... came up to him. 'Tell us by what authority you are doing these things?' they said. 'Who gave you this authority?'

Jesus saw the rich putting their gifts into the temple treasury. He also saw a poor widow put in two very small copper coins... 'This poor widow has put in more than all the others.'

Some of his disciples were remarking about how the temple was adorned with beautiful stones... But Jesus said, '... the time will come when not one stone will be left upon another.'

Luke 19:45-47; 20:1–2; 21:1–3, 5–6

The heart of the nation

No visitor to Jerusalem in the first century could ignore the Temple; nor would they wish to. Recently rebuilt and expanded by Herod the Great, it made up nearly a fifth of the total square area of the city. Some have said that Jerusalem in Jesus' day was not a 'city with a Temple', but rather a 'Temple with a city' – in other words, the Temple was in both physical and spiritual terms the heartbeat of the city, its *raison d'etre*.

So, as Jesus approached the city, it was clear where he was headed. 'Jesus entered Jerusalem and went to the Temple'; on this occasion, however, because 'it was already late', he simply 'looked around at everything', giving it an inspection (Mark 11:11). The next day he was back. And that was when the sparks began to fly.

This so-called 'cleansing of the Temple' is one of the most dramatic events in the Gospels (in John's account Jesus even uses a 'whip of cords' to drive out the 'sheep and cattle'). For more radical scholars this is one of the assured points in the ministry of Jesus: Jesus clearly kicked up a commotion in Israel's central place of worship, and this then triggered his arrest and subsequent execution. What made him do it? What exactly was he criticizing about the Temple? What was he intending to achieve?

The Temple in Old Testament thought and practice

To answer this we need to know something of the Temple's history. Its origins lie in the desert. The Israelites had wandered through the wilderness with a portable 'tabernacle' or tent. At Mount Sinai they were instructed about how their God was to be worshipped and how they were to seek out the 'place' in the Promised Land which their God had chosen 'as a dwelling for his Name' (Deuteronomy 12:11).

Several centuries later, King David hoped to build this dwelling-place for the Lord – on the site of Araunah's threshing-floor in his new capital city of Jerusalem – but it was eventually built there by his son, Solomon. The mobile features of Israel's wanderings finally came home to settle; the holiness of Mount Sinai was now, as it were, incorporated into Mount Zion.

The Temple then remained at the heart of Israel for nearly 400 years. According to the Torah all male Jews over the age of twelve were to 'go up' to the Temple three times a year (for the feasts of Passover, Weeks, and Tabernacles). Around 620 BC, however, the prophet Jeremiah stood on the Temple steps and began to denounce God's people for their false trust in the Temple, asserting that they had made it a 'den of robbers' – a place of intrigue, a place where the Lord was 'robbed' of the worship due to his name. As a result, the Lord himself might destroy his own Temple. Even though it was a gift from God, this gift could be taken away if it was abused – being used, as it were, against the Giver. Within 30 years, his words had come true: the Babylonians razed it to the ground. And, a few years later, the prophet Ezekiel had a picture of God's glory leaving the Temple – God's house had been left desolate.

When the exiles returned, the Temple was in due course rebuilt, but it was only a

'I love the house where you live, O Lord, the place where your glory dwells.'

Psalm 26:8

Looking up to the southern wall of Herod's vast platform for the Temple. The dome belongs to the el-Aksa mosque.

The Herodian Temple

Herod's work on the Temple was truly magnificent. Starting around 15 BC, the work was still going on '46 years' later during the time of Jesus' ministry (John 2:20) – indeed it would continue for a further 30 years after that. This involved a mammoth influx of labourers into the city, itself causing some considerable expansion of the city towards the north-west.

Vast stones were cut from the quarries just north of the Temple Mount. The largest of these marble slabs was nearly 40 feet (12 metres) long and 10 feet (3 metres) high. One can only imagine something of the difficulty involved in rolling these massive blocks through the city and then hoisting them into position. Huge numbers of them were required. For Herod's architects were proposing to extend the area of the Temple courts by over 30 per cent, expanding them some 25 yards (23 metres) further to the south. This was no easy feat. At this point the slope of the rock falls away quite sharply, so this southerly extension involved the construction of a mammoth platform. All this had to be in place before the construction of any building in the Temple courts – for example, the porticoes on all four sides and the huge 'sanctuary' itself with the central 'Holy of Holies' rising up over 130 feet (40 metres) above the court.

We are able to reconstruct the plan of Herod's Temple with a reasonable degree of accuracy from the accounts in Josephus, *War* 5:5 (and also in the later *Mishnah*, written c. AD 200). Both of these accounts were written down after the Temple's destruction, so there is room for some error, but their general picture can be relied upon.

Two models of the first-century Temple, drawing upon these two accounts, have been particularly helpful in recent years: one in Jerusalem (now located at the Israel Museum), the other in Suffolk, England (made by Alec Garrard). Pictures of these models give us a good idea of what Herod's Temple would have looked like. It is worth noting the following:

- the clear demarcation between the various concentric courts (for priests, Jewish men, Jewish women and then Gentiles);
- the various entrances – in particular the Huldah gates on the south side, which allowed visitors to come up some hidden stairs to emerge in the middle of the Gentile court;
- the ritual baths (or *mikvehs*) to the south of those gates;
- the south-western corner where the *shofar* trumpet was sounded to announce the start of the Sabbath;
- the sheer height of the whole platform above the street level below (to the west) and the Kidron Valley (to the east).

It is quite likely that it was only during this Herodian reconstruction that provision was first made for a 'court for the Gentiles'. Non-Jews had never been allowed into the Temple's inner sanctuary. With Herod's building, however, they were now welcome onto the Temple platform and inside its outer court. Yet at a certain point they reached the *soreq* – a low fence or wall beyond which they could not pass.

Notices were clearly displayed on this fence warning the Gentile visitors that they would themselves be deemed responsible for the death which would surely occur if they trespassed beyond this line.

One of these notices (in Greek) has survived and can be seen in Jerusalem's Rockerfeller Museum. Almost certainly Paul was thinking of this *soreq* fence when he spoke later of Jesus having destroyed the 'dividing wall of partition' (Ephesians 2:14). This was one of the clearest signs of the boundary that existed between Jew and Gentile, which Paul believed had been broken down through Jesus.

Model of the Jerusalem Temple. Moving out from the large white sanctuary containing the Holy of Holies behind the curtain, we can see the Court of the Priests (Israel), then the Court of the Women and (out near the colonnades) the Court of the Gentiles. Note the four massive candelabra in the Court of the Women (specially lit at the Feast of Tabernacles) and the grand Nicanor Gate for priests going up to the altar (in the inner court to the left).

shadow of its former self – indeed some of the returnees wept when they remembered its former glory (Ezra 3:12). In some senses the exile was now over, but in other ways its shadow still hung in the air. So throughout the next five centuries there was a continual longing for God to bring Israel's national life (including the Temple) back to its previous status. There were also those (like the Essenes based at Qumran) who fell out with the Temple's hierarchy and established their own 'alternative' Temple-like community, in prayerful expectation that God would usher in a new, more glorious Temple in Jerusalem. And as hopes grew of a Messiah–King, many became convinced that he would be like a new Solomon – a royal figure building God's house in accordance with its former glory, a new king with a new Temple.

Rumours of this Jewish belief may have come to the ears of the non-Jewish Herod the Great. In any event, one of the key ways in which he sought to establish his own rule over Judea was to rebuild Jerusalem's Temple: *he* would be the king with evident authority over God's Temple. Many Jewish people were understandably in two minds about this. They desperately wanted the Temple rebuilt and could not 'look a gift horse in the mouth'. On the other hand, they deeply resented Herod's rule – not least because he himself was not Jewish. Could a 'pagan' truly build the Temple of the Lord?

Model of first-century Jerusalem, viewed from near the Siloam Pool up the Ophel Ridge (the former City of David) towards the vast Temple platform (top right).

Would this new Temple be the fulfilment of their prophetic hopes? Or should they be expecting yet another Temple when the authentic Messiah arrived? For these reasons it was possible to be thoroughly committed to Judaism and to the importance of the Temple, while being critical of *this particular* Temple and longing for its replacement.

This was the volatile mix of passionate questions that Jesus walked into when he entered the Temple. Was this truly God's Temple? What might replace it? Who truly had authority over it?

Surface meanings: Gentiles, extortion and politics

Jesus' provocative action in the Temple had many different layers to it. So we should not think that it had only one true meaning. Almost certainly Jesus intended it to signal a range of concerns. There were, after all, several different ways in which the

Temple was open to a prophet's critique. Three come immediately to mind, but underneath them all, as we shall see, there was also a deeper, more fundamental point.

First, there was Jesus' critique of how Gentiles were being treated. Jesus' action almost certainly took place in the court of the Gentiles (recently created by Herod's expansion). Isaiah's vision of the Temple as a 'place of prayer for *all nations*' (Isaiah 56:7), however, was being flouted by the money changers using the Gentiles' court as the place for their dealings. If this was the only place where Gentiles could worship the God of Israel, it was a scandal that it had been turned into a place of trade and a 'den of robbers'. This was a comparatively recent innovation, instigated some twenty years earlier by the High Priest Caiaphas; but this abuse of the Gentiles' court had to stop: Israel's God, Jesus was insisting, was to be accessible to all.

Secondly, there was a critique of financial extortion. Worshippers were required to pay for their sacrificial animals in a unique currency (the 'Tyrian shekel'). There was plenty of room for corruption here, with the charging of high exchange rates. Jesus' concern for the potential abuse of poor worshippers is clear from his comments about the tiny gift placed in the Temple's rich coffers by a destitute widow. It seems clear, then, that Jesus was being provoked, in part, by this 'daylight robbery'.

Thirdly, there was the political dimension. The Temple was increasingly becoming the symbolic focus for a hot-headed Jewish nationalism. Overlooking the Temple courts was the Romans' Antonia Fortress, from which the pagan overlords could keep a close eye on any developing political unrest within the Temple. It was an unpleasant and provocative reminder to the Jewish worshippers of who retained political control. Yet it could not stop Jewish nationalists from congregating in the Temple and using it as a place for plotting. For the Temple itself raised Jewish passions; there was an ardent desire to defend 'this place' against Israel's enemies. In the Gospels we hear the Sanhedrin (the leading Jewish council in Jerusalem) being anxious that Jesus' actions might provoke its own kind of political unrest, which would then cause 'the Romans to come and take away both *our place* and our nation'

(John 11:48). This place had to be defended against the pagan Romans at all costs; it was therefore becoming the bastion and epitome of their desire for national independence.

So Jesus may also have been putting down a marker that this kind of nationalistic devotion to the Temple was not just misplaced, but wrong. The place of divine worship was not to be desecrated by becoming no more than a political pawn. In the imagery that he himself used when quizzed in the Temple, they were to 'give to Caesar the things that belonged to Caesar' (not seeking independence) while ensuring that they truly gave 'to God what is God's' (Luke 20:25) – that is, not 'robbing' God of his worship by using *his* Temple for *their* own agendas. Forty years later, we note, this would be precisely what happened: violent clashes in the Temple and disputes about its independence and sanctity would trigger the arrival of the Roman armies.

Artist's impression of the Temple courts, overlooked by the turrets of the Romans' Antonia Fortress.

A deeper meaning: a portent of destruction?

Yet beneath all this, Jesus' action was also a prophetic warning of what would soon be happening to the Temple. He was not just criticizing certain malpractices: anti-Gentile attitudes, financial distortion, political intrigue. No, Jesus was acting out a divine judgment and giving a clear warning that the days of *this* Temple were numbered – not least because of the various ways in which it was being abused. It was a 'portent of destruction'. Jesus was announcing the imminent demise of God's Temple.

The very nature of his action forces us to this conclusion. For, as a brief protest, it was unlikely to achieve anything – presumably normal business would have been resumed in under half an hour. Instead all its power lay in its symbolism. It was similar to the 'prophetic actions' seen when Old Testament prophets did something slightly strange (such as Jeremiah smashing a pot) to teach God's people a powerful lesson. So here there was a lesson to be learnt: divine displeasure against his Temple – just as in the days of Jeremiah.

In his Gospel, Mark helps us to see this theme of imminent destruction by placing this event between two incidents relating to a fig tree (Mark 11:12–14, 20–21). On the way into Jerusalem Jesus curses a fig tree because it lacks any fruit – a strange thing indeed to do since 'it was not the season for figs'. The next day, after the Temple cleansing, the disciples comment with astonishment that the 'fig tree you cursed has withered'. What is Mark saying to us through 'sandwiching' the Temple episode in this way?

His answer, surely, would be that the cursing of the fig tree is related to Jesus' action in the Temple and was intended to point the disciples to its deeper meaning. The two prophetic actions are meant to interpret each other. Mark is teaching that the

Temple cleansing was indeed an act of 'cursing' that would lead to its 'withering'. It was also a declaration that the Temple had been found, in God's eyes, to be lacking in 'fruit'. Jesus' action is indeed, says Mark, a portent of the Temple's imminent destruction.

Jesus' stance against the Temple

This is then confirmed when Jesus actually predicts the destruction of the Temple's beautiful buildings, saying that 'not one stone here will be left upon another' (Mark 13:2). Here Jesus explicitly states what his prophetic actions had symbolized. The disciples, looking at the Temple's 'massive stones' and 'magnificent buildings', are duly horrified. Yet Jesus elaborates on the distress that will soon be coming on Jerusalem – this great Herodian edifice will soon be no more (Luke 21:5–36; see page 140).

In fact Jesus had hinted at this before. He had used the picture of a 'house' crashing to the ground and had warned that Jerusalem's 'house' would be left 'desolate'; and, on entering the city, he had wept because Jerusalem's enemies would 'dash you to the ground' (Matthew 7:26–27; Luke 13:35; 19:43–44). Moreover, in his own offering of forgiveness to various people in Galilee there had also been a veiled threat towards the Temple as the sole dispenser of divine forgiveness (Luke 5:20; 7:48). That prerogative now belonged to him, not to the Temple. Now Jesus had come, the Temple was becoming redundant. For he himself, so he claimed, was 'one greater than Solomon' (the builder of the Temple) and indeed was 'one greater than the Temple' itself (Matthew 12:6, 42).

So there are hints that Jesus saw himself as a kind of 'one-man counter-Temple' operation. The Temple had fulfilled various roles within Israel, as the heart of the nation, the place of forgiveness, the location of God's presence; Jesus was now going to fulfil these roles himself among his own people. He, not the Temple, was the true centre; he was the access point to God.

'Jesus was implicitly claiming to be and do that which the temple was and did… So when Jesus came to Jerusalem, he came embodying a counter-system. He and the city were both making claims to be the place where the Living God was at work to heal, restore and regroup his people.'

N.T. Wright

John's Gospel: Jesus the true Temple

This theme is drawn out most clearly in John's Gospel, where Jesus is found in the Temple quite frequently. John does this, not only to make clear that Jesus had been into the Temple many times prior to this final incident, but also to convey a powerful truth about Jesus: Jesus himself was the true Temple and its true fulfilment.

John conveys this in various ways. For example, during the feast of Tabernacles (when there was an elaborate Temple ritual involving water and when giant candelabra were lit within the Temple courts), he records Jesus saying: 'If anyone is thirsty, let him come to me and drink', and 'I am the light of the world' (John 7:37; 8:12). In other words, John saw a spiritual meaning or symbolism behind the ancient festival that Jesus was now fulfilling in his own person.

This symbolism is most evident in John's account of Jesus' 'cleansing of the Temple'. John places the incident near the beginning of his Gospel (John 2:13–25). This may reflect the fact that Jesus challenged the Temple on more than one occasion; or it may be John's way of emphasizing the importance of this theme for understanding what he wants to convey later in his Gospel. Either way, John includes a statement that takes us to the heart of the matter. For, when challenged about his authority to overturn the tables, Jesus speaks about the Temple as his 'Father's house' and then utters the vital words, 'Destroy this Temple, and I will raise it again in three days' (John 2:19).

It is a powerful but enigmatic statement. In fact this is the strange saying that Jesus' opponents tried (in vain) to reconstruct at his trial. His accusers remembered that he had spoken against the Temple in some way and made reference to something happening 'after three days', but they couldn't quite agree on the wording (Mark 14:58). What should be clear to us, however, is this. Jesus was using his action in the Temple as a symbol of destruction; Jesus was speaking out against 'this Temple' and he had the theme of its destruction on his mind; he was also hinting at his power to replace it.

Within some strands of Judaism, as we saw above, there was a longing for this Herodian Temple to be replaced, presumably with a new and bigger *physical* Temple. But Jesus now hints that the replacement Temple would actually be *himself*. John sees the reference to 'three days' as a clear prediction of Jesus' resurrection, which he explains must mean that the '*temple* he had spoken of was his *body*' (John 2:21–22). Now that Jesus had come, the Temple's functions would cease to be important, because there would be a new reality at work in the world – the body of Christ.

In biblical thought, the Temple manifested the presence of God among his people. John is saying that, in the same way, Jesus is the embodiment of that divine presence on earth. Truly, the Word of God has 'become flesh and made his dwelling [or tabernacle] among us' (John 1:14). In this way the Temple-motif, as expounded in John's Gospel, becomes a Jewish and biblical way of referring to what later Christians would term the 'incarnation' – that is, in Jesus, God himself was walking among us. As God formerly had dwelt in the Temple, so now he dwells in Jesus.

Jesus' authority: as Messiah and Lord

In the light of all this it is hardly surprisingly that, when Jesus came to Jerusalem and went into the Temple, there was a major confrontation. It was as though the city 'wasn't big enough for the both of them'.

For, by going into the Temple, Jesus was not acting merely as a social protester, nor even as a prophet with a devastating message. He was challenging the Temple with his own unique authority. We have seen how the Messiah was expected to be the one to rebuild the Temple, the one to exercise authority over it. Not surprisingly then, after his action, the question that was put to him by the religious leaders was this one of authority: 'By what authority are you doing these things?' (Luke 20:2). They sensed in Jesus' action a veiled messianic claim. And the same issues came together later in his trial before Caiaphas: they interrogated him about his attitude to the Temple, because they felt that this, more than anything else, would force him to make clear his messianic pretensions.

Yet deeper still there was a sense in which Jesus went into the Temple as its rightful owner – as the *Lord himself*. An Old Testament prophecy in Malachi had spoken of 'preparing the way for the Lord' (Malachi 3:1); the gospel writers believed this was fulfilled when John the Baptist prepared for the coming of Jesus. Yet the verse went on to say that 'the Lord whom you are seeking will come suddenly to his

The destruction of the Temple

Josephus gives an extended account of the destruction of the Temple and the burning of the upper city of Jerusalem in the summer of AD 70. Here are some extracts describing the moments leading up to the burning of the Temple's Holy of Holies. In coming to terms with this tragic event, he seems anxious to clear Titus of wanting to destroy the Temple (he was now writing in Rome for a Roman audience) and suggests instead that its destruction should be put down to 'fate'.

When two of the legions had completed their banks on the eighth day of the month Ab, Titus ordered that battering rams be brought and set against the western edifice of the inner temple... The soldiers had already put fire to the gates from where it spread and caught hold of the cloisters. Upon seeing this, the people's spirits sank.

Titus retired into the tower of Antonia, and resolved to storm the temple the next day and to encamp round about the holy house. God had, for certain, long ago doomed that house to the fire. And now that fatal day was come, according to the revolution of ages. It was the tenth day of the month Ab (the same day as when it was burnt before by the king of Babylon)...

Since Caesar was unable to restrain the enthusiastic fury of the soldiers, and the fire proceeded on more and more, he went into the holy place of the temple and saw what was in it. The flame had not yet reached to its inward parts, but was still consuming the rooms that were about the holy house. Titus supposed that the house itself might yet be saved, but the soldiers had a vehement inclination to fight. Moreover, the hope of plunder induced many to go on, believing that all the places within were full of money, seeing that all round about it was made of gold. Then one of them threw the fire upon the hinges of the gate; the flame immediately burst out from within the holy house itself. And thus was the holy house burnt down, without Caesar's approbation.

Now people might justly lament the destruction of such a work, since it was the most admirable of all the works that we have seen – both for its curious structure and its magnitude, the vast wealth bestowed upon it, and the glorious reputation it had for its holiness. Yet there might be some comfort in the thought that it was fate that decreed it so to be, which is inevitable, both as to living creatures, and as to works and places also.

Josephus, *War* 6:4

Temple' (Malachi 3:2). If Jesus was fulfilling this prophecy then, in coming to the Temple, Jesus was coming to it as the Lord himself. In other words, the owner was making a sudden appearance *in his own house*. As a result, the words Jesus quoted from Isaiah when cleansing the Temple take on a new light: when he quoted the words '*My* house will be called a house of prayer', was there an extra layer of meaning? God's words that came through the prophet Isaiah about *his* house seem now to have become Jesus' words about *his* house. It is a subtle hint to those who can hear that in Jesus the Temple is being presented with its rightful owner – God himself.

Leaving the Temple behind

So, according to the New Testament, Jerusalem's Temple had found its match in Jesus – its truest meaning. Now that he had come, its spiritual power had been transferred. During the next 40 years Jesus' followers would still meet there on occasions, and fulfil their obligations there as required; yet they would always be mindful of Jesus' prophecy concerning its destruction. And in the meantime, they would begin to experience the new reality that Christian believers throughout the world were now the true expression of God's new Temple in the world. Writing to the Gentile believers in Corinth, Paul can boldly declare, '*you are* that Temple' (1 Corinthians 3:17).

The New Testament writers also taught that the spread of the gospel to 'all nations' overthrew the Temple's rigid exclusion of Gentiles. So, when visiting Jerusalem later in AD 57, Paul would be accused of having taken some of his Gentile converts (such as Luke) into the Temple. In fact this was false, since Paul would have observed the customs of his day; but the logic of his preaching message was clearly pointing in that direction. In the light of a gospel that was available for all people, the Temple was now clearly a thing of the past. Its days were numbered. Or, as the writer of Hebrews would say (developing the idea that Jesus' death had replaced the need for any continuing high priests or sacrifices): 'what is ageing and obsolete will soon disappear' (Hebrews 8:13). In Christian biblical theology, therefore, there is no longer any need for a Temple because truly the 'one greater than the Temple' has come (Matthew 12:6).

'I did not see a temple in the city, because the Lord God Almighty and the Lamb are its temple.'

Revelation 21:22

Key dates: The Temple

c. 980 BC	David buys the 'threshing-floor of Araunah' (2 Samuel 24:18–25).	c. AD 8	Twelve-year-old Jesus sits with the teachers in the Temple, describing it as 'his Father's house' (Luke 2:49).	AD 333	Bordeaux Pilgrim sees a 'tower' associated with Jesus' temptation; the 'blood of Zacharias' still visible on the Temple's altar; 'two statues of Hadrian'; and a 'pierced stone which the Jews come and anoint each year' (*BP* 590–591).
c. 976 BC	Building of the first Temple by Solomon (1 Kings 5–6).	AD 30 ff	Jesus and then the apostles teach and preach in the Temple (Luke 20–21; Acts 3–4).		
c. 587/6 BC	Destruction of the Temple by the Babylonians.	AD 49	Massacre of nearly 10,000 people in the Temple courts (Josephus, *War* 2:12); possibly alluded to by Paul in 1 Thessalonians 2:16.	AD 638	Muslims arrive in Jerusalem.
c. 515 BC	Rebuilding of the smaller Temple by Zerubbabel, encouraged by prophets Haggai and Zechariah (Ezra 6).			AD 691	Building of the Dome of the Rock by Umayyad caliph, Abd al-Malik.
		AD 57	Paul visits the Temple and is arrested on false charge of taking Gentiles into the court of Israel (Acts 21:27–29).	AD 705–15	Building of the el-Aksa mosque.
c. 167 BC	Antiochus IV of Syria desecrates the Temple (1 Maccabees 20–24); reconsecrated 3 years later by the Maccabees (1 Maccabees 4:57–60; 12:37).			1099–1187	Crusaders use buildings, identifying el-Aksa as the 'Temple of Solomon' and the Dome of the Rock as the 'Temple of the Lord'.
		AD 62	James (Jesus' brother) is martyred, thrown down from the Temple pinnacle (Eusebius, *Ecclesiastical History* 2:23).		
63 BC	Pompey enters the Holy of Holies and, to his surprise, finds it empty.			1967	Israeli troops storm the Temple platform, but relinquish the site to Muslim control; development of the expanded Western Wall plaza.
		AD 67	Temple as the focus of riots in the First Jewish Revolt.		
c. 15 BC	Herod the Great starts renovation and expansion of the Temple and its platform; John says later that rebuilding has been going on for '46 years' (John 2:20).	AD 70	Roman armies under Titus destroy the Temple.	1998	Opening of an underground tunnel for visitors along the western edge of the platform causes major protests from local Muslims.
		c. AD 290	Eusebius describes Christian visitors contemplating the fall of the Temple in accordance with the Lord's words (*Demonstration of the Gospel* 6:18).		
c. 5 BC	Presentation of the infant Jesus in the Temple (Luke 2:22–38).			2000	Provocative visit of Ariel Sharon to the Temple brings about resumed *Intifada*.

The Temple Today

The Temple area, in which Jesus' actions caused a storm, has continued to be a place of controversy and tension. Few sites in the world can be as hotly and fiercely contested as are these 12 acres (150,000 square metres) of land in the heart of historic Jerusalem.

Islamic and Jewish approaches

For Muslims, who see Jerusalem as the third holiest city in the world (after Mecca and Medina), the Temple platform lies at the heart of their religion. They call it *Haram esh-Sharif*, the 'noble sanctuary'. From here, in Islamic tradition, Mohammed ascended to heaven on his 'night journey' from the 'furthermost sanctuary' (*Sura* 17). And on the site are two of Islam's most ancient buildings: the mosque of el-Aksa ('the furthermost') and the shrine known as the Dome of the Rock, both now more than 1,300 years old.

Meanwhile the Temple is also central to the history of the Jewish people. This was where Israel's temple stood for almost exactly 1,000 years – the centre of their religious and political life. Rabbinic Judaism adapted well to the loss of the Temple after AD 70, so most practising Jews see no need for the rebuilding of their Temple. Throughout their exile from the land, however, the stones of the Temple have been precious. Through the centuries the western wall of the Temple platform became a focal point for prayer and national aspirations. And there remain a vocal minority who fervently wish for the rebuilding of a 'Third' Temple on the site of the ancient Temple – something that would presumably be impossible without the destruction of the Muslim shrines that currently stand there.

It is a potentially explosive cocktail. Israeli interference on the site is interpreted by Palestinians as a bid for ownership. The Palestinians in turn try to pour scorn on Jewish claims to sovereignty. It is a recipe for strife in a place that needs little provocation to become a major flashpoint.

Christian approaches

Christians by and large 'sit out' on this particular tension. Noting Jesus' actions in the

Temple and his statements about his own body as the true Temple, the Christian church has, as a rule, not seen the need for a restored Temple. According to the New Testament, Jesus has now offered the one perfect sacrifice for sins through his own death (see, for example, Hebrews 10:10–25; Romans 3:25). The first Christians in Jerusalem were willing to use the Temple as a place for teaching, but they would have been waiting for the fulfilment of Jesus' prophecy that it would soon be destroyed. Almost certainly they fled the city before the Roman armies arrived, showing that their loyalty was no longer to the Temple, but to Messiah Jesus. There is no evidence of Christians mourning the loss of the Temple in AD 70; indeed, they saw its destruction as a telling confirmation of the Christian faith: through Jesus God had moved salvation history into a new era in which the Temple was strictly redundant.

So in AD 325, when Christians first had the opportunity to do something with the Temple site, they left it well alone. The Byzantines did not build a church on the Temple platform, but left this vast expanse in the heart of the city to be completely deserted – as a striking witness to the power and truth of Jesus' words. Before the coming of Constantine they had looked over the site from the Mount of Olives; now they could view it from an alternative hill, from the area around the church of the Holy Sepulchre. But from whichever direction they looked, the contrast was evident.

'Since the coming of our Saviour Zion has been left as a tent in a vineyard, as a hut in a garden of cucumbers, or as anything that is more desolate than these...'

Eusebius, *Proof of the Gospel* 2:3

View looking southwards over the Old City walls towards the Temple platform (covered with trees and the two domed buildings: the Golden Dome of the Rock and the grey el-Aksa mosque).

The old era had been brought to an end and the new one established.

The irony of this policy, at once quietist and yet triumphalist, was that when the Muslim forces arrived in AD 638, there was a perfect piece of land sitting vacant for their new buildings. This perhaps ensured that the churches of Byzantine Jerusalem were not destroyed, but it also meant that the Temple platform site could now be developed to make exactly the same triumphalist point – but with new meaning. If the Christians had used the different hills in Jerusalem to emblazon in stone their apparent victory over Judaism, the Muslims could do the same in reverse to announce *their* victory over Christianity. Jerusalem had become the scene of a long-term game of religious 'ping-pong'. Many centuries later, and with the return of the Jewish people to the city, the game has moved on into a yet more stormy period.

Anyone visiting the Temple area today, therefore, should be sensitive to the tensions of this place and should develop their own informed and theological response to what they see. For here we are not dealing simply with old stones from a bygone era, but with an almost living entity that continues to ask us its searching questions.

Three faiths: a Jewish tomb on the Mount of Olives, with the Muslim Dome of the Rock and (beyond) the grey dome of the Christian church of the Holy Sepulchre.

Visiting the site

In practice, getting up onto the Temple area can be difficult. Access to non-Muslims is not allowed during the Muslim times of prayer, and sometimes it is closed because of heightened local tensions. Even so, a good deal about the Temple can be learnt by viewing the platform from below.

Some visitors might start by looking up at the **south-east corner of the Temple platform** from the road that skirts closely round it. Already the sheer vastness of Herod's stones is evident, as is the incredible height of the platform above the natural terrain. Underneath this south-eastern pinnacle are the so-called **'Solomon's Stables'** – vast underground vaults, misnamed by the Crusaders but used by them for their own horses and storage. They entered them through the (now blocked up) single gate in the southern wall platform. Access from above is now rarely possible, and many have expressed concern about some of the 'excavating' and removal of historic artefacts that may be going on unobserved. But those who have seen the vaults testify to their appreciation for Herod's workmen, who were able to build up the Temple's platform in this way and to do so in a way that has lasted for generations.

Looking at the southern platform wall from below, it is worth noting the contours of the (also closed up) **'Triple Gates'**. These, together with a set of 'Double Gates' further to the left (now obscured by the foundation of the el-Aksa mosque), were known as the Huldah gates (2 Kings 21:14) and were the chief exit and entrance, respectively, for people entering the Temple. There was a one-way system. Having washed themselves in the nearby ritual bath (or *mikveh*), worshippers would go up the outer steps (some of which are still clearly visible), entering by the double gates, and would then be taken up a vaulted corridor with steps until they came out in the court of the Gentiles – just in front of the modern entrance to the el-Aksa.

To reach those **Temple steps** it is necessary to pass through the 'Dung Gate', turn immediately to the left for the ticket office for this site, and then walk eastwards. For some, sitting on the Temple steps can be a powerful experience. Although some of the steps have clearly been repaired in recent times, the ancient stones among them are one of the surest links back to the first century. These were the stones on which all Jewish pilgrims walked as they 'went up to the Temple to pray' (Jesus' words in Luke 18:10 in the parable of the Pharisee and the tax-collector). These were the steps that would have been used by Mary and Joseph as they brought the infant Jesus to the Temple for his dedication (Luke 2:22–38). And they were used by Jesus himself on numerous occasions.

It was as 'Jesus left the Temple and was walking away', we read, that 'his disciples came up to him to call his attention to its buildings', commenting on their 'massive' and 'beautiful' stones (Matthew 24:1). Walking back towards the south-western corner, visitors can appreciate what they meant. The Herodian stones, recognizable through their chiselled margins, are enormous. Transporting them and then hoisting them into

The so-called 'Golden Gate' on the eastern side of the Temple platform.

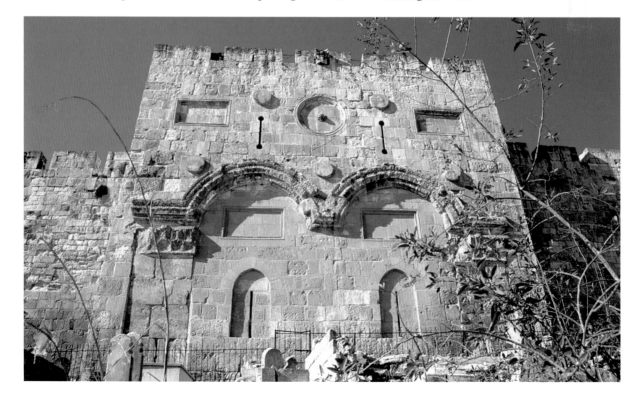

Above: The Hebrew inscription of Isaiah 66:14 on one of the distinctive Herodian stones used for building the Temple platform.

Below: Where the Temple stones fell. Ancient shops and roadways to the west of the Temple, which were crushed when the Romans destroyed the Temple above in AD 70.

position would have been a daunting task. And this was just for the platform, not for the buildings above them (about which the disciples had been speaking).

As visitors turn the corner and look northwards up the western edge of the platform there is graphic evidence of Jesus' next words: 'Not one stone', he prophesied, 'will be left upon another' (Luke 21:6). Here, lying just where they fell, are some of the **huge stones** that were thrown down by the Roman troops, crushing the shops and buildings beneath them.

This **south-western corner** was an important one. From its top the *shofar* horn would be sounded, indicating the times of sacrifice and prayer in the Temple (the corner-stone used by the trumpeter has recently been found). Then, a little lower down, there was another entrance into the Temple – a flight of steps over an arch (now known as **Robinson's arch**). The beginnings of the arch can be seen half way up the wall and some of its piers are clearly visible. When Edward Robinson first noted the arch back in 1842, however, all that could be seen was its very top. That was where 'ground level' was. The same was true for Wilson's Arch and Barclay's Gate (further along the western wall), similarly named after the nineteenth-century western archaeologists who first noticed them. Yet further evidence of the way ground level has changed through the centuries can be found in the **Hebrew inscription** (now considerably above ground level). It is a quotation from Isaiah 66:14: 'You shall see, and your heart shall rejoice; your bones will flourish like the

grass.' Almost certainly this was written by some Jews during the attempted rebuilding of the Temple in AD 361–63.

After exploring the remains of the many shops and houses in the area, visitors need to retrace their steps through the ticket office and make their way north (through some security screening) into the **Western Wall Plaza**. Until 1967 there were houses built within 5 yards (4 metres) of the wall. Now the area has been opened up as a place of historic and spiritual importance for Jewish people from all over the world. This was the so-called 'Wailing Wall', to which faithful Jews came over many centuries in order to pray near to their ancient Temple. It was not, as is often thought, the wall of the Temple itself, but was rather part of the Temple's *platform*. Visitors will want to take time to observe this place, to sense its symbolic power, and perhaps even to pray themselves.

For now, however, the focus is on discovering more about the first-century Temple. Standing at the Western Wall it is possible to see to the right (above the women's section) the outline of **Barclay's Gate**; and to the left (in the section reserved for men) the entrance to a **tunnel**. This has recently been opened to visitors and goes the full

The Western Wall Plaza, with the Dome of the Rock above.

length of the Temple platform. (The exit is by the entrance to the Umariyya School, deep inside the Muslim Quarter.) Those who have time to walk through the tunnel can see various vaulted chambers and the excavations done by Warren in the 1860s, especially his two deep shafts. The shaft nearest the Temple goes down 60 feet (18 metres), revealing fourteen courses of Herodian stones. It is yet another fascinating glimpse into the skill of Herod's workmen and the extent of this mammoth building project. No wonder people commented that work had been going on 'for 46 years' (John 2:20). Indeed, there is some evidence that work was still continuing right up until the 60s AD.

Many will want at this point to go onto the **Temple Mount**, which means going back through some more security screening. Once through the ticket office, visitors are often taken aback by the sheer extent of the area. In ancient times the Temple constituted 20 per cent of the city's total square area. Now it is a great haven from the busy streets below.

The **el-Aksa mosque** on the right was restored in the 1940s. Unlike the Dome of the Rock, this building is not on bedrock and has suffered from numerous earthquakes. Some mosaics survive from the eleventh century, but otherwise much is from more recent times. During the Crusades this was the king's palace and it was then handed over to soldier–monks thereafter known as the 'Templars' (see page 90).

Far more impressive is the **Dome of the Rock**. Built in AD 691, it stands unrivalled as an example of classical architecture – an octagon and dome of precise mathematical exactness. Its outer mosaics were replaced by tiles in the sixteenth century and again in its latest restoration (1962). Inside, however, are the original mosaics, beautifully designed by Syrian Christians but avoiding any representation of living creatures – hence the focus on garden motifs.

Strictly speaking, the Dome of the Rock is not a mosque, but rather a shrine remembering Mohammed's 'night journey'. Yet Abd al-Malik the caliph also had other purposes in mind. For example, the building covers the rock which, according to an ancient Jewish tradition, was where Abraham nearly sacrificed his son Isaac (Genesis 22:2 had located this on 'Mount Moriah' without making it clear where this mountain was). It is unclear exactly when this merging of the Temple and Abrahamic traditions took place, but the caliph certainly built here to make a point: it was a statement that Islam had appropriated the story of Abraham and was superior to Judaism.

Similarly he wished to show Islam's supremacy over Christianity. Part of the building's long founding inscription – which runs for nearly 700 feet (210 metres) around the top of the internal octagon – was a clear message addressed to Christians, countering their faith in the Trinity and the Incarnation: 'O you People of the Book, overstep not the bounds of your religion, and of God speak only the truth… Say not three. It will be better for you. God is only one God. Far be it from his glory that he should have a son.' In the contest of the three faiths, all represented in Jerusalem, this striking monument sends out its own strong, if silent, signal.

For this or other reasons, some Christian visitors may chose not to go onto the Temple Mount. There are also rules forbidding orthodox Jews from going onto the site – though for quite a different reason. This is because there is a danger that they might, unwittingly, tread on the area once covered by the **Holy of Holies** in the former Temple. The exact location of this is the subject of ongoing lively debate. There is a strong case for arguing that the Holy of Holies would have covered the highest rock on the site – namely the one now at the centre of the Dome of the Rock. However, there are those who think it may have been further to the north-west, perhaps in line with

the 'Golden Gate' (in the platform wall on the east). If this is the case, the tiny 'Dome of the Spirits' may in fact mark the correct site.

From a Christian perspective, the exact location is comparatively unimportant. Far more significant is the New Testament view that at the moment of the crucifixion the curtain covering the Holy of Holies 'was torn in two' (Luke 23:45). Any barrier between a holy God and sinful humanity, Luke suggests, was broken down by Jesus' death on the cross. And, according to the book of Hebrews, Jesus has 'entered into the most Holy Place' and encourages believers to follow him there: because of Jesus' sacrifice, access into God's awesome presence is now available to all (Hebrew 10:18–25).

So we leave our visit to the Temple, newly aware of just how vast and significant it was in the Jerusalem of Jesus' day; yet also aware, therefore, of how startling Jesus' challenge was to this enormous institution. He claimed to be the true Temple, and single-handedly, both in powerful action and prophetic word, signalled its imminent demise. Who did he think he was? And why did his coming somehow lead to this key transition in God's dealings with his people?

'Therefore, since we have confidence to enter the Most Holy Place by the blood of Jesus… and since we have a great priest over the house of God, let us draw near to God with a sincere heart in full assurance of faith.'

Hebrews 10:19, 21–22

Jerusalem

Great is the Lord and most worthy of praise,
in the city of our God, his holy mountain.
It is beautiful in its loftiness, the joy of the whole earth.
Like the utmost heights of Zaphon is Mount Zion, the city of the great King.
God is in her citadels; he has shown himself to be her fortress...
Walk about Zion, go round her, count her towers;
consider well her ramparts, view her citadels,
that you may tell of them to the next generation.

Psalm 48:1–3, 12–13

The 'holy city'?

Jerusalem – the 'city of peace', the 'holy city', beloved 'Zion'. The Old Testament is full of praise for this small city, nestled in the Judean hills. Founded by David on the site of an earlier Jebusite town around 1000 BC, it became the mother city of the Jewish nation and gradually expanded over the centuries. By the time of Jesus it is estimated to have had a population of around 40,000.

Old Testament 'Zion'

'Glorious things of thee are spoken,
Zion city of our God...
Solid joys and lasting treasures
none but Zion's children know.'

John Newton, 'Glorious things of thee are spoken'

Like any city, it had experienced moments of great celebration and joy – for example, the return of the ark from Philistine captivity (2 Samuel 6); the dedication of the Temple (1 Kings 8); its rescue from the siege of Sennacherib (Isaiah 37). Yet it had also had its fair share of sorrow, shame and disaster – the idolatrous rule of King Manasseh (2 Kings 21); its burning and destruction by the Babylonians (2 Kings 25); and its reversion to pagan rule under the Romans.

The Old Testament writers knew full well that, like any city, Jerusalem could be a place where evil and intrigue flourished: 'I see violence and strife in the city; destructive forces are at work within it; threats and lies never leave its streets' (Psalm 55:9–11). Yet they also encouraged people to have a great love for the city and to have strong hopes for its future glory. Isaiah had prophesied its restoration after the exile: 'Burst into songs of joy together, you ruins of Jerusalem; for the Lord has comforted his people, he has redeemed Jerusalem' (Isaiah 52:9). The Psalms sung in the Temple often celebrated the city and its role in God's purposes: 'He has set his foundation on the holy mountain; the Lord loves the gates of Zion more than all the dwellings of Jacob' (Psalm 87:1–2).

In such ways the people of Jesus' day were inspired to have a great love, not just for the Temple where their God was to be worshipped, but also for the city surrounding the

Temple. Jerusalem lay at the very centre of their national life. The Psalmist could say, 'If I forget you, O Jerusalem, may my right hand forget its skill. May my tongue cling to the roof of my mouth if I do not consider Jerusalem my highest joy' (Psalm 137:5–6). And the famous words of Psalm 122 may often have rung in their ears, not least whenever they travelled to Jerusalem and entered through its gates:

I rejoiced with those who said to me, 'Let us go the house of the Lord.'
Our feet are standing in your gates, O Jerusalem.
Jerusalem is built like a city, that is closely compacted together…
Pray for the peace of Jerusalem: 'May those who love you be secure.
May there be peace within your walls and security within your citadels…'
Psalm 122:1–3, 6–7

Aerial view of Jerusalem from the south-west. Most of the area to the south of the Turkish 'Old City' walls was within the city in Jesus' day: both the Upper City ('Mount Sion'), now marked by the conical dome of the Dormition Abbey; and the Lower City ('City of David'), the spur going southwards from the Temple Mount.

Jerusalem from above, with the eastern half of the Old City (*bottom*) and the foot of the Mount of Olives (*top*). Note the vast area of Herod's expanded Temple platform (making up 20 per cent of the city's square area at that time). Other features, clearly visible, include: the Western Wall Plaza, the church of the Holy Sepulchre (*bottom middle*) and the deep contours of the Kidron Valley (*going away to the right*).

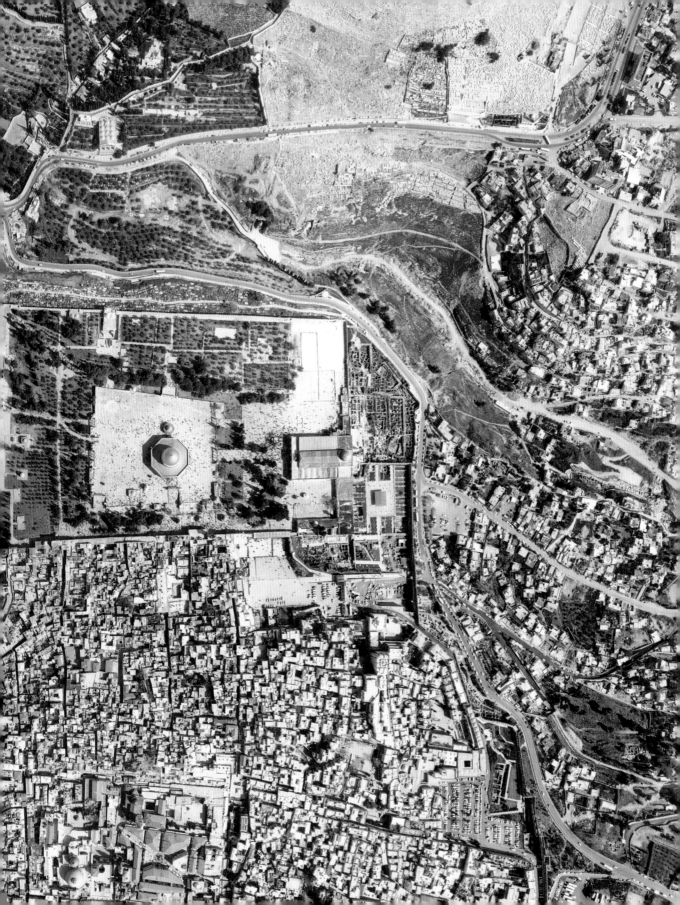

The Herodian city

In the years preceding Jesus' arrival, the city had been undergoing a major transformation. Herod the Great's plans for the city included not just the vastly expanded Temple area. For example, there was an expanded Antonia Fortress for the Roman garrison overlooking the Temple (named in honour of Mark Anthony), a new palace for Herod himself (on the western side of the city), and a new bathhouse over Siloam's Pool. Many old buildings would have been restored. The number of labourers required for these building operations would have necessitated more housing, probably in the Tyropoean Valley in the north-western quarter of the city. Meanwhile, the aristocracy were evidently investing in their own properties (on the western hill). According to some interpretations of Josephus, there is even possible evidence of the construction of a new hippodrome and theatre (previously banned from this Jewish city).

So although the city, with its religious history and mountainous location, would have a different feel to some of the more cosmopolitan and commercial cities of the empire, we are not to imagine it as some old-fashioned backwater. The 'holy city' was a thriving, bustling place. Herod was giving it a vibrant 'new look'.

Model of first-century Jerusalem, viewed north-eastwards from near the wealthy upper city towards the Temple. Note the poorer housing on the slopes down to the Tyropoean Valley. Also clearly visible is Robinson's Arch (the bridge-entrance at the south-west corner of the Temple), the Holy of Holies and the Antonia Fortress.

And, although Jesus' primary focus was naturally on the Temple, we know he also walked around the city's streets. On a previous visit, for example, we find him 'in Jerusalem near the Sheep Gate' (just to the north of the Temple) at a pool called 'Bethesda, which is surrounded by five colonnades' (John 5:2). Almost certainly this was one of the places that had recently been renovated. It was a place with supposed healing qualities (some have compared it, for example, to the cult of Asclepius, practised in other parts of the empire). In any event, disabled people congregated here in the hope of a cure. Jesus visited it one Sabbath – despite its strange, even pagan associations – and promptly healed a man who had been an invalid for 38 years. Jesus, says John, is the true source of holiness and healing.

Now, on this last visit to Jerusalem, Jesus would again be walking through the city's streets; but some of that would be while he was under arrest. For in focusing on Jesus' movements inside the city, we find ourselves concentrating on the last 24 hours of Jesus' life and on the three main events that occurred within that short period: the Last Supper; Jesus' night-time trial before the religious leaders; and the trial before Pontius Pilate the next morning. Quite conceivably, because of the mounting political pressure he was under, Jesus limited his movements within the city, preferring to focus on the Temple or otherwise to be at some distance from the city somewhere on the Mount of Olives. But, when the time was right, he entered the city resolutely.

Jesus' Last Supper

Then came the day of Unleavened Bread on which the Passover lamb had to be sacrificed. Jesus sent Peter and John, saying, 'Go and make preparations for us to eat the Passover... As you enter the city, a man carrying a jar of water will meet you. Follow him to the house that he enters, and say to the owner of the house, "The Teacher asks: Where is the guest room, where I may eat the Passover with my disciples?" He will show you a large upper room, all furnished. Make preparations there.' They left and found things just as Jesus had told them. So they prepared the Passover.

When the hour came, Jesus and his apostles reclined at the table... He took bread, gave thanks and broke it, and gave it to them, saying, 'This is my body given for you; do this in remembrance of me.' In the same way, after the supper he took the cup, saying, 'This cup is the new covenant in my blood, which is poured out for you.'
Luke 22:7–8, 10–15, 19–20

This element of necessary caution and secrecy can be sensed in the way Jesus made the preparations for his 'Last Supper' with his disciples. It was customary, if at all possible, for Jews to celebrate the annual Passover meal *within the walls* of the city. So Jesus needed a location somewhere inside the city. Yet, because the religious authorities were now looking for an opportunity to arrest him (Luke 19:47), the location needed to be secure and secret. So Jesus gave his disciples some rather coded instructions. The result, however, was that they encountered a discreet owner who provided them with a 'large upper room' – probably somewhere on the slopes of the city's more wealthy western hill. Jesus had secured the necessary privacy that he needed, despite the menacing presence of his enemies not so far away within the city. He would be able to spend some final precious hours with his friends.

Few meals can ever have received as much subsequent attention as has Jesus' Last Supper with his disciples. The Synoptic Gospels describe it fairly succinctly but John's Gospel devotes five whole chapters to this one meal. Even so, we are left with numerous questions, for example: were the number of disciples limited just to the Twelve?

Celebrating Passover in Jesus' day

Passover was one of the three major festivals within first-century Jewish practice. The Feast of Weeks (or *Shavuot/ Pentecost*) was in late May; the Feast of Tabernacles (*Sukkot*) was in October. The Feast of Passover (*Pesach*) was celebrated on the fifteenth day of the month Nisan (normally falling in late March/early April) and marked the beginning of a week-long holiday – the Feast of Unleavened Bread.

The origins of Passover lie way back in Israel's experience of release from captivity in Egypt during the period of the exodus. The Israelites were commanded to slaughter a young lamb or goat and smear its blood over their doorway so that the 'angel of death' might *pass over*, sparing their homes from the final plague that was being visited on the Egyptians – the death of their firstborn sons (Exodus 12–13). In subsequent centuries this sacrificial meal was remembered and re-enacted every year.

By the time of Jesus the meal had become central to Israel's self-understanding: it was celebrated as a communal event within family homes, giving everyone an opportunity to recite the national 'founding' story of their deliverance by God. People were encouraged to identify with those original Israelites and to see *themselves*, as it were, as those rescued by God from Egypt. It became a season when first-century Jews also longed for God to rescue them again – this time not from Pharaoh but from their pagan Roman overlords.

Passover was celebrated throughout the 'Diaspora' (wherever Jewish people were 'dispersed' from the land of Israel). Many however would have tried to go up to Jerusalem for the feast. Josephus suggests that the population of Jerusalem could rise to 3 million during Passover, but modern scholars suggest more conservative figures of up to 180 thousand. Such an influx would still cause major accommodation problems – hence the number of Galileans who would have bivouacked on the slopes of the Mount of Olives. It was also traditional to enjoy the meal itself within the city walls – hence the disciples' anxiety over where Jesus would find a vacant room in the busy city.

A later Jewish document (the *Mishnah*, compiled c. AD 200) gives details of how Passover was celebrated at that time. This may well reflect some of the practices of Jesus' day. Each family 'head' selected a lamb on Nisan 10, which was then slaughtered in the afternoon of Nisan 14. The Temple courts were busy with vast numbers of priests passing basins of blood along a line until the last one threw them on the burning altar. The man would then return to his family with the lamb wrapped in hide and hanging over his shoulder.

Meanwhile, families and guests (always ten or more) were gathering. The children would have helped ensure that any 'leaven' had been removed from the home by midday. Sunset marked the beginning of Nisan 15. Everyone then sat down for the meal, which followed a set order (or *seder*) and involved ritual actions such as hand-washings. The meal would include the lamb, unleavened bread, bitter herbs and a sweet-tasting mixture (*haroset*). The latter was a reminder of the 'mud' from which the Israelites had had to make bricks in Egypt and the other items reminded them of their bitter slavery there, eating the 'bread of affliction'. During the meal there was a set recital of the Exodus story (the *haggadah*) and wine was sipped at indicated moments to celebrate different aspects of the story.

By changing the set words said over the unleavened bread and the wine Jesus was dramatically placing himself at the centre of Israel's national story, hinting that the new exodus for which they were longing was now being accomplished at last – through him and through his death. Almost certainly the cup over which he proclaimed the words 'this is my blood' was the so-called 'cup of redemption' – hence the later New Testament imagery of people being 'redeemed' (or set free) through Jesus' blood.

The gospel writers affirm that Jesus' Last Supper was indeed focused on the Passover (Luke 22:15). Yet there were some ways in which Jesus was clearly making this a Passover meal 'with a difference'. Most importantly, he may well have held it a day ahead of schedule. There are clear suggestions in John's Gospel (13:1; 18:28; 19:31) that Jesus' crucifixion took place during Nisan 14 (not 15) – around the time when the Passover lambs were being slaughtered in the nearby Temple.

That may be part of John's point (Jesus, he was implying, was now the true Passover lamb). Yet it would also have made sense historically for Jesus to celebrate it 24 hours early. Conceivably this altered schedule brought Jesus into line with other Jewish groups (the Essenes or Pharisees), who may have been operating on different calendars. Yet the main reason may have been starkly practical: Jesus knew that, if he waited another 24 hours, it would be too late. He would be dead.

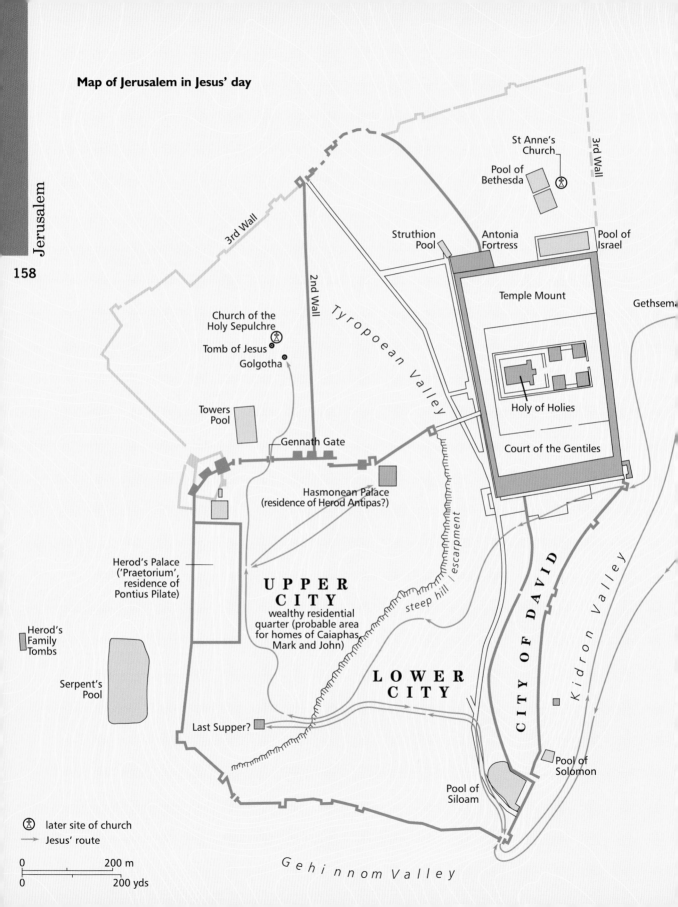

Map of Jerusalem in Jesus' day

Jerusalem

158

St Anne's Church

Pool of Bethesda

3rd Wall

3rd Wall

Struthion Pool

Antonia Fortress

Pool of Israel

2nd Wall

Tyropoean Valley

Temple Mount

Gethsem

Church of the Holy Sepulchre

Tomb of Jesus

Golgotha

Holy of Holies

Towers Pool

Court of the Gentiles

Gennath Gate

Hasmonean Palace (residence of Herod Antipas?)

steep hill / escarpment

CITY OF DAVID

Herod's Palace ('Praetorium', residence of Pontius Pilate)

UPPER CITY
wealthy residential quarter (probable area for homes of Caiaphas Mark and John)

Kidron Valley

Herod's Family Tombs

Serpent's Pool

LOWER CITY

Last Supper?

Pool of Solomon

Pool of Siloam

Ⓧ later site of church

→ Jesus' route

0 ⟼ 200 m

0 ⟼ 200 yds

Gehinnom Valley

Did Jesus lead them through the traditional Passover liturgy? And, though a Passover meal in its shape and intention, did it actually take place a day ahead of schedule (thus without a lamb), because Jesus knew that in 24 hours time it would be all too late? The answer to all these questions is probably 'yes'. Meanwhile, why does John devote almost all of his account to Jesus' teaching about his imminent departure and omit to refer to the crucial words he spoke over the bread and the wine?

Yet the general picture is clear. Jesus intended this evening to be etched deeply on the memories of his followers. Every word and action was important. It was an unrushed few hours before the gathering storm. It was a time for enjoying friendship and privileged intimacy; a time for his followers to be formed into a unique team; a time for dramatic symbols and actions – for example, Jesus taking a towel, fulfilling the role of the servant, and washing his own disciples' feet (John 13:4–17). It was also a time for some memorable teaching: about Jesus' love for those he chose to call his friends (John 15:13–15) and his new command that they should now love each other in the same way (John 13:34); about the coming of the Holy Spirit; and about Jesus' own glory, which he shared with God himself (John 14–17).

But above all else, it was the opportunity for Jesus to establish a new meal through which his followers could remember him in the coming years. Taking the bread and the wine, Jesus dramatically changed the expected Passover words. No longer just the 'bread of affliction' or the 'cup of redemption', Jesus said his followers were now to see the bread and wine as his own 'body' and 'blood'. It was shocking, indeed horrific – not least in a Jewish context where people had been trained never to drink the blood of any animal, let alone a fellow human being. But Jesus required them all to eat and drink these strange gifts, now coloured with a whole new meaning.

Jesus was telling them that his death was imminent and unavoidable, and that it was for their benefit: it would seal a new 'covenant', he said, between God and his people which would secure the 'forgiveness of sins' (Matthew 26:28). He was insisting that his followers in the future should focus on his death as his greatest achievement. He was giving them a powerful symbol to remember him by. Yet, more than that, in a strange, unique way, he was also giving them himself: just as he would give himself to them in his death, so now in the bread and wine he was pledging something of himself to them for the future – that he would always be with them and that his Spirit would live in them.

No wonder his followers ever since have done this 'in remembrance of him'. Whether in the simplicity of breaking bread or in a more elaborate setting, never has a command been so obeyed. Sunday by Sunday (indeed daily) this act is repeated throughout the world. And it all goes back to an upper room in Jerusalem when a young rabbi placed himself at the very centre of his nation's hopes and destiny, and then wrapped that destiny around himself. He was the true Passover lamb, sacrificed in the place of his people (1 Corinthians 5:7). He was the one through whom God would perform a new exodus, by rescuing his people from slavery to sin. He, not the Temple, was now the true place where people could find God's forgiveness – precisely because his death would be the ultimate sacrifice that restored their broken relationship with him. And, having overturned the tables in the Temple a few days earlier, Jesus now established a quite different table – a place where his followers could be sure to meet and encounter him in the future. From now on Jesus, not the Temple, would be the place where God's healing presence was known and felt.

'Was ever another command so obeyed? For century after century, spreading slowly to every continent and country and among every race on earth, this action has been done, in every conceivable human circumstance, for every conceivable human need from infancy and before it to extreme old age and after it, from the pinnacles of earthly greatness to the refuge of fugitives in the caves and dens of the earth.'

G. Dix

The long night

Then seizing him, they led Jesus away and took him into the house of the high priest. Peter followed at a distance...

At daybreak the council of the elders of the people, both the chief priests and teachers of the law, met together, and Jesus was led before them. 'If you are the Christ,' they said, 'tell us.' Jesus answered, 'If I tell you, you will not believe me, and if I asked you, you would not answer. But from now on, the Son of Man will be seated at the right hand of the mighty God.' They all asked, 'Are you then the Son of God?' He replied, 'You are right in saying I am.' Then they said, 'Why do we need any more testimony? We have heard it from his own lips.'

Luke 22:54–55, 66–71

First-century steps leading down from the Upper City (near the modern church of St Peter in Gallicantu) to the Lower City and the Siloam Gate.

Despite the positive light in which Christians now view the event, at the time the evening was heavy with tension and grief. It was remembered as the 'night when Jesus was betrayed' (1 Corinthians 11:23). For at some point during the meal one of Jesus' own disciples, Judas Iscariot, left the table, intent on giving the religious authorities the information they needed to find and arrest Jesus. And Jesus himself was in a solemn mood as he spoke mysteriously about his 'departure' and commented that he would 'not drink again of the fruit of the vine until it finds fulfilment in the kingdom of God' (Luke 22:16).

We can imagine this small, sombre group, perhaps at around 11 o'clock in the evening, making their way down some of the steep steps from the Upper City towards the Siloam Gate. Nearby was the historic Siloam Pool, recently renovated by Herod, where Jesus had sent the blind man to wash when he had healed him of his blindness (John 9:7). Also close by was the place where eighteen people had been killed when a tower had fallen on them 'in Siloam' (Luke 13:4). Now, however, something far worse was about to fall upon Jesus.

Jesus and his followers made their way through the gate and down into the Kidron Valley. Then they made the steep climb up the length of the valley on their way to Gethsemane. It would have taken them about half an hour and, as they did so, each alone with their thoughts, they would have passed several tombs cut in the valley's rock-face on their right,

looking somewhat eerie in the light of the full Passover moon. It was a night when death was in the air.

And then, some two or three hours later, the whole journey back into the city was being reversed. This time, however, Jesus was under arrest, and was being led by guards from the high priest, with just two of his disciples following him sheepishly at a distance. We don't know the exact route taken by the guards (possibly *via* the southern end of the Temple, but not impossibly, back *via* the Siloam Gate); nor the precise location of the house of Caiaphas the high priest – though it would have been somewhere back in the Upper City, the quarter inhabited by the aristocracy. Jesus was led first to Annas (the previous high priest and Caiaphas' father-in-law) and then taken before Caiaphas himself (John 18:12–24).

Almost certainly this was not a formal trial but a preliminary hearing, in which Caiaphas hoped to secure evidence that could be used after sunrise before a larger gathering of his ruling council (the Sanhedrin). After all, this was around 3 or 4 o'clock in the morning, when few council members were awake – and indeed when formal trials were deemed illegitimate. Yet Mark and Matthew focus on it because from their point of view it was more significant than the official trial (described in Luke), which merely repeated and rubber-stamped what had effectively been decided in the still hours of the night.

Mark and Matthew are thus able to focus on the long-awaited personal encounter between Caiaphas and Jesus – a meeting full of irony as the official high priest met the one who would later be called by his followers the 'true high priest' (Hebrews 4:14). We see too the first attempts of the religious authorities as they try to build up their case against Jesus.

The Kidron Valley (c. 1880), looking northwards past the Temple Mount (*top left*), before the extensive building of houses (modern Silwan).

Jesus' questioners concentrated first on those puzzling words that Jesus had said in the Temple: 'Destroy this Temple and I will raise it again in three days' (John 2:19). Yet they could not agree on the exact wording. They had started there because it seemed to show Jesus' radical and dangerous opposition to the Temple (as seen in his act of 'cleansing' the Temple), but also because it was the role of the Messiah (when he came) to rebuild or restore the Temple. Was Jesus thereby implying he was the Messiah?

When this charge collapsed, and when Jesus remained obdurately silent, Caiaphas himself came to the point: 'Are you the Messiah, the Son of the Blessed One?' (Mark 14:61). Jesus then spoke: 'I am; and you will see the Son of Man sitting at the right hand of the Mighty One...' It was a solemn declaration of his identity as Israel's Messiah and as the exalted 'Son of Man' figure – the One who truly represented God's people.

For Jesus it was a moment of honesty, and also of implicit warning. For Caiaphas it was a moment, as he had half hoped, of 'blasphemy'. This was a charge that would surely be upheld by the full Sanhedrin with their religious concerns. Yet it could also be usefully used against Jesus when he came before Pilate: for any would-be 'messiah' could easily be portrayed as a political troublemaker and insurrectionist. Jesus had walked, deliberately, into the trap.

The sentencing before Pilate

Then the whole assembly rose and led him off to Pilate... Pilate said to them, 'You brought me this man as one who was inciting the people to rebellion. I have examined him in your presence and have found no basis for your charges against him. Therefore, I will punish him and then release him.' With one voice they cried out, 'Away with this man! Release Barabbas to us!' Wanting to release Jesus, Pilate appealed to them again. But they kept shouting, 'Crucify him! Crucify him!' So Pilate decided to grant their demand.
Luke 23:1, 14, 16–21

In due course, Jesus was brought before Pilate. From the high priest's house in the Upper City it was not that far to the former palace of Herod the Great, where (almost certainly) Pilate would have been staying during his Passover visit.

Some suggest that Jesus would have been taken to Solomon's Portico (in the Temple courts) for the official trial before the Sanhedrin council, but a sufficient number of council members could easily have gathered in the kind of spacious courtyard found in the wealthy houses of the Upper City. Meanwhile, others have suggested that Pilate may instead have been staying in the Roman garrison of the Antonia Fortress (overlooking the Temple from the north). Though not impossible, the governor is more likely to have availed himself of the spacious accommodation in the palace than to have suffered in army barracks. He did not especially enjoy his visits to Jerusalem, so he was unlikely to have made things even more troublesome than they needed to be – as long as he was adequately protected.

When the religious authorities first brought Jesus before him, Pilate deliberately annoyed them by insisting on a proper trial with a formal 'accusation'. They had hoped he might simply 'rubber-stamp' the Sanhedrin's decision. Then Pilate questioned Jesus

Pontius Pilate

Were it not for what happened on that Friday morning in Jerusalem in AD 30 few people (except readers of Josephus) would have heard of Pontius Pilate, the procurator of Judea at the time. As it is, his name is mentioned by thousands of people every Sunday of the year as they recite a Christian 'creed' (or statement of belief) in Jesus, who was 'crucified under Pontius Pilate'.

What do we know about this man? Until June 1961 there was no archaeological evidence for his existence. Then an inscription was discovered at Caesarea Maritima with its clear reference in Latin to '*Pontius Pilatus*'. This confirms that he was indeed in Palestine during this period. He probably spent most of his time in Caesarea (the province's administrative capital), only coming up to Jerusalem on business and at critical times such as Passover.

Our chief source on Pilate, however, is Josephus. Judea had been under direct Roman rule since AD 6, when the first procurator was sent out to the province from Rome. Josephus indicates that Pilate had been governor of Judea since AD 26 and that during his time of office there were several episodes when he showed his antagonistic stance towards local sensitivities. For example, he brought the flags (or 'standards') of the Roman legion into the city by night, even though their symbolism was highly offensive to the Jewish population. The Jewish leaders went down to Caesarea to plead with him to remove them, which eventually he did (*Antiquities* 18:3). Then he funded the building of an aqueduct into Jerusalem by taking money that was dedicated for the Temple. In the ensuing riot he sent soldiers into the crowd with hidden daggers which they then used when he gave the signal (*Antiquities* 18:3). In due course (in AD 36) he would put down a Samaritan revolt in such a barbaric fashion that even the emperor Tiberius was appalled and recalled him to Rome (see page 84.)

Here, then, was a man who was not afraid to cause offence. He was not initially given to compromise, though he found he had to back down on some occasions. And eventually he would lose his job because of the opinion of Caesar. It all fits well with what we see in his encounter with Jesus.

The area of traditional Golgotha as it might have appeared at the time of Jesus (according to Pixner). This view is taken from the north-east and assumes that the 'second wall' was indented.

Key

1 Region of today's Jaffa Gate
2 Herod's Upper Palace (Citadel)
3 Hezekiah's Pool
4 Mausoleum of John Hyrcanus
5 Agora (Market Halls)
6 Jerusalem's oldest 'Way of the Cross'
7 Gennath Gate
8 Quarry
9 Hill of Golgotha
10 Tomb of Jesus
11 *Kokhim* tombs
12 Private Garden
13 Second Wall
14 Outline of today's Holy Sepulchre

privately. His accusers had evidently translated 'Messiah' into more political colours to mean 'the king of the Jews', for Pilate's questions focused on this: 'Are you the king of the Jews?' Jesus' answer ('my kingdom is not of this world') was enough to cause Pilate to question whether Jesus really was a normal political rebel and insurrectionist. But this only gave him the opportunity to come back to the religious authorities and annoy them once more: 'I find no basis for a charge against him' (John 18:29–19:4).

The accusations then went wider and deeper. 'He stirs up the people all over Judea by his teaching' (Luke 23:5). 'He claimed to be the Son of God' (John 19:7). This latter charge was the original religious one of 'blasphemy', but now shorn of some of its political trappings. It gave Pilate cause to hesitate. He tried the ploy of a Passover amnesty, but the gathering crowds preferred to see a revolutionary figure called Barabbas set free, not Jesus (Mark 15:6–11). He then played for time by sending Jesus round to the court of Herod Antipas (the ruler of Galilee, also in Jerusalem for Passover: Luke 23:6–12). Eventually, the authorities played their ultimate card: 'If you let this man go, you are no friend of Caesar. Anyone who claims to be a king opposes Caesar' (John 19:12). Pilate was cornered.

Pilate knew the real basis of the charge was not political – he suspected that it was 'envy' (Mark 15:10); and he knew the authorities were being insincere in claiming that *they* had 'no king but Caesar' (for Jews, the true king was God, not the emperor). Yet there was simply too great a risk that news of his releasing a supposed king would get back to Caesar. Weighing his political options, he took his position 'on the judge's seat at a place known as the Stone Pavement' and sentenced Jesus to flogging and crucifixion (John 19:13). According to Matthew (27:24), he even washed his hands as he did so.

Simon of Cyrene and John Mark

When Jesus was too weary to carry his cross, the Roman soldiers requisitioned a man called Simon to carry it for him. He was a native of Cyrene in North Africa, so he may well have been a Jewish man visiting Jerusalem for Passover (there is another reference to Jewish visitors coming from Cyrene to Jerusalem in Acts 2:10). Maybe at that moment he was just arriving in Jerusalem for the very first time – we read that he was 'coming in from the country just then' (Luke 23:26) – or perhaps he was simply going about his day's business. Either way, there is some evidence that this chance event just outside Jerusalem's Gennath Gate may have changed the whole direction of his life.

Mark's Gospel adds the interesting detail that he was the 'father of Alexander and Rufus' (Mark 15:21) – a phrase which suggests that Simon's sons were well known to some of his audience. As many scholars believe that Mark wrote his Gospel in Rome, this then makes a reference in Paul's letter to the Roman church all the more intriguing: 'Greet Rufus, chosen in the Lord', he writes, 'and greet his mother, who has been a mother to me too' (Romans 16:13). If this was the same Rufus, Paul seems to have known Simon's wife and at least one of his sons. From this it seems likely that the whole family had become Christian believers – almost certainly influenced by the way Simon's life had intersected with Jesus' at that critical moment.

Yet there is more. For in 1941 an ossuary was found in a tomb in the Kidron Valley with the following inscriptions: 'Alexander of Cyrene' (in Aramaic) and 'Alexander, son of Simon' (in Greek'). Alexander, Simon, Cyrene – it is a telling combination. Could this small box have contained the bones of the man whose father carried Jesus' cross? If so, we have an insight into four members of this one family: the father who was visiting Jerusalem on that fateful Friday, a mother who later on extended her care to the apostle Paul, and two sons (both known in Rome), one of whom was in Rome in the early 50s AD, while the other died in Jerusalem.

We also have insight into another Jewish family who may have had links with both Rome and Jerusalem. For, even though he was probably writing in Rome, the author of Mark's Gospel originally hailed from Jerusalem. He is normally identified with the 'John Mark' who travelled with Paul on his first missionary journey (Acts 12:25). But Acts also tells us that the early Christians had met in the 'house of Mary, the mother of John Mark' (Acts 12:12). This would have been somewhere within the city of Jerusalem.

If Mark's family home was in Jerusalem, then he may well be referring to an embarrassing moment in his *own* life when he refers to a 'young man' who 'ran away naked' (Mark 14:51–52). From this some have conjectured that Mark was sleeping in Gethsemane that night because his father was the owner of this olive grove. With Jerusalem overcrowded with visitors, John Mark's father had suggested that the younger members of Jesus' entourage slept outdoors, while the older members (for example, Jesus' mother) could stay in his home in the Upper City.

The evidence suggests, then, that both Simon's family and Mark's family were caught up in the events of the first Good Friday and found themselves in later years travelling around the Mediterranean and to Rome telling their story to others.

So, after some further flogging, Jesus was led out through the Gennath (or 'Garden') Gate located in the north-west corner of the city walls. Leaving behind him the city of Jerusalem, he made his way towards his place of execution. It was indeed a *via dolorosa* – a way marked with grief.

Initially Jesus was forced to carry his own cross-beam (or *patibulum*) but, exhausted by all he had recently been through, he collapsed under its weight. So the soldiers requisitioned the help of a passer-by, Simon of Cyrene (Mark 15:21).

Then, along the way, Jesus passed some women in the crowd who were beginning to weep at what they saw. But Jesus told these 'daughters of Jerusalem' instead to 'weep for themselves and their children' (Luke 23:27–31). For even in this moment of agony for himself, Jesus was aware of another tragedy. What the Romans were doing to him was only tiny compared with what they would one day do to Jerusalem. The 'holy city' would be destroyed; Zion would be covered in shame. Jerusalem itself, Jesus implied, was on its own *via dolorosa* – headed in a direction marked by grief.

Key dates: Jerusalem

c. 1000 BC	David makes the Jebusite stronghold of Jerusalem his capital; 'city of David' established on southern spur (Ophel Ridge).	100s BC	Upper hill to the west brought within walls of Jerusalem.	c. AD 450	Transfer of tradition concerning the site of David's tomb (from 'City of David' to Byzantine 'Mount Sion').
c. 960 BC	Solomon's building of the Temple to the north of David's city.	63 BC	Jerusalem brought under Roman rule.	c. AD 614	Sion Church burnt down during Persian invasion.
597 BC	Jerusalem first besieged by the Babylonians; prophetic ministry of Jeremiah (627–580 BC).	c. AD 41–44	Under Herod Agrippa, Jerusalem expands northwards (construction of the 'third' wall).	c. 1335	Franciscan rebuilding of Sion as monastery (the Cenacle), now understood to be the site of the Last Supper (not just the Descent of the Spirit at Pentecost: Acts 1:13; 2:1).
587/6 BC	Siege and destruction of Jerusalem, with its king and some of its population taken into exile to Babylon (2 Kings 24–25; Jeremiah 52).	c. AD 70	Romans under Titus destroy Temple (August); city of Jerusalem burnt and southern walls pulled down (September).		
		c. AD 135	Emperor Hadrian destroys the city after the Second Jewish Revolt and refounds it as a Roman city called Aelia Capitolina. Much of the Upper City now left *outside* the walls of Hadrian's military 'camp'.	c. 1537–42	Suleiman the Magnificent builds the 'Old City' walls (including the Damascus Gate).
538 BC	First return of exiles to Jerusalem.			1917	General Allenby enters Jerusalem on behalf of the Allies.
515 BC	Rebuilding of the Temple on a smaller scale; ministries of Haggai and Zechariah.	c. AD 340	Construction of the 'Upper Church of the Apostles' (later known as 'Sion, Mother of all the Churches'); upper hill now known as 'Mount Sion' (following confusion in Josephus about the original city of David).	1948	Declaration of the State of Israel (East Jerusalem lies under Jordanian control).
c. 450 BC	Further return of exiles and rebuilding of the walls of Jerusalem under Nehemiah.			1967	Six Day War, resulting in Jerusalem being under Israeli control.

And ever since there have been those who have sensed a possible connection between that later tragedy and this one. For perhaps in this moment, as we watch this solitary figure make his way outside the city gate, we see in its most acute form that the 'holy city' was not so holy after all, and that the 'city of the Great King' may have been involved in rejecting the one who was truly her greatest king.

*'I will not cease from mental fight,
nor will my sword sleep
in my hand,
till we have built
Jerusalem
in England's green and
pleasant land.'*

William Blake, 'Jerusalem'

Jerusalem Today

Visiting any unknown city can be a bewildering experience, but this is even more the case with Jerusalem. Here is a city with over 3,000 years of continuous inhabitation. Here ancient Israelites have clashed with Jebusites, Assyrians and Babylonians; Jews have clashed with Romans; Byzantines with Persians; Crusaders with Mamluks; the British with Jews and Arabs; and Israelis with Palestinians. Visitors wanting easily to find the 'Jerusalem of Jesus' day' – preserved for them in some kind of time warp – are going to be peculiarly disappointed. In some places the street levels of Jesus' day are now buried by up to 20 feet (6 metres) of rubbish and 'fill', accumulated over 2,000 years of ordinary (and sometimes, not so ordinary) city life. Jerusalem has moved on.

Indeed, you could say, it has moved! The first thing visitors to Jerusalem need to

get clear in their minds is that the present walls of the 'Old City' (built 1537–42) are not in the same place that the line of the walls had been in the first century. The city has moved some 300 yards (270 metres) to the north (see diagrams on page 169). Some sites in the north of the Old City were *outside* the northern city walls in Jesus' day; meanwhile some things now outside the southern walls were *inside* ancient Jerusalem. So, in this present section (where we focus on Jesus' last night in Jerusalem), we will find ourselves quite often *outside* the walls of the Old City.

There is no straightforward way to visit Jerusalem. So many different layers of history are superimposed upon one another that it becomes impossible to focus simply on the movements of Jesus without being made aware of other historical episodes before and after his time. And, for practical reasons of geography and transport, one cannot be endlessly criss-crossing over the city. On page 130, however, there is a suggested itinerary, which some have found a helpful way of dividing up the material, and which allows time for the initial overall orientation that is necessary before the individual sites can make sense.

The Mount of Olives in 1900, showing the Garden of Gethsemane (in the foreground) and the recently built Church of St Mary Magdalene. Jesus' disciples would have fled over the hill towards Bethany beyond. The summit is the traditional site of the ascension.

A First Overview

The itinerary suggests that visitors gain their first **view of Jerusalem from the Mount of Olives**. This is not the time to visit all the particular sites on the Mount (see pages 126–130), but rather to enjoy the panorama of the city and thereby to get a sense of Jerusalem's complicated topography.

From the viewing platform in front of the Seven Arches Hotel, visitors can see how ancient Jerusalem was surrounded on three sides by steep valleys (the **Gehinnom**

Valley on the south and west, the **Kidron Valley** on the city's eastern side); so Jerusalem has only been vulnerable to attack from the north-west. Here again the vast size of Herod's Temple compound can be sensed. It is also possible to make out the spur of King David's tiny Zion/Jerusalem (running away southwards from the Temple area), chosen partly because of its access to water from the Gihon Spring; and to sense how this **'City of David'** and the higher hill beyond (the **'Upper City'** of Jesus' day) could both have been *within* the walls of first-century Jerusalem.

It is good to start here too for a quite different reason. It enables visitors to capture the feeling of expectancy that ancient pilgrims would have had as they came over the crest of the Mount of Olives and gained their first view of the city. There is something about Jerusalem that causes many a heart to pulsate with anticipation and excitement. Here on the Mount one can sense why. Coming up through the desert, perhaps reciting the words of Psalm 122 ('I was glad when they said to me, "Let us go to the house of the Lord"'), modern visitors can sense something of what people in Jesus' day (and ever since) have felt about this unique city. Arriving shortly before sunset can be an unforgettable experience – the ideal introduction to the city and its complexity.

A model of ancient Jerusalem

Model of first-century Jerusalem, showing traditional Golgotha outside the 'second wall' but now surrounded by dwellings in Agrippa's new development (AD 41–44).

Strangely, the next most helpful visit for purposes of orientation is some distance away in **modern 'West' Jerusalem**. Between 1948 and 1967 Jerusalem was a divided city – 'East' Jerusalem was within the Hashemite Kingdom of Jordan, 'West' Jerusalem within Israel. Since the Six Day War in June 1967 and the 'unification' of the city, the dividing wall (and 'No Man's Land') that was built between the two halves of the city has been removed, and there are now few traces of it to be seen. Yet the terms 'East' and 'West' may still be useful, both for ongoing political debates as well as to help the visitor.

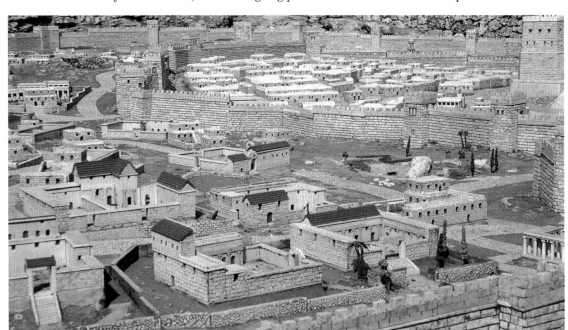

Jerusalem's moving walls

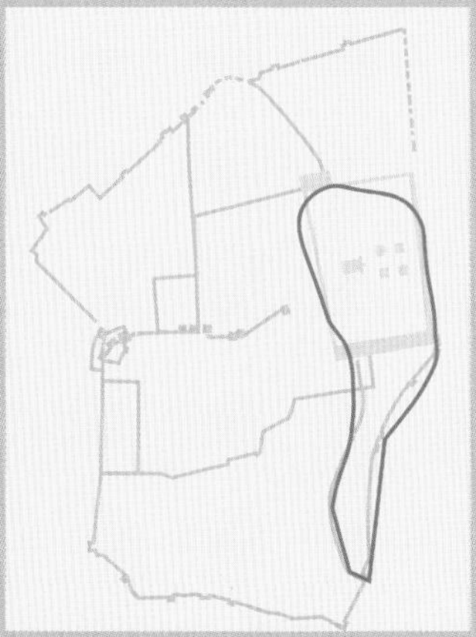

1. In the time of David and Solomon (tenth century BC).

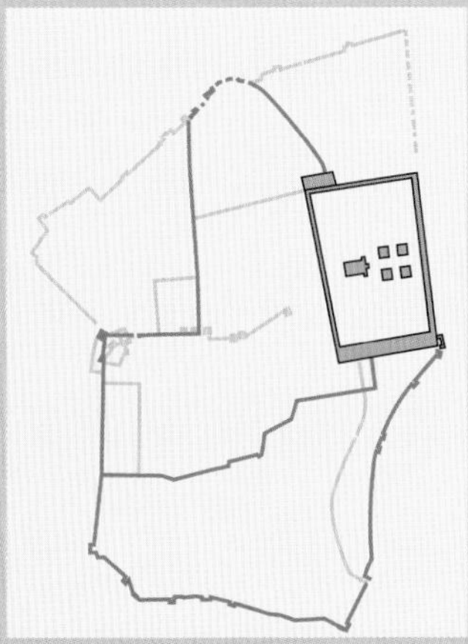

2. In the time of Herod the Great and Jesus (until AD 41).

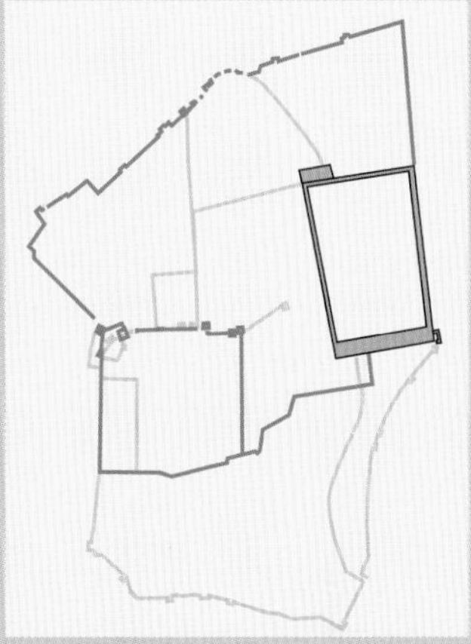

3. After Agrippa's expansion of the city (AD 41–70).

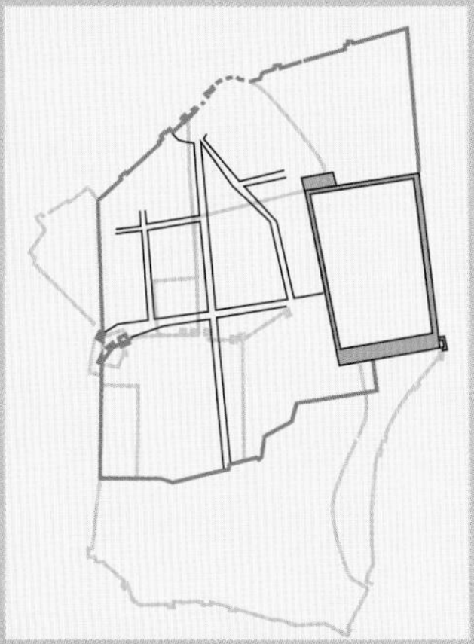

4. Hadrian's refounding of the city as 'Aelia Capitolina' (AD 135–325).

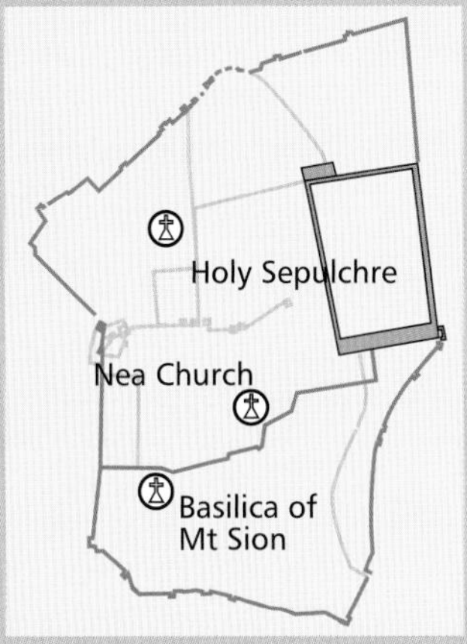

Holy Sepulchre

Nea Church

Basilica of Mt Sion

5. Later Byzantine Jerusalem with some of the walls built by Empress Eudocia (AD 440s); the Nea Church and the Basilica of Mount Sion were built c. AD 525 and c. AD 345 respectively (see model on page 189).

West Jerusalem has many key things to do and see which should be on a visitor's itinerary: shopping on Jaffa Road or in Ben Yehuda street; a guided walking tour around the Orthodox Jewish area of **Mea Shearim**; a few hours' reflection at the Holocaust Museum at **Yad Vashem**; or a visit to the fascinating **Israel Museum** – not least because of its preservation of some of the texts discovered at Qumran (housed in its 'Shrine of the Book'), including a complete copy of the prophecy of Isaiah.

Also at the Israel Museum is the **model of ancient Jerusalem**, which is our focus for now. This gives visitors a brilliant opportunity to imagine the city in the first century. The model, which is designed to portray Jerusalem just before its destruction by the Romans in AD 70, is kept up to date by Israeli archaeologists as more is learnt year by year about ancient Jerusalem. Again it is helpful for visitors

Looking down into the ruins of the Pool of Bethesda.

to begin by standing, as it were, on the Mount of Olives, viewing the city from the east, and imagining what Jesus and his disciples might have seen as they overlooked the city on that first Palm Sunday: the Temple in all its glory (see page 134); the poorer housing in the small 'city of David', spreading up towards the larger and wealthier housing in the Upper City (see page 154); the depth of the Cheesemakers or 'Tyropoean' Valley, which cuts between these two hills and then moves north-west through the rest of the city.

There is considerable controversy about the correct line of the northern wall in AD 70. Josephus refers to this wall, built from the 40s onwards, as the '**third wall**' (*War* 5:4); he gives quite an extended description, but working out its exact route still remains difficult. This model adopts a 'maximalist' position. This means, for example, that the Garden Tomb and its 'Skull Hill' (currently outside the Old City walls) are brought well *within* the city. Others argue with good reason for a 'minimalist' position, which suggests that the north wall would have followed roughly the line of the present Old City walls (see plan 3 on page 169). This would still represent quite a significant expansion of the city since the time of Jesus a generation earlier. The line of the inner wall – the '**second' wall** – can still be seen in the model, showing how even the traditional site of Golgotha would have been outside the wall in AD 30 (see page 168).

There are disputes about the line of the 'second wall' to the north of the Temple, but the **pool of Bethesda,** visited by Jesus on an earlier occasion (John 5:2), may have been *within* the city. John describes this as a pool 'near the Sheep Gate surrounded by five covered colonnades'. For some time this unusual description caused biblical scholars to doubt the reliability of John's account, but the pool was duly uncovered in the 1930s – with four colonnades around its edges and one across its middle. The (slightly confusing) remains can clearly be seen to this day in the enclosure next to the Crusader Church of St Anne's – just inside the 'Lion Gate', known also as 'St Stephen's Gate'.

An overview of Jesus' last hours

For now, however, our focus is on the last 24 hours before Jesus' crucifixion. So, before leaving the model, we note Jesus' likely movements (see also map on page 158):

- Jesus walked to the **Last Supper** somewhere in the Upper City. The 'upper room' may not have been as luxurious as some of the more wealthy houses shown here in the model; yet it may well have been in a house that was considerably larger than some of the poorer houses in the Lower City. Jesus needed a reasonably sized room for his disciples and, providentially, he had some key contacts within this part of the city.
- He walked down from the Upper City, making his way towards the **Siloam Gate**. Note how steep some of this descent would have been.

◆ He then returned under arrest to **Caiaphas' house**. Almost certainly this would indeed have been one of the largest and wealthiest in the Upper City.

◆ Finally, he appeared before Pilate, not in the Antonia Fortress overlooking the Temple, but rather in what had been **King Herod's Palace** (see page 162). This is the large, extravagant building that, according to Josephus, was 'wondrous beyond words' (*War* 5:176). It is just inside the western gate and is overshadowed by the **three big towers** built by Herod in honour of his family and friends (known as Hippicus, Phasael and Mariamne).

Looking at the model, visitors can sense how – with the exception of Jesus' chosen 'detour' to the quiet Garden of Gethsemane – Jesus spent much of those last hours in Jerusalem's **Upper City**. In other words, he was at the heart of Jerusalem's political and civic life, surrounded by the aristocracy and their trappings – a far cry from the poor, rural setting where his ministry had begun in Galilee.

Mount Sion: scene of the Last Supper?

Returning to East Jerusalem, visitors should go to the area outside the Old City walls now known, confusingly, as **Mount Sion**. We now know that David's city (the biblical 'Zion') was on the much lower hill to the east. But probably by the time of Josephus (and certainly by the Byzantine era) it was wrongly assumed that this higher hill to the west had been David's Zion – hence its modern name. This was part of Jerusalem's Upper City – where Jesus spent that long Thursday night. But trying to locate Jesus' movements here turns out to be quite difficult.

We cannot secure the **location of the Last Supper** with any certainty. Some argue that it may have taken place in the home of John Mark (referred to later in Acts 12:12). This may well be correct, but where was *that*? The tiny Coptic Church of St Mark's, for example, is suitably named for a church in the Old City, but it has no real claim to authenticity.

From around the fifth century the location of the Last Supper has been identified with the spot now marked by the Franciscans' **'Cenacle'** (or 'dining-room'). Yet originally this site was almost certainly remembered by Jerusalem's Christians as the site, not of the Last Supper, but of the coming of the Spirit at Pentecost. This too had occurred in an 'upper room' (Acts 1:13; 2:1), so it was not unnatural for later Christians (in the fifth century) to suggest they had been one and the same venue. This remains possible. One of the arguments against it, however, is precisely the strength of the early church's tradition that this spot was associated *only with the events of Pentecost*. If they had wished to do so, they could easily have located the two biblical events in the same place, but they seem not to have done so – presumably because they knew it to be false.

If so, when visiting the Cenacle, you may in fact be in the authentic location of a quite different biblical event – the 'birth' of the Church – as Jesus' followers first received the gift of the Holy Spirit and then Peter spoke to the assembled crowds (Acts 2:1–41).

The Cenacle itself is confusing for yet another reason. Because the Byzantines wrongly identified the upper hill with the 'Zion' of the Old Testament, there came a point when this basilica on Sion became associated with the **burial place of King David**. A suitable tomb was built as a place of commemoration, which since 1948 has

Jerusalem in the book of Acts

Luke's second volume describes the movements of Jesus' followers in Jerusalem and mentions places not touched on in his Gospel.

He says that the believers met 'all together in one place' on the day of Pentecost. Although traditionally identified with the 'room' mentioned in Acts 1:13, this could have been a more public place – perhaps, some have suggested, even the Temple itself or the steps below its southern entrance.

The Temple is mentioned explicitly on several occasions in Acts. For example, Peter and John performed a healing miracle at the 'gate called Beautiful' (Acts 3:2) and then explained their actions to the crowds gathered in 'Solomon's Colonnade' (Acts 3:12–16). It is possible that their interrogation in front of the Sanhedrin council also took place nearby (for the Sanhedrin sometimes met in the Royal Stoa on the south side of the Temple platform). Over twenty years later, Paul went into the Temple (Acts 21:26), but when a riot ensued he was soon whisked away by the Roman soldiers to their 'barracks' (presumably the Antonia Fortress), from where Paul spoke to the crowd (Acts 21:34–22:29).

More generally, Luke says the first Christians met regularly and 'broke bread in their own homes' (Acts 2:46). We only know the name of one host family, however: when Peter escaped from prison (somewhere in the city) he went to the 'house of Mary, the mother of John, also called Mark' (12:12). This may also have been the secret location for Jesus' Last Supper (see page 171), made available by Mark's parents.

been guarded by Israeli Jews. This is on ground level, but it is *underneath* the Cenacle, and needs to be visited *via* an alternative entrance.

Close to the Cenacle is the large church of the **Dormition Abbey**, built in 1900 to commemorate the Catholic belief that Jesus' mother Mary was 'assumed' into heaven. Within Protestant thought, Mary is presumed to have died a natural death – whether in Nazareth or perhaps in Ephesus, where she may have travelled with the apostle John. None of this has prevented visitors to Jerusalem from identifying a site as her supposed 'burial-place': the **Tomb of the Virgin**, near Gethsemane, which dates back to the sixth century. The coexistence of these two sites so close to each other (one commemorating Mary's death and burial, the other her 'assumption') is just one of the unresolved paradoxes to which Jerusalem is ever prone.

Also in the region of Mount Sion (kept under lock in the Protestant cemetery) are some remains of what may be the **'Essene Gate'** mentioned by Josephus (*War* 5:145). If so, the Last Supper may have taken place in a quarter of the city populated by Essenes. Some have wondered if this might explain why Jesus apparently celebrated Passover ahead of schedule – was he perhaps following an alternative Essene calendar (see page 156)?

Nearby too is the modern **church of St Peter in Gallicantu** (which means the 'crowing of the cock'), built to commemorate Peter's denial of Jesus in the high priest's courtyard. Underneath there are a series of rock-cut cisterns and cellars dating back to the first century. They are unlikely, however, to have been part of Caiaphas' house. What we may have here, instead, is the remains of a monastery, built in the sixth century as a memorial to the unnamed place to which Peter went out weeping bitterly. From its outside balcony, however, there are excellent views down towards the Lower City; and nearby are some steep steps, which quite possibly were used by Jesus on that Thursday night as he made his way down to Gethsemane (see page 160).

Where were Caiaphas and Pilate?

Locating **Caiaphas' house** presents similar difficulties to finding the site of the Last Supper. The whole of this area was badly destroyed in AD 70 and again in AD 135, so certainty must elude us. As the high priest, Caiaphas would presumably have lived somewhere along the top of the hill, where the wealthy could enjoy the south-westerly breezes. Yet we do not know if it was somewhere *outside* the Old City walls or further north.

Excavations since 1967 underneath the Old City's Jewish Quarter, however, have revealed a variety of first-century houses which can give us a much clearer idea of what we might be looking for. The **'Burnt House'** gives a good impression, for example, of the terrible destruction this area experienced at the hands of the Romans in September AD 70. And the extensive **'Herodian Mansions'** make clear how large and ornate some of these houses were. Standing in one of the large reception rooms, adjacent to a courtyard, visitors suddenly sense what those events involving Jesus and Peter might have looked like – the surroundings may have been quite palatial. Yet there is no evidence that this was actually the house of Caiaphas (some instead suggest it may be the Hasmonean Palace, used perhaps by Herod Antipas during his visits to Jerusalem).

In fact, the closest archaeological contact with Caiaphas can be found instead at the **Israel Museum**, where his family's **ossuary box** is on display. Though disputed by some, its graffiti markings seem clearly to refer to 'Caiaphas bar-Joseph'. Discovered only in the early 1990s, this funeral object has brought us uncannily close to the man who interrogated Jesus on that night.

The ossuary box associated with Caiaphas, the high priest.

Jesus was then taken to Pontius Pilate in **the Praetorium**. This was in fact the former palace of Herod the Great, which the procurators had now requisitioned for their own use when in Jerusalem. **Herod's Palace** would have extended southwards from the three large towers (near the modern Jaffa Gate) all the way to the present southern walls of the Old City. So the exact location of the trial cannot be determined with any accuracy. According to John 19:13, Pilate 'sat down on the judge's seat at a place known as the **Stone Pavement** (which in Aramaic is Gabbatha)'. Recently, archaeologists have wondered if they have found this, but the area is currently closed off to visitors.

Visitors must content themselves instead with a visit to what is called **'David's Citadel'**. From the second century BC onwards this high point of the city has been a natural place for a citadel (later wrongly associated with King David). The remains of Herod's massive towers can be seen here, together with the northern end of his palace. Again one can sense something of the wealthy, sumptuous surroundings in which Jesus was tried. The buildings were designed to speak of political power and influence. They also spoke loudly of pagan rule – such that Jesus' Jewish accusers preferred not to compromise themselves by entering the palace (John 18:28). It was in this place of pagan power that Jesus, a poor Galilean from tiny Nazareth, was sentenced to death as the unlikely 'king of the Jews'.

Visitors to Jerusalem in the nineteenth century

Travel to the Middle East was opened up from the 1830s onwards when the Levant came under the rule of the Egyptian pasha, Muhammed Ali. The number of Europeans visiting Jerusalem began to increase markedly, with people coming for a wide variety of reasons.

There were those who came, for example, with missionary concerns for the local population. CMJ (an organization set up in 1809 to foster the Church's Ministry among Jewish people) began to send people to minister among Jerusalem's small Jewish population. Eastern Orthodox Christians also found themselves being persuaded to embrace new forms of faith: the Anglicans and Lutherans established a joint bishopric in Jerusalem in 1846, when Christ Church was built in the Old City (initially as the chapel for the British consulate).

Others came simply as interested travellers. One of the most famous was the American Mark Twain, author of *Huckleberry Finn*; his subsequent account in *The Innocents Abroad* contains some scathingly honest and amusing opinions about what he found. Jerusalem was a small Turkish village in visible decline and the rest of the land was in an equally impoverished state.

One famous visitor came with a passion for artistic work – David Roberts. Travelling through Sinai, Jerusalem and Galilee in 1842, he drew some lithographs (such as the one below). They helped people in the West to imagine the biblical land; and today they give us an idea of how the landscape has changed in the last 160 years.

Others came with a keen interest in the emerging science of biblical archaeology. The Palestine Exploration Fund (set up in 1865) produced *Quarterly Statements* with constant new discoveries and questions. The Fund sent out numerous archaeologists, for example: Charles Warren, who investigated the Temple Mount in 1867 and gave his name to 'Warren's Shaft' (see page 148); and Charles Conder, who published his important *Tentwork in Palestine* in 1878. Other parts of the Temple Mount retain the names of such nineteenth-century archaeologists: 'Barclay's Gate' was named after the archaeologist Joseph Barclay (who visited in 1852); 'Robinson's Arch' after Edward Robinson (subsequently professor of Bible Studies in New York, who visited Jerusalem in 1838). Another important archaeologist was a Swiss-German musician called Conrad Schick.

They found the city in a very poor state. Centuries of debris had filled up the Tyropoean Valley and many historic buildings had been abandoned. The church of the Holy Sepulchre, in particular, was in a decrepit state (following the earthquake in 1808) and failed to impress visitors – especially those with Protestant beliefs and tastes. Robinson saw this church building as reflecting an age of 'credulous faith' and 'legendary tradition'; he wondered repeatedly if it was simply a 'pious fraud'.

So visitors began to suggest alternative possibilities for the site of Jesus' crucifixion. For example, Fergusson (who founded the Palestine Exploration Fund) suggested the Dome of the Rock. In 1842, however, a German called Otto Thenius suggested the skull-shaped hill to the north-east of the Damascus Gate. This caught the imagination of subsequent visitors: the Americans Fisher Howe (1853), Charles Robinson (1867) and Selah Merrill (1875–77); Henry Tristram from England (1858); and also the famous Frenchman Ernst Renan who wrote the influential 'liberal Protestant' *Life of Jesus* in 1863.

They were then followed by Conder and, most famously, by General Charles Gordon. Gordon stayed in what is now known as Spafford House by the Damascus Gate in January 1883. He had a perfect view of this 'Skull Hill' from his balcony and began to refer to it in his letters as 'my Golgotha'. His account of this visit (*Reflections in Palestine 1883*) was published shortly after his death in battle at Khartoum in January 1885.

By the end of the nineteenth century, Jerusalem had been transformed by this surge of Western interest in the city. The major European powers were all developing key properties and institutions in and around the city: the French built the Ecole Biblique; the Italians built Notre Dame; the Russians catered for their many Orthodox pilgrims in several compounds. Meanwhile the Anglicans and Lutherans went their separate ways: the Anglican Cathedral of St George was consecrated in 1898 – the same year as the Lutheran Church of the Redeemer in the Old City. Something of the nineteenth-century approach to Jerusalem was perhaps epitomized in the visit of the German Kaiser Wilhelm. In order to attend the Lutherans' dedication service he wished to enter the Old City on horseback, but could only do so if the ancient Jaffa Gate was destroyed – which it duly was.

The way to the cross (the 'Via Dolorosa')

From here it was quite a short distance to the probable site of the crucifixion – the traditional site is in the church of the Holy Sepulchre (see page 190). Only sparse remains of the 'Gennath' (or Garden) Gate have been found, but there would certainly have been an exit through the walls at this point. The route of the medieval '**Via Dolorosa**', with its Stations of the Cross, was determined on the basis of a false assumption: that Jesus was sentenced in the **Antonia Fortress** (which is situated to the north of the Temple compound).

The area of this fortress was excavated in the nineteenth century. Some ancient paving came to light, which was presumed to have been the Stone Pavement mentioned in John's Gospel. Some markings in the stones (of a dice game known as the King's Game) further suggested an identification with the place where Jesus

was mocked by the soldiers. The area is now owned by the Sisters of Sion and their convent is known as the '**Ecce Homo**', which is Latin for 'behold the man' (Pilate's words in John 19:5). Yet archaeology firmly dates the pavement to the second century AD: it was part of the forum (or marketplace) built here by Hadrian when he redesigned the city. Meanwhile the archway that is visible across the 'Via Dolorosa', and which continues inside the convent, also dates to after Jesus' time: it was originally part of a three-part gate built by Herod Agrippa (AD 41–44). The site is worth a visit, as it gives a sense of the streets of ancient Jerusalem, but it does not strictly take us back to the events of Jesus' Passion.

It is time now to focus directly on the place at the climax of the Passion, the site of Jesus' crucifixion.

Pilgrims, led by Franciscan monks, follow the cross along the 'Via Dolorosa' under the 'Ecce Homo' arch.

Golgotha and the tomb

The escarpment (aptly called 'Skull Hill' by some) near the Garden Tomb just to the north of the Old City walls.

When they came to the place called the Skull, there they crucified him, along with the criminals – one on his right, the other on his left. Jesus said, 'Father, forgive them, for they do not know what they are doing.' And they divided up his clothes by casting lots. The people stood watching, and the rulers even sneered at him. They said, 'He saved others; let him save himself if he is the Christ of God, the Chosen One.'... There was a written notice above him, which read: THIS IS THE KING OF THE JEWS. One of the criminals who hung there hurled insults at him... But the other criminal rebuked him... Then he said, 'Jesus, remember me when you come into your kingdom.' Jesus answered him, 'I tell you the truth, today you will be with me in paradise.'

It was now about the sixth hour, and darkness came over the whole land until the ninth hour, for the sun stopped shining. And the curtain of the temple was torn in two. Jesus called out with a loud voice, 'Father, into your hands I commit my spirit.' When he had said this, he breathed his last. The centurion, seeing what had happened, praised God and said, 'Surely this was a righteous man.'

Luke 23:33–39, 42, 44–47

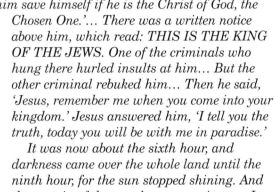

From death to life

Crucifixion was indeed a barbaric form of death, invented by the Romans some centuries before, and used particularly for slaves and those who had revolted against Rome. The Roman general Crassus had famously crucified some 6,000 slaves when he crushed a rebellion led by Spartacus in 71 BC. So most people in the Roman empire would have been familiar with its threat, even if they had not seen a crucifixion for themselves. Nevertheless, despite its quite frequent use, crucifixion was thought to be so disgusting by some of the Romans themselves that, according to Cicero, the use of the word for 'cross' was banned as a topic of conversation in polite Roman society (*Pro Rabirio* 16).

In Palestine itself there had been some 2,000 crucifixions in the year 4 BC, when the Roman general Varus put down a rebellion in Galilee (see page 34). So when Jesus encouraged people to 'take up their cross', the imagery was shocking. How frequently crucifixion was used by the Romans in their ongoing administration of the southern province of Judea is less clear. One skeleton of a man crucified in the first century has come to light in the Jerusalem area, but there may have been many more. However, the delicate politics of administering Judea may have caused the Romans to use a less offensive means of execution on occasions. For, in the eyes of the local Jewish population, there was something doubly shameful about being executed in this way. First, in their Old Testament Scriptures there was the understanding that anyone put to death 'on a tree' was under God's curse (Deuteronomy 21:23). Secondly, they understood human nakedness in public to be especially shameful. Yet those who were crucified were normally hung naked. The gospel writers do not make it explicit that this practice was employed in the case of Jesus, but their reference to the soldiers casting lots for his clothing (Luke 23:34) may be their subtle, discreet way of hinting that even Jesus was not spared this indignity.

The innocent rebel

So Jesus was treated just like any other slave or rebel against Rome. There is profound irony in the Gospels at this

Crucifixion in the ancient world

Crucifixion was a form of punishment used by the Romans for the lower classes – for slaves and violent criminals, and especially for those involved in rebellion and sedition against the empire. Judea was littered with crucifixions in each of its major uprisings against Rome: in 4 BC (see page 34) and again in AD 70 and AD 135. Victims were normally crucified naked and frequently were never buried, their corpses simply being left to be eaten by birds of prey.

The bones of a crucified man were discovered in 1968 at Giv'at ha-Mivtar just north of Jerusalem. Medical examination revealed that the man was crucified in his mid-twenties some time during the middle of the first century AD. His forearms had been nailed above the wrist and his legs had been broken. Even nearly 2,000 years later his heel bones were still nailed together.

From this it has been deduced that victims were made to stand against the cross for the nails to be hammered through their forearms. Their legs were then pushed up (almost certainly to one side), so that their arms were now carrying their body's full weight. This then caused the nails to tear through the flesh of the forearm till they reached the wrist. If there was a slight 'seat' on the vertical post on which the victim could rest, this only prolonged their agony. Eventually they would die of suffocation, unable to pull themselves up sufficiently to breathe.

point. Luke in particular has been at pains to show how this is precisely what Jesus was *not*. His opponents expressly accuse him before Pilate of 'opposing payment of taxes to Caesar' (Luke 23:1), but Luke 20:25 shows that the truth was the precise opposite: 'Give to Caesar what is Caesar's,' was what he had said. Pilate concluded in due course that, although Jesus had been brought to him 'as one inciting people to rebellion', he could 'find no basis' for these charges (23:14). Indeed on several occasions Jesus had expressly warned his hearers – even as he stumbled to the cross – what would soon happen to Jerusalem if it persisted in its anti-Roman policy: 'your enemies will encircle you and dash you to the ground' (Luke 19:43–44). Jesus was no rebel in the nationalistic cause.

Yet, because he was executed on a Roman cross, this was what Jesus was identified with in the public arena. Understandably, then, Luke tries to help his readers to see the deeper truth behind this. Five times in his account he makes the point that Jesus was reckoned to be 'innocent' of this political charge of being a rebel – by Pilate and Herod, by one of those crucified with him, and by the centurion on duty (23:4, 14, 22, 41, 47). By contrast it is Barabbas, a man whom Luke describes twice as 'imprisoned for insurrection in the city and for murder', who goes free. For Luke Jesus is the non-rebel who allowed himself to suffer in a rebel's place, and, on a deeper level, was the truly innocent one who took the place of the truly guilty.

Luke's perspective on the cross

All the gospel writers show remarkable restraint as they describe this event that must have meant so much to them. Contrary to later books and films, there is little attempt to draw out the pathos of the narrative or to enter into the feelings and emotions of those involved. Nor have they written a 'commentary' on the text, inserting subsequent theological ideas. The basic early Christian 'creed' was that 'Jesus died for our sins' (1 Corinthians 15:3). Yet even this is not expressly slipped into the story – however much they would have fully agreed with it. Instead they have tried simply to let the story, unadorned, speak for itself. It is left to the reader to pick up their clues.

In Luke's case, in addition to his theme of Jesus' innocence, there are a string of other themes:

- Jesus is the 'king of the Jews' (as the placard over the cross indicates) and 'God's Messiah' (as the crowds jeer). Yet he is never crowned or welcomed by his own people. Even so, he will indeed, as the thief realizes, 'come into his kingdom'.
- He is the Saviour who has brought 'salvation' to others (Luke 2:1; 19:10). Yet he now brings about that salvation through the very act from which he seems unable to 'save himself': 'He saved others; let him save himself!' (Luke 23:35).
- He is the one who brings 'forgiveness of sins' to people. He achieves this by dying as the innocent one in their place, and releasing forgiveness to those who so manifestly sin against him: 'Father, forgive them, for they know not what they do' (Luke 23:34).
- He is the one who had signalled by word and deed the imminent demise of Jerusalem's Temple. Now by his death he somehow brings about the rending of the Temple's curtain, thereby opening up God's holy presence to all who approach God through his death.
- And this is indeed an event of cosmic significance. For although in many other

'He cannot preach Israel's hope, but he can die for it; he now becomes a Zealot, identifying himself with the national disease he himself had diagnosed so it might be healed.'

N.T. Wright

respects this was just another ordinary day in Jerusalem, there was a period of profound darkness in the early afternoon when the 'sun stopped shining'. Possibly caused by a desert sandstorm, this eerie phenomenon only confirmed to Jesus' followers that in Jesus' death there was something that deeply affected both the spiritual and the physical worlds.

All this is conveyed in a seemingly artless way. And it is certainly enough to cause any reader of the Gospel to pause at the cross, and to press behind the outwardly visible events to the deeper story that is powerfully at work beneath the surface. We are brought to a halt at this place of execution outside Jerusalem's walls.

From the cross to the grave

Now there was a man named Joseph, a member of the Council, a good and upright man, who had not consented to their decision and action. He came from the Judean town of Arimathea and he was waiting for the kingdom of God. Going to Pilate, he asked for Jesus' body. Then he took it down, wrapped it in linen cloth and placed it in a tomb cut in the rock, one in which no one had yet been laid.
Luke 23:50–53

Yet our journey must continue, for the story itself moves on. Jesus' body was taken down from the cross by a man called Joseph 'from the Judean town of Arimathea' (a village some 5 miles or 8 kilometres north-west of Jerusalem). He was a member of the Sanhedrin who 'had not consented' to the council's decisions (Luke 23:51). Even if he could not have spared Jesus from his death, he could at least ensure he received a decent burial. Sometimes corpses were left to rot on a Roman cross for days; others were simply thrown on a pile, to be scavenged by dogs. All this would have been anathema within a Jewish context and now, with the Jewish Sabbath day fast approaching, there was not a moment to lose.

So, late on the Friday afternoon, Joseph, together with Nicodemus and a few others, wrapped Jesus' corpse in some spices, and then placed it in a rock-cut tomb of his own which was conveniently nearby. All this was watched by some of Jesus' most loyal followers – 'the women who had come with Jesus from Galilee', who 'saw the tomb and how his body was laid in it' (Luke 23:55). To keep out birds and dogs, a rolling stone was placed across the tomb entrance and then all those involved made their way quickly to their lodgings in the city – just in time to keep a Sabbath-rest that would be coloured by grief and gloom.

On this occasion the corpse may well *not* have been placed in its final resting place but rather laid temporarily on any suitable ledge in the front part of the burial chamber. After all, this was a hasty operation, a temporary expedient, with those involved committing themselves to come back on the Sunday to embalm the body at a more leisurely pace and to place it in an appropriate final location. Jesus was indeed 'buried', but not necessarily buried 'properly' – that is, in the manner that his mourners intended for his final, undisturbed resting place. Instead Jesus' corpse seems to have been laid on a slab in the front burial chamber in a position that was visible from the front entrance and probably towards the right-hand side (John 20:5; Mark 16:5).

'There is a green hill far away, outside a city wall, where the dear Lord was crucified, who died to save us all.'
Cecil Alexander, 'There is a green hill'

First-century burial practices

The last 30 years of archaeology in and around Jerusalem have given us quite a comprehensive picture of burial practices in the first century. During this period the Mount of Olives was still being developed as a burial site. Also popular, however, was the area a little to the west of the city where the limestone rock was sufficiently soft for cutting.

A common design in the first century was for a tomb chamber to be cut out from the rock. Spanning out from this would be a string of shafts (going further into the rock face at ninety degrees from the chamber). These shafts, known as *kohkim*, would receive the corpse for 'primary burial'. The body would be wrapped in linen and anointed with suitably sweet-smelling spices, which could be augmented again later as necessary. In Jerusalem's comparatively dry climate it would take 18 months to 2 years for the body to decompose. At that point the bones were gathered for 'secondary burial', being placed in a stone urn or box known as an 'ossuary'. The name of the deceased would normally be placed on the ossuary and the box preserved somewhere else in the chamber (see page 173 for the ossuary of Caiaphas).

Sometimes there would also be an antechamber, for use by the mourners. Almost always the entrance would be fairly low, requiring people to stoop or crawl inside. This was so that a rolling-stone of a manageable size could be placed securely across the entrance, preventing scavenging dogs and birds from gaining access to the tomb. The stone would also be a deterrent (though not a total one) against grave robbers. The ground outside the tomb would normally be dug in such a way that the rolling-stone sank into position and therefore could not easily be removed by someone single-handedly.

Above Entrance to a first-century tomb near Jerusalem, showing a rolling-stone.

Kohkim tombs were popular from c. 100 BC to the fall of Jerusalem in AD 70. Another, less frequently used, style was the *archesolium*. This was a flat ledge on the side of the chamber wall that was normally cut out under a suitable arch formation. The strong impression we gain from the gospel accounts is that Jesus' body was never placed in a *kokh* shaft, even if that was his followers' ultimate intention. Instead it was left on a ledge of some kind.

The first Easter

The plan was that the women should return first thing on the Sunday morning to complete the task of burying Jesus properly. Waking before dawn, meeting somewhere in the city, quietly going through the Garden Gate in the city's wall, they made their way out to the disused quarry – a place now associated in their minds with barbaric torture, political injustice and human tragedy. It was likely to have been a damp, chilly April morning. They were a small group – probably four of them (Mary Magdalene, Joanna, Susanna, and another Mary). They hoped that they would not draw attention to themselves, and that their combined efforts would be sufficient to roll the stone away.

Although a tiny expedition, it was destined to become perhaps the most famous of all time. For, when they came within sight of the tomb, they could see that the stone had already been rolled away. And then, when fearfully they dared to go into the burial chamber, they found that Jesus' corpse had disappeared – though his grave clothes were still there.

The story of what happened next is so well known, and is best left to the gospel writers themselves. They are fully aware that the events they are describing are unique and bizarre, but again they write with unadorned simplicity. There is a raw, unpolished freshness about the accounts:

...they did not find the body of the Lord Jesus. While they were wondering about this, suddenly two men in clothes that gleamed like lightning stood beside them. In their fright the women bowed down with their faces to the ground, but the men said to them, 'Why do you look for the living among the dead? He is not here; he has risen! Remember how he told you, while he was still with you in Galilee: "The Son of Man... must be crucified and on the third day be raised again." ' Then they remembered his words.

They told all these things to the Eleven and to all the others... But they did not believe the women, because their words seemed to them like nonsense. Peter, however, got up and ran to the tomb. Bending over, he saw the strips of linen lying by themselves, and he went away, wondering to himself what had happened.

Luke 24:3–9, 11–12

It is the beginning of a long, memorable day – the first Easter day. By the end of it, Luke claims, the risen Jesus had appeared to Cleopas and his friend as they walked to Emmaus, to Peter, and to the disciples gathered in the upper room (Luke 24:13–49). Despair had been turned to hope, grief to joy; loss and bereavement had been replaced by renewed contact with Jesus.

Along with the incredible joy of the resurrection, Jesus' disciples would also have had a dawning realization of what this unique event would mean for their *own* future. Yes, it meant that death was not the end, that there was life beyond the grave; in

raising Jesus' body, God had revealed something of the resurrection that all his people would one day enjoy. Yes, it meant that Israel's God had at last done what he promised to his people, bringing in a new age and revealing his power at work in the midst of his creation. Yes, it meant Jesus could now be seen for who he truly was: the Messiah, indeed the Lord. Yet it also meant that they now had a key responsibility, and a new role that would change their lives forever: for they alone were the chosen 'witnesses of these things' (Luke 24:48). It would be up to them to pass on to the wider world the news that it did not yet know.

So the resurrection of Jesus just outside Jerusalem's walls will in due course cause many of Jesus' first followers to travel to the four corners of the earth, proclaiming the name of God's appointed king. Their journeying, even if it had found its heartbeat and its joy in Jesus' resurrection, had only just begun.

'The Day of Resurrection, earth tell it out abroad!'

John of Damascus
(c. AD 790)

Key dates: Golgotha and the tomb

AD 30	Crucifixion of Jesus (April 7; or April 4, AD 33), probably north-west of Gennath Gate in a disused quarry (last used in 100s BC).	AD 348/50	Cyril, bishop of Jerusalem, delivers his *Catechetical Lectures* to baptism candidates in the Holy Sepulchre; he includes frequent references to the 'wood of the cross' now transported 'throughout the world'.	1185	Reversion to Muslim control of the Holy Land; ever since the keys of the Holy Sepulchre have been kept by a Muslim family.
AD 41–44	Inclusion of this area in an expanded suburb of Jerusalem; (area itself left undeveloped?). Possible subsequent visits of Paul and other Christians to the site.			1808	Fire in the rotunda; attempted renovation of the 'aedicule' over the tomb.
		c. AD 355	Completion of the rotunda over the tomb (the 'Anastasis').	1838	Visit of Edward Robinson from USA, who criticizes the Holy Sepulchre.
AD 70	Roman destruction of the city; this area remains within the ruined city walls.	AD 384	Death of Bishop Cyril; end of Egeria's visit to Jerusalem (see page 114).	1842	First suggestions of alternative 'Skull Hill' to the north-east of Damascus Gate (by Otto Thenius).
C. AD 290	Eusebius refers in his *Onomastikon* (74:19–21) to Golgotha being 'pointed out in Aelia to the north of Mount Sion' (*i.e.* Byzantine Mount Sion).	AD 631	Heraclius returns the 'true cross' to Jerusalem (stolen by the Persians in their attack of 614).	1867	Discovery of the 'Garden Tomb'.
AD 325	Macarius, bishop of Jerusalem, attends the Council of Nicea; Constantine orders the site to be excavated.	AD 638	Patriarch Sophronius invites Caliph Omar to pray in the Holy Sepulchre but he declines. Instead the mosque of Omar is built to its south.	1883	Visit of General Charles Gordon and his support of alternative 'Skull Hill'.
AD 326	Discovery of the tomb; also of some wood, later identified as the 'wood of the cross'.	1009	Basilica and tomb largely destroyed by Caliph el-Hakim.	1894	Formation of the Garden Tomb Association.
AD 333	Bordeaux Pilgrim (*BP* 593–94) refers to Constantine's new basilica, Golgotha and the tomb.	1042–48	Partial rebuilding under Constantine Monomachus, with the former courtyard now becoming the church (facing east).	1953	Development of an Arabic bus station in front of alternative 'Skull Hill'.
AD 335	Dedication of the church of the Holy Sepulchre (in Constantine's absence) with readmission of Arius to fellowship of the Church; Eusebius gives the main address.	1099	Arrival of Crusaders in Jerusalem; a bloodbath ensues as they enter the Holy Sepulchre, singing the *Te Deum*.	2000	Completion of the restoration of the roof of the rotunda in the church of the Holy Sepulchre.

Golgotha Today

The search for Golgotha

The Gospels all locate Jesus' crucifixion at a place 'called the Skull' (Luke 23:33). They also give the original Aramaic name 'Golgotha', which (when the Bible was translated into Latin) was rendered as 'Calvary'. It is unclear how the place got its macabre name: was there a rock formation there that resembled a skull? Or was it just a regular place of execution? Either way, it was fairly close to the city and its gates – the Gospels speak of people jeering at Jesus as they 'passed by'.

But where is it? For many visitors to Jerusalem this is one of their key questions. For Christians, in particular, this event has already been etched into their thinking and has perhaps marked their lives deeply. So naturally they want to know whether it is possible to locate the exact site of the crucifixion and resurrection. Indeed we can well imagine that the same question has been uppermost in many visitors' minds throughout the last two millennia: where is the authentic Golgotha?

For a much fuller discussion of this important question of authenticity, readers might like to consult my earlier book *The Weekend that Changed the World* (1998). There you will find separate chapters looking at the history of the two main sites (the church of the Holy Sepulchre and the Garden Tomb) and a further chapter weighing up their respective claims.

The Mount of Olives?

In recent years, however, some tour guides have become interested in another possibility: might Jesus instead have been crucified on the Mount of Olives? This theory, chiefly propounded by the late Ernest Martin in his book *The Secrets of Golgotha* (1996), made much of the Roman centurion's reaction to Jesus' death. Did the centurion make his comments because he was able to see *simultaneously* Jesus' death and the way the Temple's curtain was torn in two (Luke 23:45–47)? If so, he must have been standing on the Mount of Olives – the only place in Jerusalem where someone outside the Temple could see what was happening in the centre of the sanctuary.

Yet there is nothing in the text that requires the centurion *himself* to have seen what was going on in the Temple. And the other arguments used by Martin are pure conjecture, including a significant misreading of the patristic evidence. There never was a rumour in the early church that the Mount of Olives was the correct site. And the theory is extremely unlikely on strictly pragmatic grounds: the Roman authorities wanted their executions done as soon as possible and in locations much closer to and more visible to those in the city.

So visitors would do well to focus on the two main alternatives: the one, a quiet garden; the other a bustling, often confusing church. According to John's Gospel, 'at the place where Jesus was crucified, there was a garden, and in the garden a new tomb, in which no one had ever been laid' (John 19:41). So we are looking for a site of execution with a tomb close by, both of which are just outside the city wall. Which of these two alternatives is the more likely site?

The Garden Tomb

The Garden Tomb site has the clear advantage of having been outside the city walls in Jesus' day. It has an ancient tomb that resembles the description in the Gospels; and nearby is a remarkable cliff face that in certain lights resembles a skull.

A visit to the site can act as a real oasis in the midst of a busy schedule. Despite the noise of the streets nearby, once through the gate the visitor is ushered into a quite different world. Its calm and beauty, together with the kind welcome of the volunteers who are on hand, can provide the space that many visitors need to gather their thoughts. After visiting many sites and listening to endless historical discussions and debates, here is a chance to pause and think.

On arrival, visitors are likely to be conducted first to the viewing platform at the eastern edge of the garden. Here, if they can ignore the bustling Arab bus station beneath, they can get a good view of the cliff face, which at certain times of day resembles the shape of a skull. For this reason some call it **Skull Hill**. Especially in the early afternoon, the shadows cause two 'eye sockets' to stare out in a macabre fashion.

The approach to the Garden Tomb. Almost all this area was buried beneath ground when the tomb was first discovered in 1867.

There is an ancient tradition associating this hill not only with the lamentations of the prophet Jeremiah, as he wept over Jerusalem's destruction, but also with a Jewish place of execution ('by stoning'). If so, the condemned persons would have been placed at the foot of the cliff, about 10 feet (3 metres) below the current tarmac level; if they were being stoned, those throwing the stones may even have done so from the cliff-top. So, even if it is not the place of Jesus' crucifixion, it might yet be the place where, a few months later, Stephen was stoned to death as the first Christian martyr (Acts 7:54–60).

Visitors retrace their steps into the main part of the garden and may then be shown the **large cistern** underground or the **ancient winepress**, showing that the area was used for horticulture in the biblical period. Next they find themselves in front of **the tomb** itself, with its distinctive vertical rock face, its long channel or groove along the bottom and its small, enticing entrance. Some of the rock-cutting may date from the Crusader period (when this area was used as an area for stabling horses and mules), but much will date back to ancient times. The large stone bricks to the right of the entrance were inserted almost immediately after the tomb was discovered in 1867, but they may well have restored the entrance to something of its original shape.

Entering the tomb

Two of the three burial *loculi* inside the Garden Tomb. Note the grooves which used to contain vertical slabs.

To go inside the burial chamber can be a powerful experience. The tomb fits the gospel accounts well: there is ample room for several mourners, and the chief burial *loculus* is indeed visible from the entrance and to the right – it used to have a vertical slab in front of it, so any corpse might have been placed on a horizontal slab about 2 feet (half

a metre) above floor level. Most visitors try to be quiet inside the tomb, feeling its coldness, considering its antiquity, and trying to imagine what might have happened on the first Easter day.

Coming out once more into the daylight, visitors know they have seen something very ancient and powerfully evocative – a tomb just outside Jerusalem's walls. Could this be the actual site of Jesus' burial? Even if it is not, many feel that they are closer to that event here, at least in their imagination, than perhaps anywhere else on earth.

There are significant archaeological and historical questions that some might then like to pursue. On the positive side this is an ancient tomb located outside the city walls; against this is the current archaeological opinion which suggests that, for stylistic and other reasons, the tomb itself might be considerably older (dating back to the Iron Age?), and therefore would not strictly have been a 'new' tomb at the time of Jesus.

Yet for many the precise authenticity of this particular tomb is not the most critical point. For them the event of Jesus' resurrection is more important than its precise location; or, as some have said, his Person is more significant than the Place. What this tomb does is to jolt the sceptical into realizing that the gospel story is a story rooted in real history and involving a real death. And it helps people to connect with that factual, earthy story in ways that may be ultimately more important – the imaginative and personal.

Christ in the garden

This is why it is significant that the area has been preserved as a garden rather than being occupied by a church or an enclosed place for worship. For this helps the visitor's imagination to leap back across the intervening centuries to that first Easter morning. Many find that the colourful and evocative accounts in chapter 20 of John's Gospel come into particularly clear focus – not least because John had explicitly described the area as a 'garden'.

Taking their seat somewhere further back in the garden, with the tomb front still visible, visitors can imagine Peter and John running, out of breath, to the entrance of the tomb. They can also imagine Mary standing outside the tomb, crying in her distress, not knowing where the body of her master has been taken. According to John, the risen Jesus stands behind her and gently asks her why she is weeping. But she supposes him to be the gardener. 'If you have carried him away,' she says, 'tell me where you have put him, and I will get him.' At that point Jesus speaks to her a single, simple word – her own name, but spoken with a knowing love: 'Mary!' She turns to face the one speaking to her, believing neither her ears nor her eyes. And in that moment she recognizes him: 'Master!', she cries. It is not the gardener, but Jesus – the one who himself brings new life and is indeed Life itself.

The Garden Tomb brings all this vividly to life and in its gentle way opens people up to the possibility of experiencing, even after all these years, their own encounter with the risen Christ. So there are many people throughout the world for whom a time of reflection in this garden has been very significant, giving them a new determination to follow 'in the steps of Jesus'.

'Peter arrived and went into the tomb. He saw the strips of linen lying there, as well as the burial cloth that had been around Jesus' head. The cloth was folded up by itself, separate from the linen…'

John 20:6-7

Eusebius' description of Christ's tomb and Constantine's buildings

The church of the Holy Sepulchre is difficult to understand today without the aid of Bishop Eusebius. As the archbishop of Palestine at the start of Constantine's reign (and later as Constantine's biographer), he gives us a first-hand account of what was done to the site in the years after AD 325. In the quest to find Jesus' tomb, Constantine ordered the destruction of the forum and the pagan temples built there in the second century – which they presumed, possibly incorrectly, had been built by Hadrian as a deliberately anti-Christian act.

Eusebius' account captures the relief of local Christians. Their risky insistence that this was the correct site had paid off after all. One of the few known 'archaeological digs' of ancient history had been gloriously successful. Here is his account of the tomb's discovery:

Constantine decided that he ought to make universally famous and revered the most blessed site in Jerusalem of the Saviour's resurrection... This very cave of the Saviour some godless and wicked people had planned to make invisible to mankind... They brought earth from somewhere outside and covered up the whole place... and so hid the divine cave beneath a great quantity of soil. Then... they built a gloomy sanctuary to the impure demon of Aphrodite... [Constantine] did not negligently allow that place to remain smothered by all sorts of filthy rubbish... At a word of command those contrivances of fraud were demolished from top to bottom, and the houses of error were dismantled and destroyed...

The Emperor gave further orders that all the rubble of stones and timbers from the demolitions should be taken and dumped a long way from the site... [and] that the site should be excavated to a great depth... As stage by stage the underground site was exposed, at last against all expectation the revered and all-hallowed Testimony (Martyrion) of the Saviour's Resurrection was itself revealed, and the cave, the holy of holies, took on the appearance of a representation of the Saviour's return to life. Thus after its descent into darkness it came forth again to the light, and it enabled those who came as visitors to see plainly the story of the wonders wrought there, testifying by acts louder than any voice to the resurrection of the Saviour.

Life of Constantine 3:25–28

For Eusebius the uncovering of the tomb, buried for nearly 300 years, was itself something of a 'resurrection' experience, which paralleled the burial of Jesus for three days. No wonder local Christians felt that they were at the threshold of a new age – not least because they had just been through a period of violent imperial persecution. Their Christ was being publicly vindicated. No wonder too that Eusebius breaks out (for the first time in his writings) into this exalted language about the tomb being a 'sacred' place. It is a silent, but powerful, witness (or 'testimony') to the gospel.

Eusebius then quotes from Constantine's letter to the bishop of Jerusalem, Macarius, which gives practical instructions for the building of the basilica. The emperor speaks of this 'present miracle' and confirms his desire that:

'...this sacred place, which I have now relieved of the hideous burden of an idol which lay on it like a weight, hallowed from the start by God's decree, and now proved holier since it brought to light the pledge of the Saviour's passion, should be adorned by us with beautiful buildings. ... It is right that the world's most miraculous place should be worthily embellished.'

Life of Constantine 3:30–31

Constantine himself would never be able to visit the site, but we see here not just something of Constantine's personal commitment to the Christian faith, but also his own focus on the supposed sanctity of particular places (which may then have influenced Eusebius). Intriguingly, we may also have evidence here of the discovery of some wood (presumed to be that of Jesus' cross). For some scholars think that Constantine's letter, with its language about the 'Saviour's *passion*', not the resurrection, might mean he is referring not to the discovery of the resurrection-tomb but to a second 'miracle' – the survival of the wood of the cross.

Eusebius then proceeds to describe Constantine's buildings. The 'principal item' was the 'tomb full of age-long memory', which Constantine 'decorated with superb columns, brightening the solemn cave with all kinds of artwork'. In front of this was a paved area, surrounded by colonnades – 'a very large space wide open to the fresh air'. And then to the east there was the royal house (*basilica*) adorned with marble columns and roofed with lead.

Eusebius' account is florid, leaving historians with numerous unanswered questions. He fails to refer clearly to the rock of Golgotha which (as can be seen from the plan opposite, figure 9) formed a challenging but important part of the design for Constantine's architects. This layout also takes into account the depiction of the Holy Sepulchre in the Madaba Map mosaic (see page 199). Note the steps going up to the three main doors that faced eastward onto Jerusalem's main street. Note too that the 'rotunda' was not built until after Eusebius' time (c. AD 355).

Eusebius also gives tantalizingly few details about the appearance of the tomb itself. Cyril, a later bishop of Jerusalem, helpfully adds a few more details (*Catechetical Lectures* 10:19; 13:39; 14:5, 9, 22). At the time of the discovery, he says, the rolling-stone had been visible, as had some traces of the original 'garden' (some natural soil?). In front of the tomb's entrance there had also been a natural 'covering' 'hollowed out from the rock', but this ante-chamber had now been removed by Constantine's workmen. This would match Eusebius' only other comment (written soon after the tomb's discovery), when he had spoken of the tomb's 'standing erect and alone in a level land, and having only one cavern within it' (*Theophany* 3:61). Evidently Constantine's architects had decided to reduce the tomb to a solitary cave and cut it free from the surrounding rock.

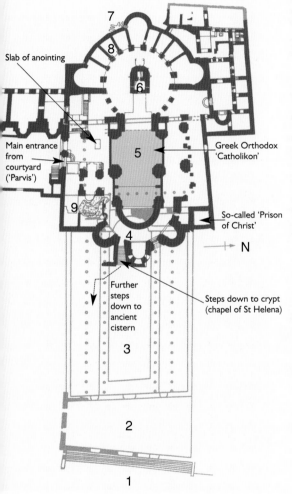

Slab of anointing

Main entrance from courtyard ('Parvis')

Greek Orthodox 'Catholikon'

So-called 'Prison of Christ'

N

7
8
6
5
9
4

Further steps down to ancient cistern

Steps down to crypt (chapel of St Helena)

3

2

1

The church of the Holy Sepulchre in the late fourth century (after Corbo [1981] and Biddle [1999]). The 'Martyrium' church (3) was entered from the main street or 'Cardo' (1) on the east through a narthex (2). Its main focus was the western apse or *hemisphairion* (4). Beyond the martyrium was the courtyard (5) facing the tomb (6). The other *kokhim* tombs (7) were partly destroyed in the building of the rotunda (8). Note how the whole complex is 'out of line' – almost certainly the result of needing to incorporate within it the large rock of 'Golgotha' (9).

Model of Byzantine Jerusalem in the grounds of St Peter in Gallicantu. The general view (*Top*) is from the north-east, showing the two collonaded streets converging in the area of the modern Damascus Gate. In the distance can be seen Justinian's sixth-century 'Nea' church. To the right is Constantine's church on the site of Golgotha: note (*Middle*) the fine entrance and five steps from the 'Cardo Maximus' (main street). The church unusually for its time faced west, not east. When viewed from the north-west (*Bottom*) you can see the courtyard between Golgotha (marked by the large cross) and the rotunda over the tomb.

The church of the Holy Sepulchre

The church of the Holy Sepulchre is quite a contrast to all this. A dark church, set deep within the city, hardly seems to be a likely site for Golgotha and the tomb, both of which were clearly *outside* the walls in Jesus' day.

Yet the evidence suggests that this area *was* outside the walls in the first century. There may be hardly any traces of this wall but there are some first-century *kokhim* tombs nearby. This indicates that the area must have been outside the city at some point during this period. In fact, we know from Josephus that Herod Agrippa expanded the city during his reign (AD 41–44). Almost certainly, then, this area has been within the walls since just a decade after Jesus' crucifixion.

The early Christian tradition in favour of this site is also quite strong. Local Christian memory seems to have been successfully passed on through to the time of Constantine, when his builders cleared the area and indeed found these *kokhim* tombs. This was itself quite a confirmation that the local Christian memory was not misplaced. Why had they taken the risk of requesting that Constantine destroy a pagan temple (built by one of his illustrious predecessors, Hadrian) unless they had good reason for believing that this alone was the true site?

There is also some interesting evidence from a second-century visitor called Melito, who came from Sardis to Jerusalem in the second century. Strangely, he refers to Jesus' being crucified in the 'central square' of Jerusalem. Why did he contradict the gospel accounts? Quite probably he was reflecting on what he had seen during his visit. The site of Jesus' crucifixion was pointed out to him, but it was now covered by a Roman forum and a pagan temple close to the centre of Hadrian's refounded city of Aelia Capitolina. Eusebius later follows in this tradition when he refers in his *Onomastikon* to Golgotha being 'pointed out *in* Aelia'.

There are good reasons, therefore, for concluding that the church of the Holy

The church of the Holy Sepulchre (from the north-west), showing the main dome (the rotunda) above the traditional tomb of Jesus. Constantine's church would have extended a further 50 metres to the east towards the line of the main street (note the shaded line from left to right). The buildings to the right are the mosque of Omar and the white tower of the Lutheran Church of the Redeemer (1898).

Sepulchre may well mark the correct general vicinity for the events recorded in the Gospels. And Constantine's builders clearly selected one of the tombs they uncovered as Jesus' tomb – quite probably because it was the only one to match the gospel accounts.

If so, then we are to imagine this area of Golgotha in the first century as a rough piece of land. It was the remains of a disused quarry, covered now with loose soil and some light vegetation. Within it there was at least one piece of rock that protruded above the floor of the quarry, left unquarried because it had a fissure running down its centre. Perhaps this rock conjured up the image of a skull and gave the place its

eerie name. The area would be ideal for the Romans for their occasional crucifixions: an otherwise useless piece of ground, conveniently close to the city gate, and clearly visible to all. And about 40 yards (35 metres) away, cut into a shallow escarpment that surrounded the disused quarry, there were some tombs – one of them the property of Joseph of Arimathea.

Preparing to visit: adjusting the mindset

In contrast to the Garden Tomb visitors may find the Holy Sepulchre to be quite difficult. The building's confusing layout, bearing the marks of so many different centuries, can leave people confused. And the sight of many different Christian denominations seemingly competing over their respective territories can provoke some strong reactions and hard questioning: if this is the correct site of the resurrection, is this really a good witness to that message?

True, the church of the Holy Sepulchre certainly bears all the hallmark of human frailty; but even this, paradoxically, only reveals the reality of the very human sinfulness for which – in Christian belief – Jesus died here. And we should not be too harsh and critical towards a building that, precisely because its location and significance has meant so much to so many people through so many years, has been at the centre of conflicting desires and intentions. After all, human beings often fight most keenly over that which they value most.

Taking a different attitude to this church, visitors can begin to see it as a unique witness to what Christ has meant to so many. It is a living 'history book' of how people have responded to his death in their different ways. And its messy buildings may serve as a reminder that the God of Christian thought is not far removed from human weakness but is the one who – perhaps in this very location – has himself been involved in such mess.

Moreover, although its long history bears witness to the power of death and destruction, it remains the one church in the world in which the central focus is an *empty tomb*. It is, yes, the church of the Holy Sepulchre, but it is also (as the Eastern church more aptly calls it) the church of the Resurrection.

Visitors might well have had a far more positive reaction to the building if only they could have visited any time between AD 335 and 1000. For nearly seven hundred years they would have been able to enter from the main street on the east, going up some steps into an enormous, spacious church. Then, proceeding westwards, they could have gone round and beyond into a colonnaded courtyard, open to the sky – there to look across to a tomb, cut free from the rock with a walkway all around it, and covered by an enormous dome (see model on page 189).

Constantine's buildings on Golgotha were truly impressive, giving space for both private devotion and grand liturgical celebration. They proclaimed that this was the place where the King of Kings had been buried in abject poverty and disgrace – they were a way, as it were, of giving to Jesus the honour that no one had been able to give him at the time. They were also built in order to declare throughout Constantine's empire that this place of suffering and death was also the place of death's defeat and God's victory.

Conceivably, some people might have preferred the area to be redesigned to look like a first-century quarry with a bit of natural scrubland. Yet such desires for the original,

'If Jesus is not raised, redemptive history ends in the cul-de-sac of a Palestinian grave.'
G.E. Ladd

'authentic feel' are a remarkably recent sentiment. In any case, the area had already been built over and 'ruined' for posterity in that sense by Hadrian in the second century, so Christians in the fourth century *had* to build something fresh. Almost certainly, if we had been in their shoes, we would have attempted to do something remarkably similar. The tragedy is that, by building something so magnificent, they made the place an object prone to attack by extremists – which is precisely what happened in 1009 when Caliph el-Hakim sent troops in to reduce it to rubble.

The building has never recovered from the shock. What visitors enter now is predominantly a ramshackle Crusader attempt to restore some order out of the chaos. So, when entering the church, visitors are in fact entering into what would have been Constantine's courtyard, with his large church and the site of Golgotha to the right, and the tomb a little distance to the left. Constantine's courtyard became the Crusaders' church.

With these perspectives in mind, visitors may begin to have the patience and sympathy to understand this building, and let it do for them as much as any historical building can. It is time now to enter the church, remembering how many thousands have come here previously to be in the place where Jesus died.

Key sites before entering

There is only one public entrance to the building, but before entering many people start their visit to the site somewhere else – just over 100 yards (90 metres) to the east in the narrow market *souk* called **Khan es-Zeit**. This *souk*, running due north–south, follows the line of Hadrian's colonnaded 'Cardo Maximus'. Constantine's building stretched all this way, and some of the entrance's stonework can still be seen at the back of Mr Zelatimo's sweet shop (and in the large building built by the Russians, entered from the south side).

If, however, visitors make their way up the zigzag steps from the *souk*, they can get a great view of the rotunda in the distance; this can give a good idea of how vast was the length of Constantine's great church. They then enter into a small courtyard. Suddenly they are in a different world, surrounded by Ethiopian monks and their cells. The Ethiopians were 'evicted' here (by the Copts) sometime in the seventeenth century, and ever since they have kept the area as a place of comparative serenity. On Easter Saturday evening the courtyard is filled with worshippers as the Ethiopians celebrate the resurrection, ululating and dancing around the cupola in the middle of the courtyard, as though looking in vain for the body of Jesus.

This cupola gives light down to the Crypt of St Helena. So, confusingly, although visitors here are 'on the roof', they are roughly at the *floor* level of Constantine's basilica – being only on the roof of its underground *crypt*. Walking respectfully through the Ethiopians' church (noting their distinctive prayer sticks and also the murals of Solomon being visited by their heroine, the queen of Sheba), visitors come down some steps and find themselves in a large courtyard – **the 'Parvis'**.

Often busy with pilgrims, at Easter time this courtyard is packed with people (especially Greek Orthodox visitors from Cyprus). The Greek footwashing ceremony is early on Maundy Thursday. Two days later, on Holy Saturday, they will be waiting with their candles for the torch of the 'Holy Fire' to be rushed out from the church. The great bell in the bell-tower opposite will be booming, everyone will be shouting 'Christ

Ethiopian monks outside their cells in the area above the 'crypt' of the Holy Sepulchre.

is risen!' and many will take the flame (symbolizing Jesus' resurrection) in their lamps back to their homes – some to their graves.

Going up to Golgotha

Once inside, visitors normally go straight up the steep steps on the right to the traditional **site of Golgotha**. It is a dark area, lit with candles on the Armenian and Greek altars. The rock of Golgotha is preserved beneath a glass panelling. This is the large piece of unquarried rock that stood up some 15 feet (5 metres) above the floor of the quarry in Jesus' day. Quite possibly it would have been covered with some soil, making a little hillock or knoll, but it is only conjecture that Jesus would have been crucified on its top. There is no reference in the Gospels to any 'hill', let alone to Jesus being crucified 'on' it. Despite the preferences of popular piety, the crucifixion may well have taken place somewhere nearby, at 'ground level'.

Coming down the alternative flight of steps and making a right turn, visitors pass a glass panelling which shows the crack or 'fissure' in Golgotha's rock. Archaeologists suggest that this explains why the rock was never quarried. Other interpretations make a connection with the drama of the crucifixion and the earthquake that occurred at the time (according to Matthew 27:51).

The wood of the cross

At this point there is a semi-circular 'ambulatory', built around the apse of the Crusaders' church (used each afternoon by the Franciscans as they remember the Stations of the Cross). Before they are half way round, visitors normally make a detour down into the **Crypt of St Helena** (recently redecorated by the Armenians). Indeed there is a further crypt at a yet lower level on the right, which is worth visiting because of the good view of Golgotha's natural rock and some quarry marks. Both these crypts – certainly the lower one – will have been cisterns at some point in the biblical period, later covered over by Hadrian when he levelled this area for the building of his forum or marketplace.

The association with Constantine's mother, Queen Helena, arose when she became linked with the story of the discovery of the wood of the cross – thought perhaps to have been discovered in these cisterns. She certainly visited Jerusalem in AD 326 and within twenty years Bishop Cyril says the 'wood of the cross' has 'now been sent all around the world'. However, there is no early, reliable evidence that Helena herself was personally involved with this discovery; and some of the accounts later in the fourth century have developed some obviously legendary components – for example, she discovered three crosses and was able to tell which was Jesus' (rather than the thiefs') by a corpse being raised from the dead after coming into contact with it.

The original discovery may have been far more prosaic. Some workmen, clearing the site and having already discovered the tomb, also found wood in the sub-fill and quickly jumped to some conclusions. There is some evidence that Eusebius, the local archbishop, was not convinced about its authenticity. Yet the local Christians were soon promoting it and sending parts of this relic to churches elsewhere, with Bishop Cyril being greatly in favour.

'The whole world has been filled with the wood of the cross, piece by piece.'
Cyril of Jerusalem

Preparing to see the tomb

Returning to floor level and walking round the ambulatory anti-clockwise, visitors pass a **few tall columns** which are very close to each other. The Crusader weight-bearing columns can clearly be distinguished from the more slender ones with their basket capitals. These latter ones go back to Constantine's time. They are all that remains of the colonnaded walkway that surrounded his courtyard. Standing here, in the midst of an enclosed church, it is hard to imagine this as a place open to the sky and full of space. Yet exercising such imagination can help visitors sense what it might have been like to approach the tomb for those 700 years after AD 325. For just out of sight, around the corner, is the traditional tomb of Jesus, which Constantine's excavators were so thrilled to discover and which they then cut free from the rock so that it could stand out in all its strange splendour.

In reality, however, seeing **the traditional tomb of Jesus** for the first time can be something of a shock. It is a nineteenth-century aedicule, propped up by metal girders to prevent its collapse. Few would term it beautiful. History has indeed taken its cruel toll: Constantine's well-intentioned workman removed some of its frontal features in AD 326; Hakim destroyed their work as much as possible in 1009; the roof above collapsed upon it in a great fire of 1808; the building was shaken with a violent earthquake in 1927... After all this, it is amazing that there is anything left to see!

However, some of the natural rock can be seen from behind, through the small Coptic 'chapel' at its rear; and recent archaeological surveys – some using highly technical equipment – have revealed that there is more of the original rock beneath the later adornment than had been supposed.

Many people believe, not implausibly, that this was the burial place of Jesus. And, despite its ugliness and structural weakness, they stop to consider the original event celebrated here, perhaps going inside and thereby joining with the thousands who have prayed here in thanks for the resurrection. The good news of this particular tomb, however, is precisely that it is empty. We are not, according to Luke, to be looking for the 'living among the dead'. So, if visitors half imagined that they might sense a special presence of Christ here, rather than elsewhere, they are almost certainly going to be disappointed. 'He is not here! He is risen!' (Luke 24:6).

No visit to the church of the Holy Sepulchre should end without a brief detour to the

The traditional tomb of Jesus, surrounded by the 'aedicule', built by the Greek Orthodox after the fire of 1808.

Syrian chapel (further to the west beyond the aedicule). Here, with the help of a candle or a torch, some first-century *kokhim* **tombs** can clearly be seen. The shafts, in which the bodies would have been laid, have been cut through by the massive Constantinian wall. This one scene therefore makes clear that this area was indeed outside the city wall in Jesus' day. It also reveals that Constantine's builders found several tombs; yet they evidently selected the one they did for some good reason.

Other features to note before departing include: the splendid roof of the **rotunda** (only completed in AD 2000, but a sign of the cooperation that can exist between the different Christian denominations who share the building); the Greek Orthodox Church or **Catholicon**; some of the beautiful **Armenian mosaics**; and, near the entrance, the **'stone of anointing'**.

This again dates only from the nineteenth century, but it commemorates the slab on which the body of Jesus may have been laid so that it could be anointed before burial. Recalling this, people now bring their own perfumes and oils. In so doing, they also repeat the action of Mary Magdalene at the feet of Jesus, some days before his burial, in Bethany (see page 111). Jesus said on that occasion: 'She has done a beautiful thing. And wherever the gospel is

The *kokhim* tombs discovered by Constantine's excavators, which suggest this area was outside the city walls in Jesus' day.

The 'stone of anointing' near the entrance to the church.

preached in all the world, what she has done will be told in memory of her.' This act of anointing can be a powerful sign of devotion to the person of Christ, which often leaves visitors with an important question in their minds: 'In the light of Christ's death, have I done anything "beautiful" for him in response?'

Christian celebration in Byzantine Jerusalem

The years following the discovery of Jesus' tomb in AD 325 witnessed a dramatic transformation in the way Christians responded to Jerusalem and the Holy Land.

By the end of the fourth century there was a veritable trail throughout the land which took pilgrims round a series of marked sites (as seen in Jerome's account of the pilgrimage of his friend, Paula: *Epistle* 108). The pilgrim trade was booming. The notion of 'holy places' had become deeply embedded in Christian thought; so too the idea of Jerusalem as a 'holy city'. While Church councils were debating the divinity of Christ, Palestine was being celebrated as the land that had witnessed his incarnation and endorsed this high view of Jesus' identity. Politically, the Christian emperors followed Constantine's lead in seeing a Christian Palestine as a useful symbol of their new Byzantine empire.

A key figure in this was Cyril, bishop of Jerusalem from c. AD 348 to his death in AD 384. His *Catechetical Lectures* give us a fascinating window into his passion for the emerging Holy Land.

Frequently he refers to Jerusalem as a 'holy city'. The events of AD 70 had done nothing to alter its special place within God's purposes; it therefore had a natural 'pre-eminence' within Christian life and thought. Similarly the gospel sites were 'all-holy' and 'blessed'. They were important historical 'witnesses', but they also had an almost sacramental potency to evoke faith and to convey a sense of God's presence. They had the power to 'shame' and 'confute those opposed to Christ', while 'all but showing Christ to the eyes of the faithful' (*Catechetical Lectures* 14:23).

He also refers five times to the relic of the 'true cross': it had been 'given away' to the 'faithful, so that it might 'fill the whole world'; just as the apostles had taken the *message* of the cross to the world in the first century, so now key visitors had been allowed to go out from Jerusalem with some of its physical remains (*Catechetical Lectures* 4:10; 10:19; 13:4). Cyril then ensured that those remains retained by the Jerusalem church were put on display each year on Good Friday, so that they could be venerated and kissed. Yet, apparently he held on to these remains tightly with both hands because some time earlier a visitor had 'bitten off a piece of the holy wood and stolen it' (Egeria 37:2)!

For those who are inclined to be totally sceptical about this whole episode, a man in the nineteenth century named de Fleury, himself a sceptic, went round all the cathedrals which claimed to have some of the 'true cross'. He discovered, contrary to his expectation, that the amount of such surviving relics made up only about a third of the volume of wood required for a crucifixion. So the legend may not have expanded as far as the cynical surmise. And it is conceivably possible, though statistically fairly remote, that the surviving relics were indeed in use on the first Good Friday.

Cyril's promotion of Jerusalem would have inevitable repercussions within church politics. Up until AD 325 Jerusalem had been known by many by its pagan name of 'Aelia', and the bishops of Aelia were expressly under the jurisdiction of the archbishop in Caesarea. By AD 451, however, Jerusalem had become one of the five 'patriarchates' in the worldwide church (after Rome, Alexandria, Antioch and Constantinople). It was a meteoric rise.

Yet Cyril's promotion of Jerusalem had even more long-lasting repercussions. For Byzantine Jerusalem would also transform Christian worship and the shape of the liturgy. Bishop Cyril pioneered a pattern of prayer around the gospel sites that was deeply sensitive to both place and season. In this way the Church's year took shape, with appropriate celebrations taking place, for example, in Bethlehem at Christmas and on the Mount of Olives for Ascension Day. Visitors to Jerusalem were suitably impressed by how things were done, and this seasonal pattern was soon being followed all around the empire. So it is to Byzantine Jerusalem (and probably to Bishop Cyril) that many modern churches owe the shape of their year: Advent and Christmas, Epiphany and Lent, Holy Week and Easter, Ascension and Pentecost. Just as Jerusalem had been the source in the first century for the first message about Jesus, so now 300 years later Jerusalem would prove to be the source for a common pattern for worshipping him throughout the world.

Egeria was one such visitor to Jerusalem. From her diary we gain an idea of what it was like to celebrate the 'Holy Week' in the final years of Cyril's episcopate. Here is a list of (just some!) of the services on offer:

- **Lazarus Saturday (1pm)** — Services at Lazarium in Bethany
- **Palm Sunday (1pm)** — Procession from *Eleona* down into city
- **Tuesday (after dark)** — Reading of Apocalyptic Discourse in *Eleona*
- **Wednesday (after dark)** — Reading about Judas Iscariot in *Martyrium*
- **Thursday (2pm till 5pm)** — Eucharist offered 'Behind the Cross'
- **Thursday (7pm till 11pm)** — Hymn singing and readings in *Eleona*
- **Thursday (11pm till 1am)** — Hymn singing and readings at *Imbomon*
- **Friday (before dawn)** — Candlelit procession down to Gethsemane
- **Friday (8am till noon)** — Wood of the Cross on display at Golgotha
- **Friday (noon till 3pm)** — Passion readings 'Before the Cross'
- **Saturday (8pm–early hours)** — Paschal Vigil in *Martyrium* (welcoming newly baptized)
- **Easter Sunday (noon till 8pm)** — Services at *Eleona* and *Imbomon*; then procession to *Anastasis* for reading from John 20:19–25 (the risen Jesus appears to Thomas).

Detail from the mosaic floor in Madaba (in Jordan), depicting the 'Holy City of Jerusalem' in the early seventh century AD. Clearly visible are the two main colonnaded streets (meeting close to the modern Damascus Gate) and the three main churches (see plan on p. 169). The entrance to the church of the Holy Sepulchre is best observed by turning the map upside down.

Emmaus

Now that same day two of them were going to a village called Emmaus, about seven miles from Jerusalem. They were talking with each other about everything that had happened. As they talked and discussed these things with each other, Jesus himself came up and walked along with them; but they were kept from recognizing him... He said to them, 'How foolish you are, and how slow of heart to believe all that the prophets have spoken! Did not the Christ have to suffer these things and then enter his glory?' And beginning with Moses and all the Prophets, he explained to them what was said in all the Scriptures concerning himself.

As they approached the village to which they were going, Jesus acted as if he were going farther. But they urged him strongly, 'Stay with us, for it is nearly evening; the day is almost over.' So he went in to stay with them. When he was at the table with them, he took bread, gave thanks, broke it and began to give it to them. Then their eyes were opened and they recognized him, and he disappeared from their sight. They asked each other, 'Were not our hearts burning within us while he talked with us on the road and opened the Scriptures to us?' They got up and returned at once to Jerusalem.

Luke 24:13–16, 25–33

Travelling along the way

'*While they were still talking about this, Jesus himself stood among them and said to them, "Peace be with you." '*

Luke 24:36

The New Testament writers build their case for the resurrection of Jesus on two key claims: the empty tomb and the appearances of the risen Jesus to his followers. Writing in the early 50s AD, Paul lists some of these resurrection appearances: Jesus appeared, for example, to Peter, to James, to the Twelve, and on one occasion to 'more than five hundred people at the same time' (1 Corinthians 15:5–7).

Of these appearances each gospel writer selects a sample to suit their own emphases: for John, Jesus' appearances to Mary Magdalene, to Thomas and to the disciples fishing on Lake Galilee; for Matthew, Jesus' appearances to the women and then to all the disciples on a mountain in Galilee. Luke, however, focuses his attention resolutely on what happened on that first Easter Day in and around Jerusalem: Jesus' appearance to two disciples walking to the village of Emmaus, followed by their rapid return to Jerusalem where Jesus had appeared to Simon Peter and then appeared to the disciples in the 'upper room' (Luke 24:34–49). His first volume therefore ends tidily with Jesus summarizing the 'good news' to his disciples in Jerusalem. The scene is set for his second volume when the good news will then go out to 'all nations' *from* Jerusalem.

The mysterious traveller

The story of the 'road to Emmaus' is deservedly one of the most frequently quoted accounts in the Gospels: Cleopas and his companion (possibly another male disciple, but conceivably his wife, Mary) had to leave the city around noon to go out to Emmaus – a village described by Luke as being 7 miles or 11 kilometres (literally '60 stadia') from Jerusalem. They were deeply depressed and saddened by what had happened over the weekend; with 'downcast faces' they rehearsed the events leading up to Jesus' execution. The bottom had fallen out of their world, their hopes dashed on the hard rocks of political expediency.

And then a mysterious figure appeared! Walking alongside them, he asked them to offload their story; and he then began gradually to reconstruct their world and rebuild their hopes. As he took them through the Scriptures, their hearts were 'burning within them'. They began to see how the Old Testament had pointed towards a Messiah who would suffer and 'then enter his glory' (Luke 24:26). But, at that precise moment, they still could not imagine what this 'glory' after a period of suffering might possibly mean.

And then it all fell into place. Invited into their home, their guest did what they had seen him do before on several occasions: first he prayed and then he broke bread. In that instant 'their eyes were opened'. They had been talking all this while with the risen Jesus himself! No wonder, despite its now being early evening, they immediately retraced their steps all the way back up to Jerusalem. This astonishing news was something they simply could not keep to themselves.

Luke's four concerns

Luke tells this story at some length and with lots of colourful touches. The emotions are clearly near the surface. As a result people ever since have found in this story something powerful with which they can readily connect: there is the theme of dashed hopes being turned to joy; there is the motif of Jesus walking alongside his followers on the road of life. The story is designed to work at all these different levels. Yet Luke's chief reasons for selecting this story centre on four key themes.

First, and most importantly, there is the focus on the *truth of the resurrection*. Luke's readers are to be in no doubt as to what Luke himself believed: Jesus' body had been raised physically from the tomb. This is not mere wishful thinking. The picture of Jesus walking along the road is not designed to make an imaginary, sentimental point about his 'continuing presence'. No, Luke is giving the reader something far more real than that. The following story in the upper room makes this quite clear, when Jesus displays the wounds in his hands and feet, and deliberately eats some broiled fish in their presence. In their fear and bewilderment the disciples had thought they were seeing a 'ghost', but Jesus replies that a 'ghost does not have flesh and bones, as you see I have' (Luke 24:37–39).

Of course puzzles remain within the story: for example, how did Jesus himself travel back from Emmaus to Jerusalem? Luke is openly acknowledging to his readers that he is relating extraordinary, unparalleled and unexpected events. There is no hiding the strangeness or the mystery. But he hopes, by relaying how the doubts and confusion of the disciples were turned to new conviction, to move his readers too along the same path.

Indeed one of the strongest themes in Luke's telling of the story is precisely this theme that the resurrection was totally unexpected. First, even though Cleopas knew about the empty tomb, he saw this not as an occasion for hope but rather for being yet more depressed. Then, even when the risen Jesus was talking to them on the road about the Messiah's 'glory', they could not work out who it was or what he was talking about; and later in the upper room, they were 'startled', 'troubled' and 'did not believe it because of joy and amazement' (Luke 24:41). There simply was no prior expectation that Jesus would be raised. It crashed upon them out of a seemingly open sky, smashing their expectations and only thereby rebuilding their hopes.

Secondly, Luke points the reader back to *Jesus' death*. When describing Jesus' crucifixion, Luke had simply recounted the events, with little comment on their inner meaning. Now, from the lips of Jesus himself, comes the authoritative account of what was really going on. Jesus' death, we learn, was no accident: it was a necessity, for 'did not the Messiah *have* to suffer?' (Luke 24:26). Yes, he had been sentenced to death by a combination of Jewish and Roman authorities ('the chief priests and our rulers'). Yet the deeper cause of his death was God's mysterious will, hinted at by the prophets of the Old Testament, that through the Messiah's suffering 'forgiveness of sins' could be

'He said to them, "Why are you troubled, and why do doubts rise in your minds? Look at my hands and my feet. It is I myself! Touch me and see; a ghost does not have flesh and bones, as you see I have."'

Luke 24:38–39

announced to the world. So this was a death with a purpose, achieving something vital for others, bringing blessing to 'all nations'. This was a death that dealt with human sin, absorbing its full force and removing its judgment, so that people could experience God's love and forgiveness.

Next, Luke makes some key points about *Scripture*. We might imagine that, now that the disciples had had such a vital experience of the risen Jesus, there would be no need for something as prosaic and wordy as a Bible. Yet the risen Jesus, both on the road to Emmaus and in the upper room, gave first priority to the Old Testament Scriptures: 'beginning with Moses and all the Prophets, he explained to them what was said in all the Scriptures concerning himself' (Luke 24:27). This would have been quite an awesome 'Bible study', with the One at the centre of the story explaining the plot thus far. But Jesus did this because he wanted the disciples to see that both his death and resurrection were in accordance with the Scriptures, and that in fact they were the climax of the whole biblical story. This would help the disciples as they now tried to unpack the meaning of the cross and resurrection for themselves. Yet it also served as an object lesson in how they should now view the Bible – not as something to be dismissed as outmoded, but rather as something God-given which was now seen to have an even greater authority.

And finally there is the intriguing point about the precise moment when Jesus was recognized at Emmaus: 'Jesus was recognized when he *broke the bread.*' Within a matter of weeks Jesus' followers would be 'breaking bread' in their homes as part of their response to Jesus (Acts 2:42). And ever since this has been one of the key ways to remember Jesus – by sharing in the meal known as the 'Lord's Supper' or 'Communion'. There is a hint here, then, of what later came to be referred to as the 'sacrament'.

What Luke seems to be saying to his readers is this: just as the Emmaus disciples met Jesus in that moment of the 'breaking of bread', so you may too in the future. The Scriptures are important, but so too is the sacrament. And both of these need to be set against the backdrop of the two great gospel events – the cross and the resurrection. Without these it is impossible to meet with Christ or to know his forgiveness, but once these things have been taken to heart readers will find themselves driven both to the Scriptures and to the sacrament – hungry to know Christ more.

This is indeed, then, a fitting place both for Luke to conclude his Gospel and for us to conclude this first part of our journey, following in the steps of Jesus. Luke has explained to us that, through the resurrection, this story about Jesus has the capacity to jump out of the history books into the present, and that Jesus wants to come alongside us in our own journeys.

Luke has told a story that in its first half focuses on a journey towards Jerusalem: just as Jesus 'resolutely set his face to Jerusalem' (Luke 9:51), so the reader has been forced to travel with Jesus to the city. But now the scene is set for a second part of the journey, recounted in the book of Acts, which travels in the reverse direction: just as the disciples were now ready to go out from Jerusalem into the world, so Luke's reader is invited to keep going for this next instalment. And in all this the Emmaus story acts both as a central hinge-point *within* the journey and as a pattern for the *whole* journey. For, along the road, there will be many opportunities to hear from Jesus through the Scriptures, and many resting places in which to meet him in the 'breaking of the bread'.

'This is what I told you while I was still with you: Everything must be fulfilled that is written about me in the Law of Moses, the Prophets and the Psalms.'
Luke 24:44

Key dates: Emmaus

c. 1020–1000 BC	The ark of the covenant is temporarily kept in Qiryat Yearim (1 Samuel 6:21–7:2).	
161 BC	Key battles for Emmaus in Maccabean fighting against the Syrians (1 Maccabees 3:38–4:15; 9:50).	
43 BC	Roman Cassius sells the inhabitants of Emmaus into slavery for non-payment of taxes (Josephus, *War* 1:218–22).	
4 BC	Varus, governor of Syria, burns Emmaus after an uprising (Josephus, *War* 2:60–65, 71).	
AD 68–70	Camp of fifth Legion at Emmaus (Josephus, *War* 4:444).	
AD 70	Vespasian assigns some veterans to another 'Emmaus', described as '30 stadia from Jerusalem' (Josephus, *War* 7:217), which soon acquired the new name of Colonia.	
c. AD 115	Emmaus as the probable home of Rabbi Akiba.	
AD 221	Julius Africanus (a Christian scholar) in delegation to Rome successfully requests Emperor Elagabulus to reconstruct Emmaus as the Roman city of Nicopolis.	
AD 290	Eusebius identifies this Nicopolis as biblical Emmaus in his *Onomastikon* (followed by Jerome 100 years later in *Epistle* 108).	
c. AD 500	Byzantine building of basilica at Nicopolis.	
AD 630	Nicopolis abandoned because of a virulent plague.	
1140	Crusaders (wrongly) identify Qiryat Yearim as 'Emmaus', building a large church near the military campsite.	
1500	Transfer of 'Emmaus' tradition to Qubeiba (site of a Crusader church and castle).	
1800s	Qiryat Yearim renamed Abu Ghosh.	
1948	Arab village of Qoloniya abandoned (formerly Emmaus/Colonia near the modern village of Motza).	
1967	Arab village of Imwas (the former site of Emmaus/Nicopolis) destroyed and replaced by Aijalon Park.	

Emmaus Today

For those seeking simple and straightforward identifications of biblical sites, Emmaus can seem bewildering and discouraging. No less than four different sites have been identified with the Emmaus referred to in Luke 24. Yet each of them is worth a visit.

Almost certainly, however, the authentic 'biblical' Emmaus can now be identified with the ruins in the abandoned Arab village of **Qoloniya** (overlooking the modern village of Motza, signposted as an exit at a sharp 90 degree bend on the main Jerusalem/Tel Aviv highway). Qoloniya was located on the rocky ridge above Motza and drew its name from the Roman 'Colonia', the site of a Roman colony of veterans settled here by Vespasian after the First Jewish Revolt in AD 70. But 'Colonia' was a new name; according to Josephus, the place was originally called 'Emmaus'.

This change of name then made it difficult for Christians who wanted to identify Luke's Emmaus; this tiny village of Emmaus had disappeared off the map. Meanwhile not far away a much larger town was discovered, which had also (confusingly) been called Emmaus back in Jesus' day. In the early third century this had itself been renamed **Nicopolis**, but the memory of its former name lived on well into Muslim times. So it was only natural for Eusebius of Caesarea, when compiling his list of biblical sites at the end of the third century, to identify Luke's Emmaus with this alternative Emmaus. This tradition then held firm throughout the Byzantine period and in due course a large church was built on the site.

This confident identification did, however, involve a little emendation to the biblical text. Almost certainly Luke's original had referred to Emmaus being '60 stadia away from Jerusalem' (Luke 24:13). However, some manuscripts have instead '160 stadia' –

conveniently the distance between Jerusalem and Emmaus/Nicopolis.

When the Crusaders came, there was further confusion. Emmaus/Nicopolis had been wiped out by plague in the seventh century. Looking for a place 60 stadia from Jerusalem they opted for **Qiryat Yearim**. This was a village with an interesting Old Testament background: it was the place where the ark of the covenant had been kept for twenty years, after it had been retrieved from the Philistines and before it was taken to Jerusalem by King David. The Crusaders probably selected it, however, because it was the site of a large military campsite, a good stopping point on one's journey up to Jerusalem. Later in the nineteenth century, the village was renamed **Abu Ghosh** after a local chieftain.

The Crusaders, however, were soon defeated and their 'Emmaus' forgotten. Around 1500 the Franciscans made their own identification instead at **Qubeiba**, the place of some earlier Crusader buildings constructed for agricultural and military reasons.

Returning to the first and most authentic Emmaus (at Qoloniya), we note that a further reason for its being overlooked was its distance from Jerusalem. In fact it is only 30 stadia from Jerusalem. What Luke seems to have given us, therefore, is the 'round-trip' distance. Sixty stadia (roughly 7.5 miles or 12 kilometres) is the total distance the Emmaus disciples covered that day including their hurried return (uphill!) to Jerusalem.

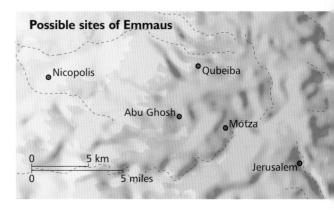

Possible sites of Emmaus

Very recent excavations on the site of Qoloniya have revealed some interesting first-century buildings, but the site is not yet readily accessible to the general public. Meanwhile those who may like to reconstruct the walk from Jerusalem to this Emmaus will find it pretty much covered with urban development. So the other three settings of Emmaus, with their quieter feel, can still be helpful alternative sites to ponder this significant story.

Qubeiba has a church, rebuilt in 1902, which is thronged with Catholic worshippers on Easter Monday. Abu Ghosh also has a Benedectine monastery, and the Crusader church is a good example of Crusader design – its peeling frescoes are Byzantine in style but have Latin inscriptions. Finally at Emmaus/Nicopolis there are opportunities to explore the ruins of this town in the Aijalon Park. Alternatively at this last site people can celebrate Communion amidst the open ruins of the Crusader church (built within the floor-space of the larger Byzantine church). It is not uncommon for groups to do this, especially non-Catholic groups who have fewer locations to chose from. Indeed it often works well near the very end of a visit to the Holy Land (even *en route* to the airport nearby) as people begin to ask how what they have learnt will travel back with them to their homes.

For, although the historic identification of these three sites is almost certainly misplaced, it can still be a powerful experience to imagine Byzantine, Crusader or Franciscan Christians worshipping on these sites, and to do in the present what they did in their own style in their own day: listen to the words of Scripture and break bread in the name of Jesus. In this way the Emmaus story, which in one important sense is totally unique and unrepeatable, *is* somehow repeated and becomes a fresh reality in our times as Christ meets us on our journey and leads us on to whatever lies ahead.

Emmaus: The continuing journey

There is an early church tradition that Luke was not just a doctor but also an artist. It is not clear how this tradition grew – it may have been a way of recognizing that Luke is perhaps the gospel writer best able to portray human beings and 'paint' human emotions. And there certainly is artistry in his account of the resurrection encounter on the Emmaus Road.

For example, he has deliberately given us in this final chapter three 'snapshots' of the resurrection, each of which is set on the very first Easter Day (with no reference to later resurrection appearances). Luke 24 is therefore 'a day in the life' of the risen Christ. It is all set 'on the first day of the week' (Luke 24:1). Luke may here be evoking the Jewish idea that the 'first day' after the Sabbath was also the 'eighth day', which was seen as the day of God's renewed creation. The resurrection of Jesus, Luke is saying, is the ultimate 'eighth day' – or the 'first day' of the new creation. A new world has been born!

There are other artistic features too: the vivid portrayal of the disciples' emotions (weary and 'downcast', dispirited and exasperated, puzzled and perplexed) contrasting with their later joy and excitement; the way Luke shows there is a time lag between their emotions and their conscious minds, with the disciples only recognizing what was going on *after* the event ('were not our hearts burning within us while he talked…?'). The theme too of a journey to and from Jerusalem picks up so well Luke's overarching theme in the two volumes of Luke and Acts – a journey which is also both to and from Jerusalem. He clearly wants his readers' journey to be one in which they meet with the risen Christ.

Noting these artistic touches causes some people to question the underlying historical component of the Emmaus story. Now that we can see Luke's theological interests, it is claimed, we can dismiss the apparently 'historical' setting of the story as pure invention – it is purely there as a vehicle for these other more 'spiritual' points. In other words, because Luke believed people could still meet with Christ, he made up a story about Christ's meeting two disciples as a mere *illustration* of this invisible reality. Such people say that in a historical sense Emmaus *never happened*, but in another sense Emmaus is *always* happening.

Were Luke still here to answer this charge, there is little doubt that he would disagree. He for one truly believed that this Emmaus encounter truly happened. The whole of Luke 24 makes the point that the resurrection of Jesus was not merely a 'spiritual' event in the minds of the disciples but was something starkly physical: 'Touch me and see; a ghost does not have flesh and bones, as you see I have' (Luke 24:39). Of course he may himself have been misinformed and wrong, but he was not deliberately intending to delude others.

Luke would probably also ask his modern interrogators why they are so convinced that history and theology must exist in separate, seemingly watertight, compartments. For, just as there is art that is 'true to life', so there is spiritual reality that can grow out of real historical events. There is nothing stopping a historian from also being an artist or a theologian – especially if, as Luke believed because of the resurrection, God has done something dramatic *in the course of real human history*.

So Luke would surely argue that meeting Christ spiritually in the here and now was only possible because of a prior historical event – namely Christ conquering death through his own resurrection. We might say, 'B is not possible without A; if B happens, it is only because A happened first.' In other words, if 'Emmaus is *always happening*', it is because once upon a time 'Emmaus *actually happened*'.

At the end of his first volume, then, Luke leaves his readers with the possibility of encountering this Christ for themselves. His whole Gospel is an extended invitation to meet this figure who is both within history and yet beyond history. It is also an open-ended invitation – his Gospel does not demand anything of the reader but leaves the page wide open, allowing time perhaps (as in the case of the Emmaus disciples) for the conscious mind to catch up with any emotions stirred through his telling of the story.

Luke has more to tell. In his second volume, Acts, he will want to explain what happened next, and how the climax of this first story was the trigger for a whole next instalment. But that second instalment will not make any sense without the first one. Put another way, his readers cannot appreciate what it means to travel away *from* Jerusalem if they have not first travelled *to* Jerusalem. For the dramatic events of Jesus' death and resurrection in Jerusalem stand as the hinge-point of the whole story, and only those who have truly gone *in* to those events are able then to go *out*.

Jesus himself, according to Luke, had made just this point – though in different words – as he himself set out for Jerusalem: 'Those who would come after me must deny themselves and take up their cross daily and follow me' (Luke 9:23). If we wish to follow 'in the steps of Jesus', we must remember that those steps lead us inevitably to his cross. Only then, when we have ourselves travelled to the cross, can we continue 'daily' to walk 'in his steps'.

Index

Bold entries indicate main section on topic.

General References

209

212

Further reading

Primary texts quoted or discussed in this book

Josephus

See Whiston, W., *The Works of Flavius Josephus* (1737), as found in, for example, Maier, P.L., *The New Complete Works of Josephus* (Grand Rapids: Kregel Publications, 1999). For a more recent translation, see Mason, S.N., *Flavius Josephus: Translation and Commentary* (Leiden: Brill 2000).

Eusebius of Caesarea

See Richardson, E.C., 'The Life of Constantine', *Nicene and Post-Nicene Fathers* (Oxford and New York, 1890), vol. 1., pp. 481–559; also Ferrar, W.J., *The Proof of the Gospel* (London, 1920). For more recent translations, see Cameron, A. and Hall, S.G., *Eusebius: Life of Constantine* (Oxford: OUP, 1999) and Williamson, G.A., *The Ecclesiastical History* (Harmondsworth: Penguin, 1965).

Cyril of Jerusalem

See Gifford, E.H., 'Cyril of Jerusalem', *Nicene and Post-Nicene Fathers* (Oxford, 1894), vol. 7. For more recent translations, see McCauley, L.P. and Stephenson, A.A., *The Works of Saint Cyril of Jerusalem* (Washington, 1969–70) and Yarnold., E.J., *Cyril of Jerusalem* (London: Routledge, 2000).

Bordeaux Pilgrim and Egeria

See McClure, M.L. and Feltoe, C. L. (eds.), *The Pilgrimage of Etheria* (London: SPCK, 1919). For another good resource, see translations of ancient pilgrimage texts in Wilkinson, J., *Egeria's travels* (see below).

John Moschus

See Wortley, J., *The Spiritual Meadow* (CSC: Kalamazoo, 1993).

New Testament Issues

Humphreys, C.J. and Waddington, W.G., 'The Star of Bethlehem, a Comet in 5 BC and the date of Christ's birth', *Tyndale Bulletin* 43:1 (1992), pp. 31–56.

Humphreys, C.J. and Waddington, W.G., 'The Jewish Calendar, a Lunar Eclipse and the Date of Christ's crucifixion', *Tyndale Bulletin* 43:2 (1992), pp. 351–52.

McGrath, A.E. (ed.), *The New Lion Handbook: Christian Belief* (Oxford: Lion Hudson, 2006).

Walker, P.W.L., *Jesus and the Holy City: New Testament perspectives on Jerusalem* (Grand Rapids: Eerdmans, 1996).

Walker, P.W.L., *Jesus and His World* (Oxford: Lion Hudson, 2003)

Wright, N.T., *Jesus and the Victory of God* (London: SPCK, 1996).

Wright, N.T., *The Challenge of Jesus* (London: SPCK, 2000).

Biblical Theology and Contemporary Issues

Alexander, T.D. and Gathercole, S. (eds.), *Heaven on Earth? The Temple in biblical theology* (Carlisle: Paternoster, 2004).

Brueggemann, W., *The Land: Place as gift, promise and challenge in biblical faith* (London: SPCK, London, 1978).

Chapman, C., *Whose Promised Land?* (Oxford: Lion Hudson, 2002).

Chapman, C., *Whose Holy City? Jerusalem and the Israeli-Palestinian conflict* (Oxford: Lion Hudson, 2004).

Munayer, S., *Seeking and Pursuing Peace: the process, the pain and the product* (Jerusalem: Musalaha, 1998)

Walker, P.W.L. (ed.), *Jerusalem Past and Present in the Purposes of God* (Carlisle/Grand Rapids: Paternoster/Baker, 1994).

Walker, P.W.L., with Wood, M. and Loden, L. (eds.), *The Bible and the Land: Western, Jewish and Palestinian approaches* (Jerusalem: Musalaha, 2000).

Walker, P.W.L., with Johnston, P.S. (eds.), *The Land of Promise: biblical, theological and contemporary perspectives* (Leicester: IVP, 2000).

Wright, N.T., *The Way of the Lord* (London: SPCK, 1999).

Historical Issues

Bartholomew, C. and Hughes, F. (eds.), *Explorations in a Christian Theology of Pilgrimage* (Aldershot: Ashgate, 2004).

O'Mahoney, A. (ed.), *The Christian Heritage in the Holy Land* (London: Scorpion Cavendish, 1995).

Walker, P.W.L., *Holy City, Holy Places? Christian Attitudes to Jerusalem and the Holy Land in the fourth century* (OUP: Oxford, 1990).

Walker, P.W.L., with Tomlin, G.S., *Walking in His Steps: a guide to exploring the land of the Bible* (London: HarperCollins, 2001).

Walker, P.W.L. 'Pilgrimage in the Early Church', in Bartholomew and Hughes (eds.), pp. 73–91.

Wilken, R. T., *The Land Called Holy: Palestine in Christian History and Thought* (New Haven: Yale University Press, 1992).

Wilkinson, J., *Egeria's travels to the Holy Land* (Warminster: Aris and Phillips, 2nd edn., 1982).

Archaeological Issues

Barkay, G., 'The Garden Tomb: was Jesus buried here?', *Biblical Archaeological Review* 12.2 (April 1986), pp. 40–57.

Biddle, M., *The Tomb of Christ* (Stroud: Sutton Publications, 1999).

McRay, J., *Archaeology and the New Testament* (Grand Rapids: Baker, 1991).

Mare, W.H., *The Archaeology of the Jerusalem Area* (Grand Rapids: Baker, 1987).

Martin., E.L., *Secrets of Golgotha: the lost history of Jesus' crucifixion* (privately published, 1996).

Millard, A., *Discoveries from Bible Times* (Oxford: Lion Hudson, 1997).

Murphy O' Connor, J., *The Holy Land: An Oxford archaeological guide from earliest times to 1700* (Oxford: OUP, 4th edn, 1998).

Pixner, B., *With Jesus in Jerusalem: his first and last days in Judea* (Jerusalem: Corazin, 1996).

Walker, P.W.L., *The Weekend that Changed the World: the mystery of Jerusalem's empty tomb* (Marshall Pickering, London, 1999).

Travel Narratives

Dalrymple, W., *From the Holy Mountain: a journey among the Christians of the Middle East* (London: HarperCollins, 1997).

Morton, H.V., *In the Steps of the Master* (original, 1935; reprinted by Methuen in 2001).

Praill, D., *The Return to the Desert: a journey from Mount Hermon to Mount Sinai* (London: HarperCollins, 1995).

Picture acknowledgments

AKG-London: p. 137 (Peter Connolly) (sourced by Zooid Pictures Ltd).

Alamy: pp. 27 (Eitan Simanor), 119 (Trevor Smithers/ ARPS).

Alec Garrard (the Splendour of the Temple), Fressing-field, Suffolk, UK: p. 134

Bibleplaces.com: p. 34 (Todd Bolen).

Brian C. Bush: pp. 143, 151, 189, 191

David Alexander: pp. 19, 24–25, 65, 160.

Ecole Biblique et Archéologique française de Jérusalem, Couvent Saint-Etienne: p. 161.

Elia Photo Service, Jerusalem: p. 167.

Garden Tomb (Jerusalem) Association: pp. 176, 185 (top and bottom), 186 (Brian C. Bush).

Garo Nalbandian: pp. 20–21

Getty Images Ltd: p. 32 (Richard Passmore).

Hanan Isachar: pp. 79, 90, 100, 102, 105, 145, 151.

Jon Arnold: pp. 26 (Hanan Isachar), 103 (Jon Arnold).

Lion Hudson plc: pp. 133, 180 (David Townsend).

NASA: p. 8.

Pantomap Israel Ltd: p. 152–53

Peter Walker: pp. 14, 37, 39, 41 (top, middle and bottom), 46, 47, 49, 52–53, 55, 56, 58, 60, 63, 72, 77 (top left and right, bottom), 78, 91, 108, 114, 122, 126, 128, 130, 131, 135, 142, 144, 146 (top and bottom), 147, 149, 154, 168, 170, 182, 190, 194, 196, 197 (top and bottom), 198.

Photo Scala, Florence: pp. 35 (Hermitage Museum, St Petersburg, 1990), 48 (Church of the Autostrada del Sole, 1990), 98 (Pinacoteca, Vatican, 1990), 123 (Musée des Beaux-Arts, Tours, 1990), 136 (Santo Spirito, Florence, 1991), 157 (Museo de Arte Catalana, Barcelona, 1990), 163 (courtesy of the Ministero Beni e Att. Culturali, 1990).

Sonia Halliday Photographs: pp.7, 28, 40, 44–45, 67, 70, 80, 83, 88, 110, 115, 201.

Zev Radovan: pp. 25, 31, 93, 96, 117, 173, 175, 199.